Albuquerque Academy

1095

M = x = 26

D0088880

THE
GOLDEN
MAN

913.3
Von

THE GOLDEN MAN

A Quest For El Dorado

by
Victor W. von Hagen

Book Club Associates
London

SAXON HOUSE
D. C. Heath Ltd.
Westmead
Farnborough
Hampshire
England

© 1974 Victor W. von Hagen

All rights reserved. No part of this publication may be reproduced, stored in a retrieval system, or transmitted, in any form or by any means, electronic, mechanical, photocopying, recording, or otherwise, without the prior permission of D. C. Heath Ltd.

This edition published 1974 by
Book Club Associates
By arrangement with Saxon House
D. C. Heath Ltd.
1 Westmead, Farnborough, Hants, England.

ISBN 0 347 00006 1
Library of Congress Catalog Card Number 74–4864

Manufactured by Halliday Lithograph Corporation,
Hanover and Plympton, Massachusetts
First American Edition

CONTENTS

Albuquerque Academy
25765

LIST OF ILLUSTRATIONS

COLOUR INSET

EXORDIUM TO A FACTUAL MYTH

The collective madness for the search of the Golden Man and the Golden City lasted for a full century. That is from the time that Sir Thomas More published, in 1516, his *Utopia* until the year 1616 when Sir Walter Raleigh in indirect consequence lost his head. It was precisely one century.

What were the events that set the stage for this strange and haunting search? It was, firstly, that with communications being reopened between peoples and nations man began to want something beyond the mere huddle and vacuity of the then highly stratified society. There were open thoughts of an obtainable earthly paradise. Food was monotonous and dull. He longed for spices to give his daily food a bounce, a taste – pepper, cinnamon, nutmeg, ginger: so eager men went out in search for a way to the Spiceries.

The presses were now bringing out to the many that which was and had been the privilege of the few – the printed book. The tales of Amadís de Gaula, the famous Romances of Chivalry, once only obtainable in embellished manuscript, had been published in 1506. *Amadís,* widely read and equally widely dreamed-over, held the public rapturously until it was laughed to death by the publication of *Don Quixote.*

There was for long much talk of islands, mysterious islands far out into the Atlantic, islands of the blessed where "people lived happily and whose poverty no one covets". There was power in islands. Seamen returning from fishing in those far-off waters long regarded as *mare tenebrosum,* the repellent tenebrous seas, talked of mysterious islands they had seen. One was called *Antilla.* An Englishman sailed outward "intent to fynde an island called *Brasil*". Then there was St. Brendans Isle and another "which is called 'lost' . . . now and then found by chance".

Thus it came about when Sir Thomas More wrote his tale of an ideal society it was set on an island, "an isle . . . which fetching about a circuit or compass of 500 miles do fashion the whole island like to be a new moon". This was Utopia.

When South America entered the lists of the knowable, it was also believed to be an island so that when, in time, those who sought out the Golden Man on that continent came across the lake of Guatavita it answered the requirements of the myths contained in islands. It was fashioned round like a cup to catch the first rays of the sun and lay on the high, frigid, lands of the antiplano close upon Bogotá. It was in this lake that the Golden man made his ablutions, washing off the gold which was his sole raiment.

Thus began a golden lunacy which would involve, as will be seen, Kings and bankers, knight and villeins – Spanish, Germans, Portuguese, English – notables and human ciphers. Now had this book been written then and in that time it would have borne a title such as: The Golden Man A Charming and Agreeable Account of the History of the Search for El Dorado and all that Happened to those who went in its Pursuit. Briefly written and Diverting to Read.

But the word "madness" as word and state would, in all probability, never have entered text or title. The Golden man was a fact a factual myth. None of those – and there were thousands – thought themselves to be in the least mad. For what really was madness, Anatole France once asked. Was it not, could it not be, some sort of mental originality? Insanity was a loss of one's intellectual faculties, madness was only the strange use of those same faculties. Madness when not characterized by some anatomical lesion remains indefinable; psychologically the ideas of the mad are as legitimate as the unmad.

The notable fact is that there once was a Golden Man and there was a lake in which he made his golden ablutions. That is the *leitmotiv* of this history. It is as true a history as one can forge out of the existing materials: documents, printed narratives, a detailed knowledge of the crucible of geography, the description of peoples from the disciplines of archaeology and ethnology. But then what is history? It is presumably a true narrative based on past events and notable facts. And what is a notable fact? And how does a historian judge whether a fact is notable or not? He selects. He judges arbitrarily. He does it on his caprice. In sum, as an artist.

Now in the tale of the Golden Man there are many notable facts and also many non-historical facts, and on that account unknown, facts so many that even falsehood would seem often to wear the mantle of truth.

"History is not a science. It is an art. And one succeeds in it mostly by imagination."

V.W.v.H.

Begun
Bogotá 1947
Finished
Trevignano Romano, 1974.

DEDICATION

To the descendants of the Fugger and Welser who supplied
the ducats and maravedis to the electors of the
Holy Roman Empire that made possible the elevation of
Charles V as Emperor and in so doing brought about this
astounding history of the Golden Man.

Fdr-Carl Fürst Fugger-Babenhausen of Augsburg
and
Hubert Freiherr von Welser of Nürnberg

The
Welser

CHAPTER I

The Golden Lunacy

*I saw such things which were brought to the
King from the New Lands, a sun entirely
of gold, a moon entirely of silver . . .
likewise sundry curiosities, all of which is
fairer to see than many marvels . . . I have
never seen in all my days what rejoiced my
heart as these things* – Albrecht Dürer to
himself in 1520

*I*N 1519, two notable historical events occurred:
Hernán Cortés, the conqueror of Mexico, entered
Tenochtitlán for the first time and in Innsbruck,
Maximilian von Hapsburg, German King and Holy
Roman Emperor, died.

These events, so widely set apart and seemingly uncon-
nected, nonetheless formed the texture of a historical tapestry. They were the origin of a strange weaving, the skein of
golden threads to be woven into the incredible and extrava-
gant tale of the Golden Man.

3

To begin, Hernán Cortés first made his preliminary contact with the king, Moctezuma (or Montezuma, as the Spaniards called him), and sent back – to overwhelm his monarch with wonder – an astounding treasure of plumes and ornaments "all modelled in fine gold". Then he burned his ships, and marched resolutely to make his conquest.

Maximilian, by the grace of God Archduke of Austria, Duke of Styria and Carinthia, was feudal lord of the lands in Swabia, Alsace and Switzerland. As such, he had first married Mary, heiress of Charles (sometimes called "the Bold") and so acquired Burgundy and Flanders. He then drove out the Hungarians, defeated the Turks in Styria and found time to marry again, this time Bianca Sforza, daughter of Duke Galeazzo Sforza of Milan. He also was elected Holy Roman Emperor. From these varied strands of history began the tapestry of the Golden Man.

The Holy Roman Empire, which had been spawned in Europe in 800 A.D., was political, in that the Emperor ruled – at least in theory – over all Germanic lands and Italy, and religious, in so far as it drew its spiritual power from the Pope. However, the Empire which Maximilian inherited in 1493 was not the same that he yielded up in 1519. During his lifetime, printing from movable type was invented (1452) and the new learning crossed the Alps. Gunpowder (1450) changed warfare in both attack and siege. America was discovered (1492), and no matter how unrelated, Martin Luther struck at the very base on which the Holy Roman Empire had been founded and upheld: the Pope's spiritual authority.

Not that Maximilian never indulged in limited wars, but his greatest gains were not by arms but by marriage. One of his children swelled the Hapsburg realms with the addition of Hungary, while his influence in Spain came through the marriage of Philip, his son.

In 1496, Philip the Fair of Flanders took Joanna, the third child of Queen Isabella, as his bride. Fragile and afflicted from birth, she was already eccentric when she

4

married. Yet she became the mother of ample progeny, and it is two of her sons, Charles and Ferdinand, who concern our agreeable tale. Illusory or real, her husband's philandering swept her over the rims of sanity. It was a gentle madness, yet marked enough to deprive her of the throne. Queen Isabella knew Joanna could not rule, and on the advice of her ministers inserted a clause in her will that Joanna would be the "Queen-proprietress of Castille", with her husband Philip as consort, but Charles, their son, would wear the Crown.

And so at the age of seventeen, Charles, child of the Mad Queen, became King of Spain – yet not at once. Born in Ghent, a Fleming, Charles had been reared in Flanders and knew little Spanish. His French was imperfect, and he spoke the guttural German of the Lowlands. Not unnaturally, at first the Spaniards found little about his person to inspire devotion for he had the shovel-jaw of the Hapsburgs, with a protruding lower lip, and lacked the gaiety one associates with youth. Moreover his habits were gluttonous.

Perhaps worst of all, a great incompatibility of temperament prevailed between the Spaniards and the Flemings, arising from their loathing of these purse-proud, heavy drinking Lowlanders. Everything about them was the epitome of all that was hateful to the Spaniard, with their scorn for trade and industry and for *mercachufiles* in general. Few then, in either Flanders or Spain, could have foretold that Charles would emerge as a great European with a superb hold over men and events and become, one day, beloved by most of Spain.

None of this was even glimpsed when, in the cold dawn of September 1517, he was put ashore in a remote coastal village of the Asturias, there meeting the agents of the aged Primate of Spain, the Cardinal Archbishop of Toledo, who held Christendom's most lucrative preferment save that of the Papacy itself. It was he who had favoured Charles as King, and had done the groundwork for Charles's acceptance.

5

There were at that time many Spains and many royal courts, so before each of them – Castille, Aragon and the rest – Charles had to swear to observe the customs and to *withhold offices from all non-Spaniards.* He also undertook upon oath that he "would not make a further request for money during the next three years, *except for extreme necessity.*"

Thus, dutifully, the young King went from court to court, taking his oaths, receiving homage and grants, until the last – the court of Catalonia – claimed his attention. It was there, while his ministers haggled, that on 11 January 1519 the news arrived that his grandfather, Maximilian, had died. The title of Emperor of the Holy Roman Empire was now vacant.

Without completing his business with the Valencian Court, Charles I of Spain decided to go off at once to Germany to press his claim for the coveted title. But how was he to secure it? His personal funds were scanty and his oath to the courts of the Spains precluded him from requesting further funds, except for extreme necessity. Where, therefore, would he find the money?

It so happened that the means to acquire the title were available from the Fugger (the name was always written in the singular even when referring to the plural) and their rivals, the Welser. As bankers to Maximilian, the Fugger felt it their duty to extend the same financial support to his grandson Charles. Money, therefore was to be lent by both the Welser and the Fugger to bribe the Electors of the Holy Roman Empire. With this assurance, the young monarch left Valencia without even taking his oath as King.

Bankers of Augsburg, the Welser and the Fugger were a new class of men – enlightened capitalists. And in accordance with the Spanish adage – "muy poderoso caballero es don Dinero" – they obtained noble lineage and power through banking. It had not always been so. The earliest known Fugger, one Johannes, who was born near Schwabmünchen in 1348, eventually became a master weaver. Settling in Memmingen, a Reichsstadt in Swabia, he began to manufacture on a large scale, perfecting *barchent,* a cloth composed of wool and cotton, and *loden,* a waterproof fabric made from boiled wool. Both enjoyed vast trade, as did the subsequent weaving of linen. From weaving, the Fugger expanded into new spheres of capitalism; with the growth of Renaissance science and its new technologies, mining became profitable. It was an age of opportunity, for the opening up of new commercial markets and relative safety in shipping brought prosperity to Europe.

While not exactly their competitors, the Welser were the Fugger's rivals. As far as is known, the first Welser appeared in Nuremberg in the thirteenth century, so that as a patrician family they were much older than the Fugger. Indeed, the Welser engaged in overseas commerce a century before the Fugger rose to such prominence, and built in 1441 the Fonde de Tedeschi in Venice (still standing on the Grand Canal) from which they operated part of their overseas trade.

Anton Welser was controlling the Welser fortunes when the loan of 141,000 ducats was made to Charles I in 1519. Personally conducting negotiations, Anton was obviously a person of high social distinction as his portrait by Christopher Amberger clearly testifies. Portrayed in the setting of his counting-rooms in Augsburg, he is seen in a simple unadorned dress of the period, a gold chain about his neck, a flattened hat set on his head at a rakish angle. Thus he was caught by the artist, looking up from his tables, while in the act of counting his golden ducats. It was this Anton Welser, in the last act of his life, who was to negotiate with Spain the leasehold on Venezuela – the entrepôt to the Golden Man.

As already mentioned, the Fugger and the Welser operated on a world-wide basis. They had offices (or "factories") in Antwerp, Venice, Seville, Valencia, as well as in parts of Germany and Austria. They risked their capital in research as was demonstrated by Jacob Fugger who

7

financed a voyage to the Malacca Islands and applied for a contract to exploit the Spice Islands. They were creative capitalists, employing architects on both private and public buildings and commissioning the finest artists of the period – Holbein, Dürer, Bellini, and Jost Amman, famed for his wood cuts. Equally profound was their interest in literature. The Fugger built up an immense library while the more literary Welser were authors of many a book – notably Marcus Welser, who wrote on Roman antiquities and reproduced and wrote the commentary for the *Tabula Itineraria,* the only known surviving Roman road map.

The Welser fortunes were founded on goods, spices and property and the Fugger's on banking and mines in the Tyrol, Hungary and Bohemia. Thus by 1530, they could reckon their wealth at 2,000,000 Rhine florins – the equivalent of fifteen tons of gold.

Therefore, when Charles I wished to borrow 300,000 ducats with which to bribe the Electors of the Holy Roman

Bartholomeus Welser, head of the house of Welser when it began its exploration of the New World in Venezuela and beyond for the Golden Man. (Stadtbildstelle Augsburg. Private collection in Schloss Neunhof.)

Empire, the bulging purse of the Fugger was at the King's disposal. In like manner, though lacking the same largesse, was the contribution of the Welser's 141,000 ducats.

It was to be the beginning of the journey to the Golden Man.

The election of the Emperor was memorable. Never before had such sums been distributed to "persuade" the Electors, tactics made necessary to forestall the ambitions of Henry VIII of England and Francis I of France. So determined were the patricians of Augsburg to elect Charles I that a decree by the town Diet threatened any banker who loaned money to the French King with dire consequences.

For surety, the Welser and the Fugger asked Charles I, when he became Charles V of the Holy Roman Empire, to pledge almost the entire Crown property of Castille, to which he agreed.

As soon as his election was confirmed, his courtiers proclaimed it throughout Spain to the accompaniment of fanfares and rolls of drums, announcing the King's new dignity; henceforth he was to be addressed as "Your Majesty". Then he made preparations to leave Spain for Aachen in Germany, where the Coronation was to take place.

Spain was rightfully indignant. Not only had Charles recently arrived and been crowned King (amid, incidentally, considerable dispute), but now he had surrounded himself with a pomp and dignity hitherto unknown to the Spaniard; moreover, he had accepted a foreign crown. He was forsaking Spain to its present misgovernment and, meanwhile, had summoned the courts to seek fresh subsidies. All this, as can be imagined, set off hostile rebellion. The *Comuneros* rioted in many parts of Spain. Buildings were sacked and burned; Medina del Campo, one of Europe's great emporiums, crammed with trade goods, was set on fire. In near panic, Charles of Spain, the elected Emperor of the Holy Roman Empire, put out to sea with his Flemish nobles; only a few spirited Spaniards accompanied him.

Nuremberg in 1492, from the Nuremberg Chronicle. (Germanisches
Nationalmuseum, Nürnberg)

After Charles had been crowned Emperor, he moved with his entourage to visit his birthplace, Ghent, and later, with a large and spectacular train of nobles and patricians, carried on to Brussels. There, on 12 July 1520, the newly-found lands of America dramatically intruded into the proceedings: two gentlemen were waiting upon the King-Emperor, with gold from the new land, called Mexico, which was even then being conquered by Capitán Hernán Cortés. Not aware of recent events, they had sailed first to Spain, then extended their journey on being informed that the King was in Flanders.

Hernán Cortés, landing at Vera Cruz on the Mexico coast in November 1519, after an eventful journey, had there been given presents by the envoys of Moctezuma.

Bernal Díaz, an eye-witness of all that happened, described the treasure: "The first was a disk in the shape of the sun, as big as a cartwheel and made of a very fine gold. It was a marvellous thing, engraved with many sorts of figures . . . There was another larger disk of brightly shining silver in the shape of the moon. . . .

"Next came twenty golden ducks, of fine workmanship, some ornaments in the shape of their native dogs, many others in the shapes of tigers, lions, and monkeys, ten necklaces of very fine workmanship, some pendants. They brought crests of gold, plumes of rich, green feathers, silver crests . . . models of deer in hollow gold."

Albrecht Dürer was at Brussels at the historic moment when this Aztec treasure arrived. Allowed to examine these finely wrought pieces, he exclaimed he had never seen such marvels, which might well have been true, for who could have known better than he?

Albrecht Dürer was the son of a goldsmith, who after settling in western Hungary, had returned to Nuremberg where Albrecht was born. "I saw such things," he recorded in his notebook, "which were brought to the King from the New Golden Land [Mexico]; a sun entirely of gold, a

Cast gold filigree ornament, Chibcha-Muisca culture.

whole fathom broad; likewise a moon entirely of silver, just as big; likewise sundry curiosities from their weapons, arms and missiles . . . all of which is fairer to see than marvels. . . . These things were all so precious that they were valued at 100,000 gulden. But I have never seen in all my days what so rejoiced my heart as these things. For I saw among them amazing artistic objects and I marvelled over the subtle ingenuity of the men in these distant lands. Indeed, I cannot say enough about the things which were before me."

The impact of these golden Mexican ornaments on the public was, as can be imagined, most startling, for at that time, very little gold circulated in Europe. Thus the fact that some barbarous people beyond the sea – of whom they had never previously heard – owned gold in such abundance that they could make golden fishhooks prepared the public to accept the idea of golden cities in the New World.

Columbus had said he had found the new way to the spiceries. Such news was received with joy, for European food was monotonous and insipid without the flavouring of pepper and other spices. To obtain them hitherto involved a lengthy process by sea or overland routes from India. Spices were almost as costly as gold – furthermore, a Portuguese monopoly, for it was they who had first ventured round the Cape of Good Hope to India. Now Christopher Columbus had located a new route to the spiceries – at least so he related in a letter widely circulated throughout Europe.

Europe waited. But there were no spices. Hopefully, Columbus sailed once more to the Americas and this time, on the return in 1494, the sailors of one of his ships stopped briefly at Naples, then occupied by French troops, and introduced a contagious infection which, under the name of *morbus gallicus,* "the French disease", spread rapidly all over Europe. So there were no spices, no "Joyful News out of the New Founde Worlde", only syphilis. Columbus, who had talked of the gold, rubies and silver

14

("more abundant than in King Solomon's mines"), had only
fed illusions. He refused to admit that he had discovered a
New World, and it was not until 1504, when Amerigo
Vespucci (who had managed the Florentines' affairs in
Seville) himself sailed to Brazil, that he confirmed it as a
Mundus Novus. A German map-maker named it "America".
Europeans became aware that Columbus had not opened
the promised floodgates of plenty; the spiceries were as far
away as ever.

By this time, under the Treaty of Tordesillas, Spain and
Portugal had divided the New World between them. Hence-
forth all other nations were prohibited to trade or explore
America. But even with this monopoly, the opening of
American territory was timorous. The Portuguese set up a
few colonies on the immediate coast of Brazil and the
Spanish settled islands in the Antilles. Española (Santo
Domingo) was made the centre of administration. For the
next twenty years, Spaniards moved cautiously across the
Isthmus of Panama, while other expeditions skirted the
length of the American coastline.

Europe had by now almost forgotten these Americas until
the treasure ship of Hernán Cortés arrived in Spain.
Europeans responded immediately to this first influx of
gold. An anonymous printer released in 1521 a *Neue
Zeitung,* a new newspaper, dealing with the lands called
Yucatán which the Spaniards had found. Two years later,
the first letter of Hernán Cortés was printed by "George
Coci, Alemán", which told how they reached the grand and
marvellous and rich city of Tenochtitlán and the grand lord
named Moctezuma. The second and third letters of Cortés
to his King describing the conquest, with the famous map
of the plan of the city of Mexico, was printed in Nuremberg – the ancestral city of the Welser.

The Welser had already gained considerable experience in
overseas investments. In 1493, for instance, one of their
factors, Bernard Walter of Nuremberg, had organised,
financed and co-operated with King John II of Portugal for

a commercial voyage to Cathay to obtain spices. The German cosmographer, Martin Behaim, had participated as navigator. In 1505, the Welser planned an expedition, equipping three German ships to sail to India under the aegis of the viceroy, Francisco de Alameda. Four years later, they bought land in the Canary Islands where they raised cane and sugar for their European markets.

Yet until the arrival of Cortés and his Mexican gold, the Welser's main contact with the New World had been to procure the bark of a certain guaiacum tree. Now this guaiacum, called by the Welser "Indisches Holz", grew in the West Indies, a tree of hard brownish-green wood which the natives held to be an elixir for all diseases. The Welser secured the tree in quantities through their Seville contacts, and for a time it was a source of considerable trade since it was believed that it was a specific for the cure of syphilis. The Welser even sponsored publications on its efficacy: "A Prescription From the Wood Used To Cure the French Disease". One appeared in 1524 which gave an "approved prescription of a wood that is called guaiacum that grows on the islands of Spagnola . . . which heals all wounds caused by the French disease".

The Welser's theory of business was founded on liquid capital. They dealt chiefly in articles that could be consumed: sugar from their own plantations; spices from Ceylon and India; ginger, pepper, nutmeg, cinnamon, cloves; also linens, cotton, thread, silk, wool and velvets; the guaiacum bark; but rarely in metals, and then only in manufactured products of copper and iron. All this makes it hard to understand how and why they involved themselves in the bankers' lunacy of El Dorado.

Now the Fugger were dedicated Catholics. Despite their great losses of property in Hungary, Spain and the Americas, their close ties to both Church and the Spanish Court were never destroyed. The Welser also adhered to the Catholic faith but with a difference. Among them were some who backed Luther's reforms – an allegiance which

16

made them suspicious in Spanish Catholic eyes. Ulm on the Danube, the Reichsstadt from which they drew many of their agents and *Landknechte,* contained many reformists, all of whom were labelled indiscriminately *luteranos* (equating them with the Turk or Lucifer). This was not a vague theological dispute, a dialectical dialogue; it was earthy and sentient. One of the Welser would lose his head because of it.

At Burgos, on 3 January 1528, the Welser signed the famous contract or *capitulación* which would allow them the governorship of the large slice of American earth now known as Venezuela. The sequence of circumstances is now clearer: the death of Maximilian; the election of Charles V (through the aid of the Welser money); the arrival of Cortés with his golden Aztec treasure as a stimulant; and now the contract to exploit the earth-riches of Venezuela.

The King of Spain did not "sell" to the Welser the recently discovered mainland of Venezuela, as many people have implied; its governorship was given for exploitation as a guarantee of the King's ability to repay the 141,000 ducats, and as an additional security for the one million ducats of credit expected to be provided by them. Both the Welser agents who signed the contract were patricians: Heinrich (Enrique) Ehinger of Constanz (whose father had long managed the Welser interests in Zaragoza) was a member of the Order of Santiago and a *gentilhombre* of the Court, and Hieronymus Sailer, who was born in St. Gallen and had married Felizitas, one of Bartholomew Welser's daughters, and had been ennobled by Charles V three years before in 1525.

The Welser Company was to be subject to the same conditions as those imposed upon Spaniards contracting for the rights of conquest. These were minutely laid down by the Casa de Contratación, a sort of Board of Trade in Seville which handled all such matters. They were allowed to conquer and populate the lands; take the titles of Governor and Captain-General "in Perpetuity"; construct fortifications out of the King's fifth, which was the King's

17

twenty per cent share of all income accruing from the territories; introduce fifty German miners; make slaves of Indians ("should they rebel"); import horses; and, under the "Black Negotiation", they were allowed to bring in four thousand negro slaves over a period of four years. When all this had been duly witnessed, signed and sealed, the Welser expedition set out in its own ships to Española – Santo Domingo.

Since the time of Columbus, this island had been the administrative centre of the Antilles and all other known lands in the Americas. All matters – political, commercial and personal – were expected to go through its various agencies, whence they would be sent off (or not as the Governor-General thought best) to Seville for final solution. So, in 1528, Bartholomew Welser and Company settled in Santo Domingo, set up their organization and factories, and prepared to begin their own conquest of Venezuela.

It was due to this sequence of circumstances that Micer Ambrosius Dalfinger came to Venezuela.

CHAPTER II

Micer Ambrosius

WHEN Ambrosius Dalfinger took over in the name of the Welser ("his masters") the first governorship of Venezuela on 24 February 1529, he did not seem overwhelmed by the vastness of the land that lay before him, principally, perhaps, because its immensity was not yet grasped.

Micer (a hispanicized form of Messire, denoting a man of quality) Ambrosius had accompanied the Welser company (fifty miners, administrators, and one German woman to do the cooking and sewing) to Santo Domingo. The island which was Española to the Spaniards, the first among the new-found lands to be settled (in 1493), was then the administrative centre for the exploration of the New World.

Dalfinger's name (which – like most German names – defied pronunciation in Spanish) was written "Cinger" or "Alfinger" in official documents, and was finally compromised into "Micer Ambrosio". He was a Swabian from the imperial city of Ulm in Germany, a descendant of the *Suevi,* the Germanic tribe that had for centuries terrified

19

ULM an der Donau, Kunstuhr am Rathaus

the Roman legions. Ulm, first mentioned in 854, lay on the Danube at what was then the highest point of river navigation. By 1181 it had become an Imperial City and within 150 years it was one of the foremost imperial cities of the Holy Roman Empire. Its earliest economic strength was derived from iron and brass manufactures, together with textiles. Then came weaving – especially linen and *loden,* which was widely consumed in Spain under the name of *fustanias de Ulm* – to make it one of the greatest commercial cities of the Holy Roman Empire; so much so that it was allowed to mint its own coinage. *Ulmer geld* was widely circulated in trade.

By 1500 Ulm, with its 40,000 population, was one of the most populous cities in Europe, in that sense equalling London. Possessing its own society of knights – the *Ritterbund* – and its own small army of soldiers (armed with spears with convoluted, sharpened points, lovingly called *partisans*), Ulm had a high share of landed nobles many of whom – although impoverished themselves – had married into wealthy patrician families. Certain of the city's destiny, in 1377 the city fathers laid the foundation of what was to be (though taking six centuries to achieve) the loftiest Gothic church spire in Europe.

It was in Ulm that Ambrosius Dalfinger was born in 1500. Like many who advanced socially in those times, the Dalfingers amassed their fortunes as tailors, then branched out into factoring (that is commission merchants) and so entered banking. Among those who financed Sebastian Cabot's voyage in 1526, an enterprise which led to the discovery of Río de la Plata, was the name of Ambrosius Dalfinger. One can appreciate why he was appointed the first governor of the Welser contract. Young, capable, combining a command of the language with his considerable

The sixteenth-century Town Hall at Ulm, birthplace of Ambrosius Dalfinger and Nicolaus Federmann. In 1530, Dalfinger founded the city of Maracaibo on the Gulf of Venezuela, and called the stretch of lowland across the Gulf "Ulma" after his native city.

association with Spain, he was undoubtedly in sympathy with the volatile Iberian character.

The site of Coro, as the first established city in Venezuela, was set at the most northern part of Venezuela, securely tucked into the continent behind the Peninsula of Paraguana, itself thrusting into the Caribbean. This made it safe from the prying eyes of the English pirates, now beginning to appear, and protected it equally from the hurricanes or *chubascos* that periodically lashed the coast. Although it was watered by a small river, the Coro, which rose out of the mountainous hinterland, the immediate littoral was covered with sparse, arid vegetation, dry forests and dominated by fiercely-spined cacti. The coast was almost empty

Silent sand-dunes, typical of the landscape around Coro, the first established city of Venezuela, and the starting point for the journeys of Federmann, Dalfinger and Hohermuth.

of its original inhabitants, the Caquetíos, who once used the coast for fishing and salt-gathering. Many had been seized as slaves for a work force for Santo Domingo, whose original population had already been depleted. Most of those who escaped the slave-raiding had retired deep into the higher, less accessible mountain foothills.

Coro was a small and obviously impoverished place: two score of grass-thatched huts, a *cabildo,* a church and a gibbet, all standard symbols of settlement. Even then, when it had to be surrendered to the Welser (Bélzares, in the Spanish idiom), need it be said that the original settlers did not leave it in good spirit?

In the carrying out of the conquests, in the use or misuse of the native populations, the Casa de Contratación left nothing to chance nor allowed any variations of their ordinances. Located in Seville, it was founded in 1503 to manage all things pertaining to the Americas. It had then three officers – controller, secretary and business manager – and several scriveners. As America developed, so it grew, in time burgeoning into one of the most important offices in Spain. Controlling emigration to the Americas, it drew up all contracts with the conquistadors, and regulated trade. It was a court of law (its jurisdiction extending to everything or everyone connected with American trade), and finally it operated a School of Navigation, a nautical university, one of the greatest centres of mathematical and scientific research in Europe. As such it financed the publication of books on navigation which circulated throughout Europe.

In the founding of cities, it also left nothing to chance, there being a standard and set procedure with printed instructions. A scrivener kept a record of things said and done, and recorded the names of the various office-holders. First, the land was declared to be that of the Crown, dedicated to the service of the King and God. A city was laid out in rigid conformity to these rules; a mayor was appointed; aldermen and a treasurer elected or chosen.

23

Then the priests – for two such must be attached to all new enterprises – sealed everything with prayer.

As for the Indians who were present (usually some survived the first contact), the Royal Notary, by the Law of Burgos, had to read to them the *Requirement.* This opened with a brief sketch of the history of the world as viewed by Christianity. It then discussed the Papacy and its divine right through Christ, from whom the King, through the Pope, derived his legal basis to claim these lands which under the Treaty of Tordesillas had been granted by Pope Alexander VI (may God watch over his soul).

When this folderol had first been explained to one of the chieftains in the earliest days of the conquest, he had inquired how it was possible for anyone to give away lands that did not belong to him. When divine right was again submitted as the reason, he replied, "Then your Pope must have been drunk and your King an idiot."

But this was not at all humorous to the Spaniard. His belief and the convictions of his belief were deeply felt and unassailable. Their century-long conflict with the Moors in Spain and their final triumph under the banner of Christianity endowed them with an unquestioned faith. What they said they believed. The fact that they did not always act their faith was merely one of the contradictions which made man, man. Accordingly, to his understanding, the Papacy had been instituted by Christ in the person of St. Peter and those who succeeded him renewed in the Catholic Kings of Spain the authority of the Crown. It had unimpeachable authority. To all Spaniards it was unthinkable to question it.

This much being said, the Royal Notary at Coro proceeded as elsewhere to the real business at hand. The Indians must now yield themselves to the King and embrace Christianity. Should they do so there would be no hostilities. If not, they were *legally* warned that the newly-arrived would make them submit by a goodly play of blood and iron.

Ambrosius Dalfinger, Governor of the new colony of

24

Coro and founder of its city, must have exhibited his bore-
dom over all these familiar proceedings, for no sooner had
the ink dried on the minutes of the founding of Coro than
Micer Ambrosius mustered one hundred and eighty men of
the original three hundred first arrivals. With one hundred
Indian "volunteers" to carry their impediments, and of
course a monk and his *Requirement,* he set off westward to
obtain – for himself and "his masters" an idea of what the
Welser Company had acquired.

A pigeon in flight from Coro to the shores of Lake
Maracaibo could fly this distance of some sixty-five miles in
less than three hours, but Micer Ambrosius Dalfinger and
his doughty men were not pigeons and the interior was not
the free air. The eastern branch of the Andes lowered itself
to the sea covered with *cejas de la montaña* – "the eyebrows
of the mountains", as one would say in poetical understate-
ment; and it was all ups and downs. Six or more rivers,
flowing from the spurs of the Andes, had to be crossed in
this journey and while there were occasional trade-paths for
Indians who came to fish and to leach salt on the sea, these
were neither continuous nor predictable. In addition, the
littoral of the Caribbean was empty of people. For more
than one thousand, two hundred miles, from the Gulf of
Venezuela to the mouth of the Orinoco, a survey for the
Crown reported the existence of "only two miserable ran-
cherías". Spanish slave-raiders from Santo Domingo Island
had effectively depleted the population; those not taken had
fled into the interior.

The shoreline could be followed from the sea, but in the
interior it was wholly different, for the inland geography of
South America was still vague and shadowy. At first the
Germans thought that the whole of Venezuela was an
island, and almost all the pilots and cosmographers considered it as a group of islands. When, in 1500, navigators
had first sailed into the great inland lake of Maracaibo they
had thought it to be part of an island, an impression streng-
thened by the fact that they found Indian dwellings

25

perched on stilts in the lake. Thus they called it "Little Venice" or "Venezuela", its name in the Spanish diminutive.

On this assumption, the official title of the German official at first read "Governor of the Islands of Venezuela". With this concept still unassailed by geographical facts, the obsession was to find a passage to the Mar del Sur – the southern sea – since it was politically and financially important for the Spanish Crown to find the strait leading to the spiceries. Fernão de Magalhães, called Magellan, had found a way to the Southern Seas, by sailing in 1519 around the southern tip of South America and, though the Germans referred to the passage as the *Magellan-Strasse,* it was neither a street nor an easy sea-way. So the Spanish Crown financed the Genoa-born Sebastian Cabot to find a better route. This he was trying to accomplish in the years 1526–30, even while Micer Ambrosius was making his way toward Lake Maracaibo.

If the geographers could not agree on what was where, and if the King and the King's men had seen nothing of it themselves and derived all their knowledge from their experts, it was inevitable that the grants for conquest overlapped by hundreds or thousands of miles. This was a principal cause of friction in the courts of Spain, and it would take thousands of lives, countless misunderstandings and unending sessions in courts and councils to unravel the complexities of this unknown geography.

Even Amerigo Vespucci was not altogether clear what he had found on his voyage to Brazil, but a German mapmaker, Martin Waldseemüller, using his voyages when making a new globe of the world, included the new-found lands and in 1507 published it with the name of "America". His map shows an uncannily accurate shape of South America, and there is no strait at the Isthmus. Lenox, the English map-maker, who followed with his globe in 1515, depicts the whole of South America as an island, and Leonardo da Vinci, to favour a fellow Italian, drew America like a piece of floating protoplasm.

Diego Ribeiro, drew a remarkable map in 1528 (probably at the behest of the Welser and recently discovered within the ancient binding boards of a book in the Fugger archives at Dillingen) and was a well-known Portuguese cosmographer. Now whether his gross errors were deliberately aimed to aid the Welser in their claim, or were committed in the ignorance that enveloped everyone, the map, nonetheless, is a geographical horror. All distances were foreshortened to such a degree that to any of the conquistadors who used it, the Pacific south sea would seem to have been on the immediate doorstep of Coro, whereas it was about sixteen hundred miles westward, separated by six high ranges of the Andes, four immense rivers (and countless smaller ones) with swamps and jungles.

In the margin the geographer wrote in Spanish: "esta es la gobernación de la gran casa y noble compañía de Bélzares [Welser] hasta el estrecho de tierra de Magellanes" (this is the governorship of the great and noble house of Welser to the strait of Magellan). A mere geographical oversight of four thousand miles.

So in late August 1529, after duly being assured of God's blessing, Micer Ambrosius Dalfinger set off toward Maracaibo.

The precise itinerary was not marked because there was no existing map on which to mark it, but Esteban Martín kept a journal with detailed commentary which was indeed required by all such expeditions.

Esteban Martín, who will figure in all these golden quests to his end, was listed as an interpreter, scrivener and, when needed (which was always), a swordsman. He kept the journal, and eventually prepared for the King's own eyes the *Información de Servicios* of the first journey.

The high-placed Andes are not, of course, limited geographically to the west coast. The cordillera branches off and pushes throughout the north-west to the very edge and length of the Caribbean: the extreme pinnacle of the isolated Sierra Nevada, in full view of the tropical valleys, is

27

eternally snow-bound while cordilleras in Venezuela are almost as high as those in Colombia. Near to the present city of Trujillo, they rise to over sixteen thousand feet with the result that the peaks are snow-capped most of the year. The lower parts of the mountains break up into sweeping plains, in general nearly three thousand feet high. These occur between long sweeps of open grassland and jungles when water intervenes. It was through this daunting terrain that Micer Ambrosius led his hardy followers, a few on horseback, the Indians bending under their heavy loads.

Once away from the coastal area and into the well-watered savannah, Ambrosius Dalfinger clashed at once with the Jirajara. These belligerent people had so far escaped the terrors of slavery, had not yet felt the sword or arquebus, and so were hostile yet curious as to the strange creatures who had invaded their domain. The whole region was inhabited by an almost unbelievable complexity of tribes controlling specific areas – maybe a fertile savannah

Tortuous mountain road in the Cordillera.

or a fish-rich river. And, being intensely human, they were in constant war with each other. The Jirajara occupied what are now the modern Venezuelan provinces of Lara and Trujillo and were divided into various sub-tribes who held the plains and rivers in their territory. Each had a tribal chief, but when a general war broke out, they elected a war chieftain. Weapons were the club, called macana by the Spaniards, and six-foot-long arrows which, shot from long bows, were poisoned; the harpoon-shaped tip was hard to extricate and made gaping wounds in the flesh.

Woman was the agriculturist and manioc, maize, sweet potatoes formed the basic food crops. Maize was made into a boiled soup called "caza" seasoned with chile. Fish, deer, tapir, supplemented the starch diet. Fish were plentiful and were either harpooned with bow and arrow or caught in the mass when the river was poisoned by the rotinone-yielding barbasco root. As yet there were no bananas (America had to wait until Bishop Tomás Berlanga brought them in 1535 from Africa's Guinea coast) nor many fruit trees in the jungle, except those which were planted about Indian settlements. There was little that was edible in the forest except the hearts of *chonta* plants, called "the tree of life" and, let us not be over-delicate, the large grubs of giant beetles that lived within the palm-trunk. These could be eaten raw or fried. For the rest, the expedition lived off what the Indian volunteers carried: flour, rice, beans and salt-pork. When this gave out, they had to rely on whatever the Indians grew: maize and manioc, the hot, biting chile-peppers, and beans, squash, groundnuts and sweet potatoes.

Although all planted pineapples, papaya, and guava fruit about their villages, their agriculture was based on speedy consumption, not on growing surplus to be stored for any length of time. The shrubs on the montaña were plentiful, with tapir which yielded four hundred pounds of fatty flesh, large red deer, flocks of wild pigs, and monkeys. Along the rivers were crocodiles (the tail can be eaten) and long lash-tailed iguanas which, when skinned and prepared,

29

have the distant taste of chicken; in the salt-water estuaries lived the manatee, as large as a small cow, with human-like breasts with which it fed its young.

Houses were grouped about fields. In large villages houses faced each other on opposite sides of a wide street, the street being unpaved earth trampled by bare feet. The house, occupied by those related by immediate blood ties, was rectangular in shape, and thatched with palm leaf or grass. Hammocks were tied to the house posts. Women wove from spun cotton or maguey fibre a garment called a *guayuco*. This was worn long by men and short by women. Bodies were painted red and black, chieftains sported gold earrings and diadems – and also pearls if they were within reach of the sea trade. They smoked cigars and drank the sweet sap of the maguey which, when fermented by the women, became an alcoholic beverage much like the Mexican pulque.

The enmity of the Jirajara was soon apparent and Micer Ambrosius' small army was harassed most of the way through their territory. But sometimes the small wars would break off for trading – Ambrosius' men offering hawks' bells, knives, scissors and other products of Ulm, in exchange for food. The abundance of food depended on the season. Maize yielded two crops a year and was abundant in the autumn month in which they travelled; manioc, a large parsnip-shaped tuber – nourishing when boiled – grew most of the year; the sweet potato has its periods. But a force of one hundred and eighty men trekking twelve hours a day can consume one-quarter of a ton of rations daily and such did not exist in these villages. So death took its toll on both sides and did not abate until they had quit the Jirajara country and penetrated other tribal territory, all of which Esteban Martín methodically noted in his journal.

The Bobure, who occupied the lush plains around the shores of the great Lake Maracaibo, offered less opposition – and also less food, for they lived mostly off fish which they hunted from their dug-out canoes. They were reasonably safe from surprise attack, since their houses were placed on high piles far out into the water. At the town of Bobure (which name is still retained, from this tribe), Micer Ambrosius and his depleted army looked finally upon the great freshwater inland gulf. It had first been seen in 1499 and again in 1500 by Amerigo Vespucci, but it was these soldiers of Coro, under German leadership, who first examined it, sailed over its great length and founded the first colony.

Numerous streams and rivers pour their water into Maracaibo and the largest is the Catatambo river at its extreme southern end which the adventurers reached on 5 September 1529. Of such a size was the Catatambo that Esteban Martín thought it led to the southern sea. Esteban Martín was wrong by about four hundred miles; three enormous rivers and a huge land mass of impassable mountains separated Maracaibo from the Pacific Ocean.

Ambrosius obtained by trade or by seizure a fleet of dug-out canoes from the water people, called the Pemeno, then travelled along the lakeshore for a hundred and ten miles until he reached the brackish narrows. There, on the palm-studded plains, he battled with the Ontos, the native inhabitants, sent them in full retreat to the forested hinterland and, in 1530, founded the city of Maracaibo. Across the narrows, easily seen beyond its seven mile width, spread similar lowlands, fit for European habitation. Micer Ambrosius called it "Ulma" after his native city. This has disappeared yet something is retained, for it is now known as the Camp of Ambrosio.

And there was always gold – not plentiful, but always there: earrings, bracelets, diadems and pins. Either this was bargained for with Ulm-made cutlery or simply taken by force. It amounted to a rather impressive seven thousand pesos of gold, which would be well over one hundred pounds of high-carat metal. Naturally the conquistadors made intensive inquiries to trace its origin, for they saw that the technique of gold-working was beyond the simple technology of these tribes.

31

Esteban Martín extracted the information that the gold came from a people in the high interior who were also rich in green stones, which the Spaniards accurately assumed to be emeralds. They traded for raw cotton for weaving, for coral, pearls, and ornamental shells – especially the great strombus, the huge trumpet shell, which was used by all shamans "to call down the gods". In the interior, then, were a people so abounding with gold that they traded it for goods. Esteban Martín also heard that here the Indians had an animal which resembled a sheep. This was similar to the land which Francisco Pizarro had discovered in Peru the year previously where, along with the mining of gold, the natives reared animals which looked like sheep and were called "llamas".

The Golden Man was being born. Martín exchanged his views with Pedro Limpias, a man who was open to suspicion and who would continue to be prominent in the search for golden phantoms. Nothing said was of a tangible nature. So far it was a small voice, yet a voice which would swell to a siren call, beguiling and beckoning; it would in its vague way lead thousands to their death. "I am convinced," said a historian writing soon after these events, "that it was Pedro Limpias who brought the legend of El Dorado back to the colony at Coro."

After ten months of journey and discovery, time was making Ambrosius Dalfinger its numbering clock. Days, weeks, months had melted into each other and each day was like the one before – walking, often starving, sometimes dying. The only real record of time's flight was Esteban Martín's journal. Thus we learn that it was far into the year 1530 when Dalfinger and his men turned their steps back toward Coro.

In Coro itself, having heard nothing of Micer Ambrosius for almost a year, it was presumed that he and his one hundred and eighty men had perished without trace. When notified, the Welser organization on the Isle of Santo Domingo, a day's sail from the mainland, informed the

Welser in Augsburg, and a new German governor was sent out along with one Nicolaus Federmann. But barely had they been installed in office on 18 April 1530, when Dalfinger's decimated expedition stumbled into Coro. Almost all were half-dead, including Dalfinger himself – fevered, emaciated and hanging on to life only by the call of some golden siren voice. The newly-arrived governor, whose name – Johannes Seissenhofer – so baffled the Spaniards that they simply referred to him as "John, the German," promptly died so that Dalfinger was restored to office. But after naming Nicolaus Federmann in a document dated 30 June 1530 as his Lieutenant-Governor of the Realm, Captain-General of the military forces and *alcalde mayor* – that is, Lord Mayor of Coro – Micer Ambrosius was carried in delirium aboard ship to be taken to Santo Domingo to recover or die.

CHAPTER III

'I, Nicholaus Federmann of Ulm'

For a German he was small,
Yet goodly proportioned and well made.
His speech was fulsome, serious,
Grave of mien,
He seemed to have been born to
*   lead* – Juan de Castellanos

"*I*Nicolaus Federman of Ulm, the younger" was a Swabian with a red beard matching red hair. "Our Barbarossa", the Spanish called him. Young (he was only twenty-four), audacious and ambitious to earn his golden spurs, he was a no-nonsense professional sent out to Coro by "The Welser, My Masters".

This same Federmann was destined to be "one of three" who, unbeknown to each other, were to meet, as we shall see, in the realm of El Dorado. A Renaissance man, skilled in the art of letters and commerce (and the use of a steel-tipped partisan), Federmann was affable enough in his dealings with people, and disliked to be restrained. He had

34

ROUTES OF

- - - - Nicolaus Federmann 1530-1531
• • • • • • Ambrosius Dalfinger 1531-1533
───── Georg Hohermuth 1535-1538

CORO

Guajira

Sierra Nevada

Tocuyo

Valledupar

*Lake
Maracaibo*

CARTAGENA

BARQUISIMETO

Sierra de Perija

Tamalameque

Orino

Cauca

VENEZUELA

COLOMBIA

Meta

• MEDELLIN   Sogamoso •

Tunja •

Zipaquirá •

Guaviare

• **BOGOTA**

Ibagué •

CALI

San Juan de Arma •

• Neiva

Ariari

• San Agustín

Vaupés

coa

lived in Spain, spoke the language and wrote it, and maintained his Spanish friendships. *"Todos con Federmann iban contentos"* (All who went with Federmann were content), said a contemporary of his. There were those prepared to follow him even to hell, which many had occasion to do on his great treks. Agile, perceptive, yet cautious and prudent – especially with men's lives – Federmann's crimes against humanity were no more than the standard procedure of his time and place. He knew he destroyed and often was unhappy over it. Yet how could he have achieved what he did without destroying since life is destruction and we only exist in the dust of the dead?

Federmann wrote, but did not live to see published, his small book *Historia Indiana,* which was the first ethnographic study on the Indians of the hinterlands of northwest Venezuela before they were systematically slaughtered. In the main unknown, he was one of the notable figures of this period of exploration.

Born in 1506 in Ulm, the same imperial city as his compatriot Ambrosius Dalfinger, Federmann was one of its many citizens that followed the Welser banner. The records of the Federmanns of Ulm and in another neighbouring city, Memmingen – also an imperial city – are plenteous enough and there are records of his father, sister, brother-in-law and cousins, but there is nothing in particular about Nicolaus Federmann, – neither birth record nor portrait.

It did him no harm, in the wake of rising Spanish resentment against the religious reformers of Ulm, to have a relative who was an Augustinian friar – Father Alberti (Federmann), who had attended the university at Ingolstadt. There was also the cousin who, a scrivener at the court of Charles V, had translated and published Petrarch in German, and later published (in 1567) *A Description of all the cities of the Low Countries,* in which he mentions that Nicolaus Federmann – "el conquistador" – was his cousin.

Federmann's father ("The Elder") was, as the account books of Ulm show, a business man who owned a grinding mill. He voted in the "Confession of Augsburg" – which, of course, did Nicolaus Federmann no good, since his father voted for the Reformation.

It was appropriate enough that the Welser – "His Masters" – began as weavers. For in the weaving of the tapestry of the Golden Man, the fates made for Federmann skeins of blood-red and luminous gold threads. He alone of all the principal seekers of the Golden Man would leave his own account, an important ethno-geographical survey – the first to be written on the people destined to be destroyed in the search for gold and the Golden Man.

Like other ambitious men of his age, Federmann sought out the place where the action was. This was Venice – then a great entrepôt of spices from the Orient, the centre of vast international trade. The Welser had built their emporium on the Grand Canal, there still to be seen as the Casa dei Tedeschi beside the Rialto Bridge.

From Italy to Spain was but a step, since the Welser – as well as the Fugger – had huge interests in the Iberian Peninsula. In like manner, his knowledge of Italian made Spanish easy, so that it is no surprise to see Nicolaus Federmann at the age of twenty-four proficient in Spanish. He was given the usual contract – exclusive services to Welser Gesellschaft for seven years – and sailed, as he himself wrote, as second in command of a Welser ship from Spain in October 1529. He reached Santo Domingo in December and within days was in Coro.

Nicolaus Federmann had received specific instructions from the fever-stricken Micer Ambrosius and, as already explained, his *poder* of 30 June 1530 named him temporarily Lt-Governor of the Realm, Captain-General of the army and Lord Mayor of Coro – which was, in fact, the whole of Venezuela. Federmann, was to proceed to Lake Maracaibo, re-establish the settlement Dalfinger had founded in 1529 and build up and populate – "*poblar y edificar*" was the precise Spanish wording – the place he had called Ulma. Ambrosius Dalfinger imparted to him also the manner of

37

dealing with the Indians, what to carry as trade goods, how to manage his men. "Ambrosius Dalfinger told me many things about these lands," he wrote.

The one thing Dalfinger did not tell him, nor even "his Master", the Welser, was that in a high place called vaguely the Plain of Jijira (it was then written Xixira) were people who were so rich in gold that they exchanged it for shells, cotton and hard woods with the coastal peoples.

At the age of twenty-six, a Captain-General of the Welser, in a vast, still unknown land, Nicolaus Federmann took his own survey.

The German miners sent out from the German mining centres were useless because there were no mines, as such, to work. Both iron-ore and manganese were found in commercial quantities, but where were the means to exploit them? Venezuela had yielded *palo de brasil* for dye-stuffs, mahogany had been cut, and guaiacum bark for the cure of syphilis had been secured on a commercial scale. This, however, did not justify the vast expenditure of Welser money for men, materials and ships.

There remained the obsession that there must be a waterway leading to the Pacific Ocean which had been discovered by land by Nuñez de Balboa in 1514, sailed into by Magellan in 1519, and now of late (that is 1527) penetrated by Francisco Pizarro and his myrmidons. But of this last there were as yet only rumours. A ship coming from Panama had called for water at Santa Marta, the other colony to the west, and on board was Francisco Pizarro and two Indians, with a modest collection of fine weavings (the quality of which had never previously been seen in the New World), a sizable amount of golden ornaments and several large animals, called llamas, which, because of their superficial resemblance, were called the "sheep of Peru." This Francisco Pizarro was extremely cautious and vague about where his "kingdom of gold" existed, but most suspected that it lay on the *Mar del Sur,* the South Sea. He had sailed south on the Pacific Sea toward the rumoured lands of gold, made a

38

landfall at Tumbes in 1527 (the most northern boundary of the Inca Empire), sailed down the coast, returned, exchanged and bartered Spanish products for gold and weavings, secured two Indians for hostages (in return for leaving two of his own), gathered all this, sailed to Panama, crossed it and raised a passage back to Spain on a departing vessel, which then had stopped in 1528 at Santa Marta to water. He had said no more, for he was on his way to Spain to obtain the confirmation of his discoveries and to return for its conquest. So *Mar del Sur* became the burning preoccupation of all – as Nicolaus Federmann confirmed: "Here was I staying in Coro with too many idle soldiers on my hands. And I decided to travel myself towards the South Seas (Pacific), hoping I could achieve something useful there. So I prepared all that was necessary for such expeditions. I left on 16th September 1530 together with one hundred Spanish foot soldiery and sixteen cavalry."

He struck out south-westward on the first day's march, following the banks of the Coro river through dry forest which presented no problem, and travelling in the area of the Arawak-speaking Caquetíos tribe. These had dominated the entire coast from the peninsula which guarded Coro to Lake Maracaibo, but smallpox had spread with the first white contact, taking a frightful toll of tribal lives. Slave-raiding had also made great inroads. As the result of this dual onslaught, they had retired into the foothills. Yet they had known white men since 1499, acting as the official interpreters on their expeditions, as well as – to use a euphemism – serving as "the transport corps" of all such ventures.

The Caquetíos were farmers, cultivating maize, manioc and sweet potatoes. They evaporated salt from the sea, an important item of trade – since all the inland grain-eaters required it. As well as preparing fish (salted and smoked), they gathered shells – especially the large trumpet shell which was in constant demand by all tribes – and wild cotton and silk-cotton from the kapok-tree. Hardwoods, mostly the black chonta palm, were used for bows and bamboo-like canes for arrows. They made poison for arrows by growing and harvesting the barbasco root which yields a strychnine alkaloid used to stupefy fish in freshwater streams. Tobacco was cultivated.

Their life was simple: houses (usually circular) were built of wood, thatched with palm leaves, with open hearths on which crudely made earthen pots were placed to boil or broil their foods. Hammocks were universal, knives and axes were fashioned in stone until replaced by European metal ones. Warfare with other tribes was seasonal and eternal. Man was polygamous if he had wealth – a certainty if he was a chieftain.

Death was regarded as calamitous. A Caquetío chieftain when dead was subjected to days and nights of lamenting, then his corpse was dessicated over a barbecue, the bones cleaned, ground and the bone powder mixed with a fermented masasto – a corn beverage – and drunk by all. A wooden image of his likeness was carved and his house abandoned.

The Caquetío smoked tobacco in the form of cigars and drank a lightly fermented beer made from the juice of the giant maguey, a drink not unlike Mexican pulque.

Surrounded on all four sides by hostile tribes, they were valiant warriors, possessed gold, and lived in the best valleys. Invited to come in peace, the Federmann and his army proceeded to an area where there were twenty-three villages, roughly one mile apart, which together could command four thousand warriors. Federmann collected 3,000 pesos of pure gold (worth, he adds in an aside for his German readers, "about 5,000 Rheinische Gulden"). He gave in exchange the Ulm manufactures, knives, axes, hoes. The villages were highly fortified, for the Caquetío were enemies of every other tribe about them. In spite of this, they traded with the Xaguas for salt. And although he refrained from enlarging upon it, Federmann observed that war prisoners were first fattened, then killed and eaten.

40

Federmann left the Caquetío and followed on. Within twenty kilometers and three days he and his one hundred soldiers and sixteen cavalry, two monks (needed to carry out the *Requirement* and baptize), and one hundred and fifty cargo-carrying Indians, climbed the 4,500-foot slope of the Sierra de San Luis and arrived among the Jirajaras.

The Jirajaras whom Micer Ambrosius Dalfinger had encountered on his "excursion", preferred the higher region, the cooler lands with pleasant valleys between them. Their knowledge of white men was scanty, but Federmann met with no trouble. Wisely he had warned them of his coming through his interpreter whom he had sent ahead. Therefore, manioc, maize, preserved deer meat and their corn-bever awaited their arrival.

By 23 September, seven days out of Coro and thirty miles distant, they had trekked through the Jirajara country and halted on the fringe of a barren wilderness. It was, wrote Federmann, "a no-man's land and deserted." Before them sprawled the lands of another tribe, the Ayomán – dwarfs "but valiant", against whom the others were in perpetual war. Federmann compelled one hundred and fifty Jirajara to carry his ammunition and supplies across this normally forbidden territory and act as interpreter.

At the first Ayomán village – six large communal houses, called *buhíos* – Federmann made it clear that he came in peace. His troops disturbed nothing, he generously distributed those Ulm-made goods: axes, hoes, knives and a quantity of glass beads "which we," he wrote in an aside, "value little, but here among them are most esteemed."

So day after day, they went from one Ayomán community to another. Learning of their coming, the houses were empty but the occupants had placed in sight supplies of maize, yuca-tubers and sweet potatoes.

Then they met their first opposition, six hundred Ayomán dwarfs, crowded on a hill, blew their conch-shell trumpets, beat drums and shot their arrows at Federmann's small army. He waited until he thought they had exhausted their supplies of arrows, then sent in three Indians with gifts. One of the Franciscan monks (he is not named) accompanied them and read the *Requirement.* The Pope, they were told, was God's vicar on earth. He had raised Charles, king by divine right, and conferred on him all the lands of this American earth. If they submitted to the king (represented by Federmann) and accepted his God, there would be peace. But if they refused, then he (Federmann) "would make war, devastate and burn their houses, take them prisoners together with their women and children and sell them to slave-traders."

Thus the *Requirement.* Yet it had the desired effect. The chieftain submitted, and he and his people (the tallest were no more than five or six spans high) were christened by the monks, and given a sermon on the true God. "But," said Federmann, "what is the use of making long sermons to them and thus lose time . . . obedience and friendship of this tribe . . . as happens in all the Indies, only lasts as long as they cannot do anything about it."

Resistance varied from one village to the other, since all were independent of one another, each with its own chief, except in a general war when one of their numbers was chosen to lead.

On 1 October 1530, one month after leaving Coro and travelling about seventy miles, they reached the Tocuyo river "which flows in a deep and strong current." It originated in the lower heights of the mountains of the Sierra de Barbacoas and gouged a wide, and in places a deep valley before spilling into the sea. When Federmann crossed it with balsa rafts – with the horses swimming freely – he found himself at a place called Carahana, which was the name of the local chieftain. The supplies which they received included game and smoked red-deer meat. Gold was exchanged and Federmann himself was given a female dwarf – "beautiful and well-built and only four spans high, and so this little woman I took back to Coro."

After a five-day march in a southern direction, they

42

passed the last of the Ayománs, reaching Gayón territory where they immediately learnt that all men are each other's enemies. The day was 12 October.

Neither Federmann nor his soldiers, monks, and Indian interpreters could make these people understand the reason for the intrusion into their territory. Federmann, it seems certain from his official and own narrative, tried to avoid violence.

At first the Gayón, like the other tribes, presented them with gold and food. Their tribal lands included Bobaré, now a big town, and further on, Barquisimeto, the present day capital of the Venezuelan province of Bolívar. After the first meeting, Federmann was unable to maintain amicable relations. They were attacked. Seven soldiers were wounded and one was killed, the first soldier to be lost in forty-six days of trekking through unknown country and hostile peoples. "The dead soldier [un-named] was secretly buried, so that the Indios would not discover that we were mortal."

In five days' travel they had not a single peaceful moment. Forty-seven captured Indians, laced together by iron collars and chains, became their "dray animals" and in this manner they came to the Xaguas – a water people.

The Xaguas lived on the borders of the upper reaches of the Cojedes River which, flowing rapidly south-east, would have brought them in time to the Orinoco River.

"The Xaguas," Federmann wrote, "are water-people, live without clothing, more like fish than men. Since they live mostly in the water, one cannot see their pathways. When the water is high they have no fear of being attacked. For the Indios, the journey is only a day and a half by water to their village but for us it took four days with all those horses and equipment."

The Gayóns, chained by their necks, stated that these people ate human flesh and were their bitter enemies. The Xaguas, however, were impressed that the white man could chain their persistent enemies and fled on approach. Those

43

that were captured were given glass beads as presents. All Federmann wanted, he said, was safe passage through their country.

On the morning of 25 October there was a pow-wow at the place they named as Coari. Eight hundred people, both men and women, arrived with their local chieftain, offering gold, deer meat, manioc and maize – and free passage.

By the end of October, they calculated they had travelled only seventy-three miles from Coro (although twice that distance is more realistic). Suddenly they found themselves among the Caquetío again, for this tribe, which dominated the coast, had gradually forced themselves inland. Federmann was delighted to come across a tribe with whom they could speak. "I had," he explained, "only two Christian interpreters and one reliable Indian interpreter, a Caquetío. With the Jirajara I had to make myself understood through two interpreters, with the Ayomán through three, with the Gayón through four, and the Xaguas through five persons. There is no doubt that by the time everybody had understood each other and my message had arrived at the fifth language, something was omitted and something added. Thus, from ten words I had ordered to be said, perhaps not one had remained that was to my liking and conveyed what was required. This was a considerable problem which has brought us very certainly disadvantage regarding knowledge of the country through which we were travelling."

It was here among the Caquetío, where they could be understood, that Federmann wrote: "I heard news of another sea, called South or Midday Sea, which was exactly the one we hoped to find and which was the main reason for our journey. It is said that plenty of gold, pearls and emerald jewels are to be found there. The inhabitants of the villages had told us a lot about this, but they insisted that they themselves had never been to the Midday Sea; they had only heard about it through their forefathers. But we considered this only an excuse, so that they would not have to guide us."

44

The South Sea was, of course, the Pacific, which lay 600 miles or more westward. To reach it, they would have had to cross the high cordilleras, descend to one river system, then cross another, descend and cross the Cauca River, and plunge through an impenetrable jungle of another one hundred miles or so. But Federmann in mistake, was heading toward the Caribbean Atlantic. Such was the human comedy of geographical errors.

More than half of Federmann's men were suffering from sickness. Sixty were so infirm that they could not even ride a horse; the Indians carried them in hammocks. As for himself, he wrote: "I tried not to show how miserable I felt, with sick and defenceless men, who were not really fit for travelling, and amidst people in whose friendship I could no longer trust, if they had seen us weak and sick."

Two hundred Caquetíos acted as pack animals until they reached the Cuiba territory, where they quickly dropped all the impedimenta of conquest and vanished. On a wide, beautiful savannah, dotted with clusters of villages, smoke signals warned the invaders that their presence was known. Maize fields were all about them, and although the corn was not yet ripe, they ate it anyway. Deer, not knowing horses or dogs, were easily run down, yet for the sick to recover, unripened maize and tough deer meat were not the ideal diet.

Using the towering corn as a cover – for it was so high horses could not be seen moving in it – Federmann attacked with cavalry and foot soldiers, killing fifty Indians and capturing sixty more. But it was a dubious victory: for the first time four of the soldiers had been struck with poison arrows – a Cuiba speciality.

It was only when they surrounded and laid siege to one of the fortress communal houses that the Cuibas agreed to parley. The prisoners were returned, and the usual German-made geegaws were ceremoniously given and received: hawks' bells, knives and glass rosaries bartered for valuable golden ornaments and (what was then more precious) food.

45

Federmann reveals that: "During the nine days which we stayed in the village, several chieftains came bearing gifts and the time spent there gave us a chance to study their customs and habits which would be an advantage as we continued our journey. The illness continued since we had not the proper food to bring back strength to those who had been weakened by the sickness. But anyway, we started off to reach the South Sea, which I believed could not be far away."

"On December 15th, 1530," still going southward, still searching for the way to the South Sea, they "reached the large village of the tribe *Acarigua*." A modern city of the same name, the high area around the source of many rivers which flow south-east into the treeless *llanos*, still commands the view as seen by Federmann four hundred and forty years ago. Then, in Acarigua, there were over sixteen thousand Indians. Though they provided the now familiar triad of Christian progress – gold, deer meat and food – Federmann issued the command to move on, since two more of his men had died from the effect of poison arrows. Ironically, here it was that the Christians were asked to demonstrate *their* friendliness by aiding their Indian hosts to make war on another tribe. Federmann reluctantly agreed. Villages were gutted, many people were even burned alive in their houses. On both sides the slaughter of Indians was immense. The Spanish loss was also grievous. Federmann recorded the toll: "Two of my soldiers were killed, fifteen wounded, one horse wounded by a poison arrow died eight days later . . . although I regretted it, there was nothing to be done about it."

In the same month and year, January 1531, that Francisco Pizarro, with his assembled hosts of ships, men and horses, was sailing out of Panama on the Pacific to again reach Peru, on 3 January 1531, Federmann wrote: "I, Nicolaus Federmann, commanded that they continue our journey towards the South Sea, following the way the Indios had indicated to us.

46

"We travelled through the territory of the Cuiba, as the Gayón, the inhabitants, said that within three days we could reach a *pueblo* from where one could see the South Sea. So I sent five men on horseback and twenty-five on foot to go to the village, *Itabana,* if they could get there unhindered."

It is no longer possible to follow precisely this horrifying journey. The Indians at Itabana, who were of the Guaycari tribe, and whose tribal territories were twenty-five miles from the sea, were separated from it by two days' walking distance and ruthless enemies.

"On the third day," Federmann related, "my men reached a large river which separated this tribe from the next, called Guaycario and there the country of our friends ended.

"They told my men that other men had already come by, who were dressed like us and had beards just like us. These men had travelled to Itabana near the South Sea and they had sailed on the Sea with a '*big house*'. So we thought this might have been Sebastian Cabot and his men who, three years ago, had explored the Río de Solis[1], that is the Río de la Plata. He had come on a ship which apparently the Indio mistook for a big house. He had travelled about three hundred miles inland. In all probability the area that Cabot had conquered was situated towards south, near Venezuela. Upon hearing his news, we were very glad and hoped to meet the other Christians, for this would have been of help to us. Then we might get information concerning the South Sea, the habits and secrets of the country and its inhabitants. Or, if they were in trouble and had been stranded by adverse winds, we could help them. In either case, we both would increase our manpower."

Sebastian Cabot had already explored by 1529 the Río de la Plata which was, if one used a straight line of measurement, four thousand miles away. It is quite possible that he sailed along the Venezuelan coast, landed at places, and that his ships and men had been seen.

By 23 January, Federmann was trying to quicken their movements down the river to the "Midday Sea". Once more new territory, once more a different tribe – this time the Atacari, who dyeing their bodies black and living near the rivers, "held trade-markets near the water." They ruled the rivers and held the fishing rights and the chieftain, probably named Atacari, "was a large man, blackly painted and he was very haughty."

In order to travel through swamps, Federmann decided to leave the halt and the lame behind and take only the fit. Therefore, with only thirty men on foot, eight mounted, and two hundred carriers he went through village after village. "All were armed and unfriendly," but when he reached Itabana, they were given "fish and manioc bread in abundance."

Describing his conversation with an Indian, Federmann observed: "I told him that I had come to join my companions (Sebastian Cabot) who had come out of the sea in a 'house', who had been there some days before. He pretended not to understand, nor would he admit that such people who looked like us, like Christians, had been there before. They said they trade with the Guayacari who live on the shore of the sea, two days' journey from where they now were. While we were talking about the sea or lagoon or whatever it was that was supposed to be visible from Itabana, we heard a cock crowing and the clucking of hens. Now we had not seen or heard chickens since we left Coro, because the Indios did not have chickens originally. When I asked how he got those chickens, he said that he got them from the people of Hamadoa, and they had bought them from the Christians."

The Indians assured him that the sea was only four miles away but that there were no roads, no footpaths; they would have to travel by *canoa* ("as they call their boats").

"Upon hearing this, I wondered whether it was the sea or a lake that Sebastian Cabot had discovered. The Indios would supply no further information except that the body of water was fresh and sweet; further that from their mountains they could only see water. There was no land; it was all marsh and rivers."

At last Nicolaus Federmann was convinced that what they had sought after all was only a phantom of Sebastian Cabot and the South Sea. So he moved back, gathered his men and crossed to the other side of the river from where the Indian villages were located. When seen, they were showered with arrows, some over six feet long, with harpoon ends dipped in poison. Under a covering fire of arrows, many of the Indians, painted red and black, swam across the river; it was then that Federmann ordered the cross-bowmen into close engagement. "They created havoc among them," for a bolt from a cross-bow leaves a gaping wound through which an arm can be passed. As suddenly as it began, so it ended. "We must have killed the chieftain, for when they lose their leader, they feel lost, and fighting comes to an end."

Among themselves, only four were not wounded, Federmann had been hit in the shoulder, and a horse struck by a poison arrow died after six days. From that day onward, all through the month of February 1531, it was attack, plunder, retreat – the very reverse of what Federmann had sought. "The tertiary ague" (malaria) was upon him too. "And I wanted rest, to recover from the fever which made me shiver hot and cold." When they eventually reached it, they were welcomed in Acarigua where they had rested before and there, after a council, it was decided that they would move back to Coro. The date was 27 February 1531.

They passed again through Barquisimeto, reached and passed the upper reaches of the Río Tocuyo and entered again the province of the Coquetíos.

"Their villages are large," Federmann recorded, "but usually one or two small streets broad. In one house live five to eight families with women and children. These Indios were well-built, tall and strong, their women were beautiful and therefore we called it the Valley of the Women.

"So we travelled from one village to another. My fever was so heavy that I could hardly sit on my horse. So we went on and on, until we came to the last village of the Coquetíos. There were occasional fights along the way and I had to order my soldiers to stab a chieftain who would have run away and raised the alarm in the other villages against us."

After leaving the familiar villages of the Coquetíos, they had experienced the "unfriendliness" of the Ciparicoto – unfriendliness being a euphemism for independence and a refusal to furnish food, sustenance, carriers or women to intruders. This small mountain tribe lay between them and the partially subdued Coquetíos. It was vast, uneven land full of up-going and down-going, crossing and recrossing the same stream many times, of horses falling and being entangled in liana vines, with sporadic attacks by poison-dipped arrows. At one village which they besieged, the Indians defended themselves inside a high storage place called a *barbacoa.* "It collapsed and the Indios fell down. I protected myself with my shield and tried to stab an Indio with my sword. But he hit me so hard with a *macana* (as they called their wooden swords) that he damaged my shield. I tried to pierce him again, but he had noticed the damage done to it, so I could not cover myself sufficiently. The Indio hit me on my head; I fell to the ground and would have lost my life, had not one of my men come to my help and killed the Indio. I was unconscious for two hours."

Then, to worsen matters, when crossing the Sierra de Arroa, the Indian guides led them astray, deserted them and they were lost. One of them climbed a tree, observed that before them lay a large savannah, to which they tortuously made their way. Federmann learnt in those last days that a man's worst enemy was his empty stomach. Everyone was ravenous. The dogs, equally so, cornered a large jaguar. It had already killed two of the dogs, when a Franciscan monk ("whose job," says Federmann, "was to give out the *Requirement*") tried to kill it with a lance. But it was only wounded. Fortunately for the monk, in springing the jaguar caught itself in some lianas which trailed from the trees like so much rope. On being despatched, it took six men to lay the animal across a horse which was almost too weak to carry it. So the army that set out to look for the southern sea, moved down to the plains, quenched their hot throats at a stream and began to eat the jaguar.

"The meat had a strong smell," Federmann describes, "but we were so hungry we could have eaten anything. Although the jaguar was the size of a six-month-old calf, there were so many of us there, with the Indios, that each got as his share of the jaguar a piece no larger than two walnuts."

The jaguar meat failed to transmit the animal's strength to the conquistadors, who were on the verge of collapse when they entered a deserted village, where the inhabitants in their precipitous flight had left food behind.

"After two days' rest we continued on toward Coro. It took us almost a whole day to go two miles, which shows how slowly we proceeded.

"We reached another village. It was deserted, but they had left food behind in abundance, so we rested and ate for four days. I knew if we had had to go one more day without food or water, very few of us would have reached Coro. At last we found three Indios. One of them knew the *Caquetío* tongue and he said that we were only five days' journey from the Caribbean sea. They gave us gold and we released the prisoners.

"March 12th was the final step of the journey home to Coro; we had left the mountains and were on the plains leading to the sea. Those Indios who had lived near to the coast had experienced the slave-ships, Christians who came from Santo Domingo and other islands (in the Caribbean). Further on, as we marched to Coro, I sent Indios in a *canoa,* which they call their dug-out boats, by sea to Coro to inform the governor, Ambrosius Dalfinger, who must by now have been brought back to health and returned from Santo Domingo.

"On March 17th, 1531, we returned to Coro."

While recovering from the horrors of the year's journey, Federmann dictated the details of the journey "taken down by the *escribano público,* the public notary. His Majesty then ordered that it should be written in a true account. From this report, I translated a shorter version into German."[2]

NOTE: Distance and altitudes are based on the American Geographical Society's 1:1,000,000 map. Indian names and tribal boundaries are based on the accepted nomenclature as given in *Handbook of South American Indians* (Washington 1948, vol. 4, The Circum-Caribbean Tribes).

[1] Called Río Solis because it had first been entered by Juan de Solis. It was later called Río de la Plata.

[2] In 1556, ten years after his death, his brother-in-law, Hans Kiefhaber, who married his sister Elisabeth, edited and had printed *Indianische Historia* in 1557. This fore-shortened version of *Indianische Historia, Eine Schöne kurtz-weilige Historia, Nicolaus Federmann des Jüngers von Ulm* . . . Hagenau MDLVII (1557) is here translated by the present author for the first time into English from the German original.

CHAPTER IV

The Golden Quest of Micer Ambrosius

Nach Golde drängt
Am Golde hängt
Doch Alles

(Once After the Golden Urge
Everything then hangs on Gold) – Goethe

WHEN Micer Ambrosius Dalfinger, Lt-General of the Venezuela Realm, returned on 27 January 1531, healthy and robust after his six months' sojourn in Santo Domingo, it was only to be told that his principal captain, Nicolaus Federmann, without permission, and disregarding his instructions, had gone off with one hundred men. Dalfinger was understandably outraged and thrown into a Swabian fury. The note that he received in March that Federmann's expedition was returning with only a loss of ten men did nothing to calm his anger. An inquiry was set up, people gave their accounts and Federmann wrote his report, but it did nothing to alleviate his brazen flouting of orders. Dalfinger ordered him to leave the Welserian Realm and not return for four years.

Even though he had already experienced the Dantesque horrors of search and had heard from Federmann's survivors their own horrendous narratives Ambrosius Dalfinger was not to be diverted. He had heard of the place called "Xerará", where Indians were so rich in gold that they traded it for lesser things. This information he had not even disclosed to the Welser.

Dalfinger was also officially encouraged by the Royal Audience: "We entertain the hope that the governor of Venezuela, who more than one year and a half ago explored behind the jurisdiction of Santa Marta, will now continue to *search for the other sea,* and should he survive, discover much new land."

Now in the interval between Dalfinger's first expedition in 1529 and the present year of 1531 the talk of golden kingdoms to the south had taken on a certain reality.

Francisco Pizarro had landed at Santa Marta in 1528 and rumours had spread. Upon his return to Spain, Pizarro had followed Charles V from court to court, for three long years (between 1528 and 1531) to petition the Crown for the official powers to conquer the new "Peru". Wherever he went his hampers of gold and silver ornaments went with him, and the superb weavings of vicuna cloth "such a quality unseen in Spain" and three live llamas gave additional reality to Europe's obsession with "an earthly paradise". A Fugger News Letter had informed its agents of Pizarro's arrival. The Welser staff heard of it too and confirmed it. Suddenly their holdings in the Americas took on a renewed activity.

The dream of an earthly paradise had long taken hold of the European mind. The people read with avidity those booklets of Columbus wherein he spoke of the gentleness of the natives, wild birds (such as the riotously feathered macaw that lived freely in the houses), barkless dogs, of an

54

island inhabited only by women, of people who drank from golden cups, and where one picked up diamonds in the streets. Soon all this would become in turn a New World, Golden Kingdoms, El Dorado, the Golden Man, the seven cities of Cíbola, founded by the seven Portuguese bishops who had fled before the Arab invasion of the Iberian Peninsula. "America as fantasy" summed up a dream, a wish nursed by low-born Europeans who had only in recent memory lifted themselves from social misery and desired to rise above the eternal struggle around the human feeding trough.

Sir Thomas More had called that wish "Utopia". A man of the New Learning, who rose to be Lord Chancellor of England before Henry VIII deprived him of his head, More had published in 1517 his picture of an ideal state. Man had often dreamed of such a society. Was it now, in the year 1528, really within reach? "Tell us," it read, "in what part of the New World is Utopia situated?" The answer: "Which fetching about a circuit or compass of 500 miles do fashion the whole island like to the new moon?" To the conquistadors Venezuela, then, was believed to be an island. "There is a great rock", said More, meaning the Andes. "Upon the top of this rock is a fair and strong tower which they hold with a garrison of men . . . there is no household or farm in the country hath fewer than forty persons." He added: "Husbandry is a science common to them in general . . . and clothworking". This must be Utopia, the Golden City. Madness, but not quite. Just about the time when sensible men were mocking these myths, Pizarro turned up and gave substance to them with fantastic amounts of golden treasure.

In every age, humanity has always had a certain amount of folly and dullness to spend. It is a capital that is bound to bear interest in one way or another. The great thing to know is whether after all, the imbecilities that time has consecrated do not form the best investment a man can make of his own gullibility. So in time, the Golden Man would become transmogrified into a Golden City – a "land of gold and plenty".

Men had searched for the Golden Fleece and the Holy Grail. Whole peoples had been enraptured by some aspect of myths and gods. The Aztecs were actually able to coax war prisoners into waiting in long lines, each to have his heart torn out of his living body and be offered to the Gods, for which nourishment they would graciously allow the world to continue to exist.

With such rumours in his ears, Micer Ambrosius Dalfinger prepared for his golden journey. Many of those who had accompanied him before volunteered to go again – among them Pedro Limpias. The forewarning of the privations and dangers of jungle and Indians that they faced were muted by golden visions, since all expeditions had always brought back gold in some quantity. Esteban Martín, the nimble-witted interpreter of Indian languages, and a superb swordsman, who had kept the journal of Dalfinger's first expedition and who was now given the title of captain, signed on. There were also a collection of new faces, in fact many who were not familiar with the New World. Johannes Kasimir of Nuremberg (whom the Spanish called Juan de Casimires) had been chosen next in line of command after Dalfinger. These novices were christened *chapetones* by the veterans – in a word, "tender-feet". Many were so young that they reached their majority only in death.

At the first stirring of dawn on 9 June 1531, Micer Ambrosius Dalfinger formed his soldiers – one hundred and thirty on foot and forty mounted – into three companies under three commanders, and made straight for Lake Maracaibo. Carrying immense supplies were hundreds of Indians. After camping near a settlement which is marked on modern maps as Campo de Ambrosio, they were transported by canoes across more than six miles of water to the settlement of Maracaibo which Dalfinger had founded during his first expedition.

By the first day of September, with new Indian carriers, those of the Pemenos who had submitted to the *Requirement* – that is they had gone through the ceremony of christianization, and so did not impede the conquistadors but even supplied carriers on demand – Ambrosius Dalfinger's army of conquest had moved up to the Socuy river, which emptied into the Maracaibo, and began a descent by it to the montaña de Oca. First their path was through riverine vegetation, high grass, tall, feathery guaduas, a bamboo-like cane. This gave way to jungle and thus they mounted the ridges of Oca. The way was thickly matted with scrubby bush and cactus. After the highest ridge was reached at about 2,400 feet, there began the descent into the warmer valley. Brushing aside at times minor opposition from the local inhabitants, the small army – alternately hauling and hacking fought through a succession of landscapes. Always before them, rearing its white-thatched crown into the blue pellucid sky, was the snowy peak of the Sierra Nevada of Santa Marta. Perennially snow-capped, the utmost ridge was over 16,000 feet in height.

Once the passage had been effected, they moved down into the serenely lovely Valledupar, a valley created by the brawling rivers that poured down from the glaciers of the Sierra Nevada. They were not the first to be there. Francisco César, a man of skill and magnaminity, had led his myrmidons there some years before, discovered the river and had died and been buried by the river which bore his name. Then, as now, it was the Río César. Along it Micer Ambrosius Dalfinger and his small company, keeping in good discipline, followed it in its south-western course. It is natural that such a fertile, beautiful valley would be peopled and it was equally inevitable that there would be conflict. Esteban Martín, who again kept the journal and would emerge as the historian to this second expedition of Dalfinger's, affirmed that in some places the Indians were friendly and offered them gold and food; in other areas they were attacked. Although they were all grouped gener-

Tree-ferns and a strangler figtree, typical growth of the montaña.

ally as "brown and noisy", each tribal village reacted to past experience. They had been visited two years before by the "Men of Santa Marta", people from a rival colony – Santa Marta – lying at the Caribbean base of the Sierra de Santa Marta. Already the *disjecta membra* of conquest – discarded shoes, spurs, rusted breast plates and broken helments – marked the trails.

Dalfinger's people traded for or else seized food along the way. There was maize, when it was harvested, and *yuca* – that long thickish parsnip-shaped tuber which had almost a continuous growing season – was in plentitude, along with ground-nuts and potatoes. But one hundred and seventy ravenous men will consume the entire surplus of a village within days and the Indians themselves were often on the thin borderline of hunger.

Following the banks of that River César, they entered extensive grasslands and came upon large populations containing as many as one hundred *bohios* – that is, communal houses. These were the *Chiri,* after whom the present-day town of Chiriguana is named. They painted their faces, arms, and legs, wore cotton garments, draped like a Renaissance nightgown. Their nose-septa were pierced and through them small, crescent-shaped gold ornaments were inserted. Women wore necklace-amulets, in which there were small golden *chaquiras* (beads) and bracelets of green stones. The invaders had sharp, brief encounters, in which, when they occurred on the flat land, the horsemen held their lances short so that the Indians could not seize them and aimed at their faces; the infantry made good play with the long sword. Battles were short, effective and final. The Indians made their peace, and the Spaniards dressed their wounds from the rendered fat of Indians slain in battle.

It was here on the riverine plains, bordering the great river, that the word and place Jerira (or Xerira, as they wrote it then, for *x* and *j* had the same aspirant value) was heard again. This was the word and place that Ambrosius Dalfinger had heard from the Maracaibo tribes, who by

59

indirect trade received golden ornaments in barter for tropical produce. The exact locality was vague, except that it lay south in the higher reaches of land. Even though words had to go through a triple cascade of interpreters, out of it all Esteban Martín made geographical sense: and it was this. Somewhere in the mountains lived a people rich with gold, who sent down salt, gold and painted cotton cloth and a green fire-stone valued by all. They indicated that these people were rich in gold. Once more they heard that which was told them elsewhere – *that where the salt comes from, comes gold.*

With no idea of the immensity of distances involved, no knowledge of the language which changed from tribe to tribe, with Indians at war with one another and purposely giving misinformation, and without maps, they went by blind reckoning, as if without compass on the sea.

Micer Ambrosius Dalfinger, like most of the conquistadors, was a man of action. He reckoned the great part that fortune played, well knowing that all great enterprises are uncertain. He became an expert in the calculation of probabilities, learning to seize such chances as came his way without wearing out his patience.

The small army, following the scent "where the salt comes from", now spread out along the flattened landscape, following the César river until it flowed into an immense lagoon called Zapatosa. Marsh birds – ghostly white egrets, blue herons, low-flying kingfishers, roseate spoon-bills, scarlet-legged flamingoes – filled the air, while the unseen frogs raised a din throughout day and night like the hammering of an arms factory in Toledo. Sea cows, large-size mammals with small whiskered faces, munched the freshwater blue-flowered hyacinths, while along the firm ground of the lagoon, sun-seeking crocodiles lay in such number that they became more dangerous than the *Macoco* tribe which claimed the land about the lagoon.

Another day's march – they were now in their ninth month out of Coro – and they came to the banks of an

immensely wide river. It was called Yuma, but the Spaniards promptly renamed it "Magdalena". The gargantuan
river flowed the entire length of Colombia, gathering in
rivers, rills and streams until, in almost Amazon-like proportions, it flowed into the Caribbean Sea.

Micer Ambrosius' army, now considerably depleted of
soldiers and carriers, moved along the banks of the Yuma-
Magdalena, led on by the rumours that they were approaching a rich area. In this manner they came upon the ancient
trading centre of Tamalameque. Here trade lines met:
riverine and land. It was a huge market where various
tribes, internecine battle put aside, could trade peacefully.
The Spaniards bartered their gewgaws – glass beads (a
peculiar ceramic bead made in Prague in various colours),
knives, iron hoes, cotton thread (a Welser speciality) – and
in return they received foodstuffs.

At the place which Micer Ambrosius called "Pauxoto", he
decided to send back to Coro the seriously wounded and the
halt with orders to send additional reinforcements; he also
resolved to send back his golden booty taken on the way.
The Spanish accountant, Antonio de Navaro, noted carefully all the gold that was collected: ["mil setecientos y
veintitres . . ."] – "one thousand seven hundred and
twenty-three ornaments, large and small; one thousand earrings in gold filigree; two thousand, three hundred and
twenty brooches; one thousand, five hundred and three
neck ornaments; thirteen grams of gold arm bracelets; sixteen figures of eagles; four pieces called *cemies;* a golden
head of an eagle; nine golden figures of male Indians; five
figures of women in fine gold; a great head-shaped cemi
enveloping a great emerald diadem". The whole of this vast
collection of golden pendants, labrets, calf bands, arm
bands, necklaces, brassards – an amount of gold of one
hundred and ten kilos – was large in any period or epoch.
Out of it was to come the King's fifth – that is, 20 per cent
– the rest was to be divided among captains and men.

The man chosen to return to Coro with this golden booty

61

was Capitán Íñigo de Vascuña who was accompanied by twenty-eight men, including the brother of the historian-warrior, Francisco Martín. He was to be the only survivor. The Capitán insisted on taking a new route. His men perished one by one. In the end, the one hundred and ten kilos of gold was buried under a large ceiba tree. Then the Capitán died. Weeks later, Francisco Martín stumbled into Coro. He was, it was said, so emaciated that "every bone in his body could be counted."

Meanwhile, Micer Ambrosius waited. Almost a year had passed since his expedition had left Coro. Another golden booty was piling up, but in direct relation to this the spirits of the survivors were going down. Gold fever supplies a great deal of patience, for – as the poet said – "everything hangs on gold". However, on 24 June 1532, as Esteban Martín noted in his journal, he was selected with another small group to go back to Coro, bring supplies, and additional men who were to include carpenters with their tools and nails so as to build a brigantine to navigate up the great river; for Micer Ambrosius Dalfinger believed that its source led to the south, to the golden kingdoms of Francisco Pizarro. In the shortest time conceivable when one considers that Esteban Martín travelled over heights and through jungle and marsh, he was in Coro where the men were assembled and he was on his way back.

While waiting in Tamalameque for the reinforcements to arrive, Dalfinger's men, scouring the countryside for food, always came back with the same rumours; where the salt came from, there was the gold. They often saw at the trading centre the small baskets which held fine-grained, dazzling white salt. So, when Esteban Martín returned in July with eighty-two reinforcements, additional Indian carriers and new supplies of food and trading materials, Ambrosius Dalfinger ordered that they turn inward from the great Yuma river and follow the salt train onward and upward.

The Pemeno tribe, which held the territory around the

trade centre of Tamalameque, used a trail, which went into the foothills and then into the high country. This trail, moving generally in a west-north-west direction, was taken by Micer Ambrosius' army. "We went upward," Esteban Martín noted in his journal, "along the River of the Río de la Pemenos."

Now they were among a belligerent tribe living at over 8,000 feet. As all else, they were agriculturists in off moments, warriors at all moments. They were also anthropophagous; their houses were strewn with the grisly remains of human bodies.

Death was now in constant attendance. In the hotlands it came mostly with malaria and the tertiary ague which alternately chilled and fevered; the bites of deer flies, mosquitoes, ants, blood-sucking vampire bats, the sweat fly (shaped like a bee and living off sweat exudation and blood) and the *jején* (so small as to be able to pass through a needle's eye and yet with a sting like the thrust of a needle). Now as the land rose in vast terraces from the hotlands into the temperate lands, the *nigua* appeared. A sand flea that lays its eggs in the toes of animal and man, this parasite could incapacitate even the strongest. The Spanish soldier-poet, Castellanos, remembers them as: "Minutest fleas that inward drilling, Bury themselves 'twixt skins and flesh, Where feeding on the fat they grow, And wax should they be overlooked, Until they are as large as peas, They go spreading through the toes, Multiplying their generations." Then, they were beset by yellow fever, which brings the black vomit and was always fatal. Another fever, the *verrugas*, carried by a fly sting, left the body covered with suppurating wounds, horrible to behold and usually fatal and then almost every soldier who had lain with an Indian woman became infected with love's residual host – syphilis.

As they gained altitude, following the spurs of the *cordilleras*, it grew cold. Indians died or deserted, food became scarce, and horses died or were eaten. They were

63

fortunate if they were able to climb eight miles a day. Time and distance were replaced by hunger and death's ennui. The Río de Oro was passed, where Indians offered them small pellets of raw gold washed. Always they climbed.

In the high mesetas, above 8,000 feet, where Indians cultivated corn and potatoes and other tubers, the Indians gave battle. They had been harassing Micer Ambrosius for days, killing stragglers, waylaying horses; now they felt strong enough to meet the Spaniards in pitched battle. They were dressed in long cotton garments and the principal weapons were long chota-wood spears and arrows which were dipped in poison. Having disposed of them, Micer Ambrosius' people came to a vast, high (it was over 12,000 feet), unpopulated area – the *páramos* of *Cháchira*. There, in the raw cold, with biting winds, they suffered such misery and hunger that on the edge of the treeless plains, they killed a horse and ate it ["Even," as Esteban Martín recorded, "eating its hide, its hooves, and its entrails"].

A European's idea of the Indians searching for gold. These are pictured in Florida. (Mary Evans Picture Library)

Micer Ambrosius, aware that they could no longer go southward, ordered that the line of march be changed eastward. In shaping their path eastward, they were forced to climb to the pass of Cháchira, which led across the high, frigid, windswept prairies. At twelve thousand feet, there was a vast stretch of upland. Mists swirled around the tall tussock grass, and in places the bare, bleak, treeless land was swampy. At that time, it was covered with snow. ["And we were," declared Esteban Martín, "almost all ice and icicles."] As each Indian died, he was decapitated from the iron collar.

In the cold, driving hail, eight soldiers died, one being the German, Johannes Kasimir of Nuremberg; also, one hundred and five Indians. There was no longer any need for the long continuous chain of iron collars, so it was left behind, as well as much powder and ball, for there were now no Indians left to carry; those who survived could just about carry themselves. Having crossed the *páramo,* they descended rapidly – that is, 13,000 feet downward in three days – to the forest, followed the River Zulia, close to where the city of Cucuta now stands, then turned southeast, hoping to reach the place called Tibu, where "the three rivers meet". The down-going was slow and difficult until they came to the flat *llanos.* There they found Indians growing maize and there they stayed for days, eating and resting – and fighting – for the Indians attacked every day.

Two years, 1531 to 1533, had gone by. Time was marked only by Esteban Martín in his diary, which he kept up by some inner strength. He was worried about the great loss of time, and Micer Ambrosius too was anxious to push on quickly towards Lake Maracaibo, so he separated himself with a few others from the main party.

When they came up to thickening vegetation which signalled a river, they were attacked on all sides. Martín was hit in the hand by a poisoned arrow. Ambrosius Dalfinger was struck in the throat. The arrow was cut out, the wound sucked and cauterized with a heated knife; human grease rendered from a dead Indian was put on it. After two days' rest the march toward Maracaibo was continued.

Curare, this poison, is prepared from roots of plants containing strychnine, which is boiled until the substance becomes black and viscous; it is then smeared on an arrow or spear. A small animal struck with a curare-tipped arrow can die in a half-hour, a horse in eight days, a man in ......? The poison in Ambrosius Dalfinger's bloodstream was slow-acting; it took longer to begin to break down the blood – "curdling it," as Martín wrote. So at the same time that Hernando Pizarro, brother of Francisco, the conqueror of the Incas, was en route to Spain with the great golden treasure, which had been taken as ransom from the last great Inca, Micer Ambrosius Dalfinger was dying, brought on by a sickness which, as the Spaniards say, "is only curable with gold".

Having buried the founder of Coro, New Ulm, and Maracaibo under the roots of a ceiba tree, the survivors

The ceiba or West Indian cotton tree (God tree) under which one hundred and ten kilos of gold treasure were buried by Íñigo de Vascuña on his fateful return to Coro. Ceibas marked the burial grounds of at least two leaders of expeditions, Micer Ambrosius Dalfinger and Capitán Francisco César. (Nicholas Guppy)

pushed on. What was left of the expedition that set out with golden visions stumbled into Coro on 2 November 1533. They had been gone precisely two years and three months.

There were only thirty-five survivors.

CHAPTER V

Man from Speyer

*Georg Formut, as we called him, was a
man of great strength, and of lofty heart
and courage.*

THE death of Micer Ambrosius Dalfinger in 1533 may have given the Welser in Augsburg momentary pause in their plan, but pause – if there was one – and no more. While they may have pondered over the costs of their American venture and wondered if the riches of these unknown lands were after all illusory, this doubt was dissipated in January 1534.

On that date, 9 January 1534, the galleon *Santa María del Campo,* sailing out of Panama, wharfed in Seville. On board were millions of pesos-weight of gold and silver bullion with countless golden artifacts, jewel-studded and artfully cast, the ransome of the Inca Atahualpa. "I remember seeing the rich pieces of gold," wrote Pedro de Cieza, when a young boy of thirteen, "that I saw in Seville brought from Peru where the treasure of the Lord Inca Atahualpa had been collected."

The Fugger agents in Seville also saw it and were quick to send out one of their famous News Letters and another one called the *Lettre de Pizarro* which was published in Lyons in 1534 entitled *Nouvelles de certaines Isles du Peru.* The Welser also knew of the golden treasures of Peru. The response was immediate. A new expedition would be sent out to their colonies of Venezuela.

The new Welser man, Georg Hohermuth of Speyer-am-Rhein – "a man of honourable disposition" – was selected to replace the late and lamentably defunct Micer Ambrosius.

Hohermuth, whose name with such a rush of aspirates was repugnant to all ears attuned to Spanish and beyond the Spanish tongue, was called at first "Formut", then Jorge de Espira, that being their equivalent for Speyer, and further transmuted by the English into George of Spires. As such, the second Governor of Venezuela, Georg Hohermuth, entered history.

Speyer-am-Rhein, a river port on the left bank in the Rheinpfalz, had started as a Celtic settlement. It was taken over by the Romans in the time of Augustus and refounded as "Noviomagus". It had been destroyed by the Huns, recovered, and entered the Middle Ages as a prosperous community, and was made in the year 1111 an Imperial city. In the fifteen hundreds, as the Hohermuths enter our story, it was the capital of the Rheinpfalz and an imperial city of Charles V, Holy Roman Emperor.

The Hohermuths, of whom there were many, as the records reveal, were a patrician family of the minor nobility. They had for centuries flowed in and out of the history of Speyer-am-Rhein; one, Klaus, served in a high capacity in the cathedral at Speyer; another, Peter, became a dean of a convent at Strasbourg, not too far distant from his native hearth. Georg Hohermuth, according to his own *Vitae curriculum,* was born on 18 May 1508, and by 1518 was inscribed in the list of theological students at Heidelberg. It is apparent from his latter history that God did not

69

long hold him, for the Renaissance had opened many options, all of sufficient wordliness; in the wielding of arms or the intricacies of high finance. Finally, after lengthy apprenticeship, he was singled out in 1534 to replace, as Governor of the Welser realm in Venezuela, the lately dead Ambrosius Dalfinger.

Since the Welser interests were world-wide and Spain was then the centre of all the new discoveries, Micer Georg Hohermuth was quickly established near Seville by October 1534. He is recorded as living at the Welser Villa de Dueñas, near the offices of the Council of the Indies who were then preparing his "instructions".

Of the departure of Georg Hohermuth, there was in this unique instance an excellent record put down in full detail, both in prose and illustration, by young Hieronymous Köler of Nuremberg, who had accompanied the expedition; and which, by some bibliographical miracle, has survived, even though it still remains unpublished.[1]

First the Welser men complied with the laws and signed the official register of the Council of the Indies. As they emerged, there were formed on either side of the door flanks of six soldiers who displayed the banners of Charles V (red, white and blue, with the cross of Borgoña) and those of the Welser (red, white and red), and the personal flag (white and blue) of the Governor. The Welser men walked between these flags and crossed the bridge over the Guadalquivir river, where a Mass was said in the monastery on its nether side and the flags blessed. Then, after stopping at the factoria of the Welser that stood in the district of Triana, in Seville, they marched down to the ships.

All of this was told by Hieronymous Köler who accompanied the expedition as a young lieutenant. He came from Nuremberg, the original family seat of the Welser, and was born into one of its patrician families, as he says, on 31 October 1507. The young Köler went to Holland in 1534, embarked for Lisbon and then Seville, to prepare for his American journey. Although Köler was no artist, and the drawings are at times naïve, the colours are vivid and believable. Such a record is unique.

He drew the company marching to embark, preceded by musicians playing tambourines and horns, followed by Franciscan padres walking with lighted candles, then in turn, six priests of the Order of Predicatores – whose duty it would be to read the *Requirement*. Next came the leaders of the Welser expedition. On their heads squatted small sugarloaf hats, emplumed with a white feather. They effected slashed doublets of Segovia cloth and leather, ballooning knee breeches and rough skin leather boots; a shield hung over the left shoulder and by it a long Toledo blade. They were mounted on war horses which appear more like dray animals. Then came the lancers, carrying their long iron-tipped partisans on their shoulders, followed by handlers with fierce man-hunting dogs. And. finally, the arcabuceros. The impressionable young Köler of Nuremberg put down every detail of dress and armour and noted the whole company down to shoemakers, tailors, masons and armour bearers.

The cosmopolitan outlook of Charles V – "the good European" – is shown in the diverse nationalities of the expedition. Besides Spaniards and Germans, there were Basques, Flemings, English and Scots, and even Albanians numbered among crew and soldiers.

After several weeks of *contratiempos,* which prevented the small armada putting out to sea, the storms calmed and they sailed toward the new continent, arriving in the shelter of Coro in the last days of October 1535. Within several weeks they were joined by Nicolaus Federmann, who came over from Santo Domingo in a Welser ship, bringing a treasure of two hundred horses. The reappearance of the red-bearded Federmann should not have come as a surprise to the colony of Coro, for he had served out his four-year exile imposed by Ambrosius Dalfinger in 1531. The Welser had retained him under contract, and he had already acquired fame of a local nature by various readings of his

71

adventures, entitled *Indianische Historia, A Charming and Agreeable Account . . .,* which was to be published after his death. Moreover the Governor, Georg Hohermuth, had need of a man of his experience, and so he made Federmann his Captain-General. But among the Spaniards, who after all were the bulk of the population, there were mixed feelings about the return of Federmann.

Georg Hohermuth, after putting the colony of Coro in order, rebuilding the cabildo, arranging for the construction of a new church, starting a fortification, seeing that the laws regarding the Indians were carried out, now turned to the first problem, which was one of limits and boundaries. Since no geographer had yet set down the topographical verities of coast and hinterland, no one either in Spain or in Venezuela was in a position to know precisely what lands were controlled by the Welser and what was under contract to the "Men of Santa Marta".

Nicolaus Federmann was to carry out this assignment. To make certain that he would follow instructions, the Governor had drawn up a list of instructions in the greatest detail. The scrivener who made out the document was Juan Carvajal, the official scribe of the Government of the said city of Coro. This self-same Juan Carvajal will appear again later.

Nicolaus Federmann was instructed to ascertain the dividing territorial line. He was to go to that strip of tropical aridities known as "Guajira" (lying between the Gulf of Maracaibo and Santa Marta), occupy it, found a city and build a fortress. The object, apparently, was to secure the entrance into the arcadian land called "Valledupár", which lay southward, because they were told by the late Micer Ambrosius Dalfinger that this was the best approach to the highlands and to a people called the "Xerira" (Jerira) "who were rich in gold".

In August 1535, Federmann set out with many veterans, horses, and the usual long, brown line of Indian carriers. He followed his instructions, picking up the Spanish settl-

72

ers at Maracaibo – that enormous inland lake into which the lower Andes poured its waters and which reached the sea through a narrow outlet, giving the lake the appearance of a gargantuan demijohn. The small colony of Maracaibo had been founded and settled by Micer Ambrosius in 1529 as well as a smaller one called Ulma, which had fared ill in its isolation. So, following his instructions, Federmann enlisted those who were in want, included them in his group, and marched around the protruding arm of land – known as *Cabo de la Vela* (Cape of the Wind) – through the semi-desert area of Guajiro country to the first large river called the Río Hacha. Lying only 90-odd miles from the other Spanish colony of Santa Marta – which was on the sea, in sight of the snow-peaked Sierra Nevada – it was disputed land. It was a *tierra de nadie* or no-man's land.

Federmann found it a "sterile land, with little water or food plants", and possessed by Indians "ceaselessly dedicated to war"; they were "bellicose and naked, and without permanent habitation".

Meanwhile, Georg Hohermuth prepared his own expedition to cross the *llanos* at the base of the Andes to find a route to the uplands where Ambrosius Dalfinger in 1530 had heard that a people rich with gold lived in the Valley of Jerira. Being inexperienced in this type of thing, Georg Hohermuth surrounded himself with many veterans. Foremost was Esteban Martín, the captain who had followed Dalfinger on two expeditions and had himself buried his chief on the last trek. There were five Spanish captains in all. For his second-in-command, the Governor named Andreas Gundelfinger of Augsburg. (With "Gundelfinger", the Spanish contingent did not attempt to hispanicize his name; they referred to him only as "Andreas".)

The historian of this expedition, which would travel one thousand five hundred miles through the wholly unknown lands to the tributaries of the Amazon River, was to be Philip von Hutten.

73

The expedition was travelling through a *tierra incognita,* directly south across the unknown lands in search of gold. All the preparations, the exact chronology of this historically important expedition, along with a descriptive toponymy of the regions traversed, were to be known because of the letters that Philip von Hutten sent to his father. By some lapse of interest, they were not published until 1775, and then in an obscure German periodical two hundred and fifty years after the event.[2]

A cousin of the renowned poet, Ulrich von Hutten, the same who espoused the cause of Luther with customary impetuosity and vehemence and who wrote about the causes and cure of syphilis, Philip von Hutten derived from one of the oldest and most noble families of the province of Franken. Hutten was born in Birkkenfeld in 1511, the second son of Bernard v. Hutten (to whom he addressed his letters from Venezuela), who then was the king's representative of Königshofen. His eldest son was an official at the court of Charles V, and in his youth Philip had been playmate of Ferdinand II, Archduke of Tyrol and in time to be Emperor of the Holy Roman Empire. The noble birth of some of those who took part in the conquest is stressed since it was believed that *all* who went to the Americas were baser people – criminals, riffraff and the end product of the cleansing of the Augean stables.

Hutten was a good example of the sixteenth-century nobility who were drawn to the New World to participate in great discoveries and conquests. Philip von Hutten sought for honour and glory ["for after I have spent a large part of my life with my friends here (in Venezuela), I wish to return with accomplishments which all honour our name and lineage so that my motives will never be questioned!"] Hutten was young, scarcely twenty-four, ambitious, romantic and the adventure that lay ahead had an irresistible attraction. "God is my witness," he wrote to his brother, "it is the adventure that lies ahead that is my real interest; I am not motivated by the idea of riches, but to fulfil a

74

strange desire which I have had for a long time. I believe that I could not have died tranquilly had I not visited the Indies."

After careful preparation, Hohermuth ordered out a vanguard of one hundred men, under three captains. They were to move out to Barquisimeto, following Nicolaus Federmann's old trail in 1530. After covering this 135 miles of the Montañas de Xideharas, the vanguard was to set up a base camp and scout for locally-grown foodstuffs for the long trek. Hohermuth had many Spanish veterans for this business, one of whom they called Mantalvo, another captain, Lope Montalvo de Lugo, and, of course, Esteban Martín, the saturnine interpreter of discoveries.

In June 1535, Hohermuth moved out with the entire bulk of his conquest force; four hundred and nine footsoldiers, crossbowmen, pikemen, arquebusiers, and "many good guides" and joined the vanguard; together they proceeded toward the "Valley of the Women." Here they collided with their first hostilities, and young Philip von Hutten had some of his "strange desires" satisfied; yelling, hooting tenacious Indians poured in all about them, Hohermuth's horse was killed under him. The women they captured in battle at Guarjibo village, Hohermuth offered to return to the chieftain in exchange for his friendship. While all this talk-talk went on, they remained six days resting at the village – "neither in peace nor in war," said Hutten. "They did not make war on us, but neither was there peace."

After this, they began to grope their way toward the lower spurs of the towering *cordilleras* in order to find a passage to the heights. Failing at each probing in this, they returned, joined the main group and began again to cross the plains. They were now no longer following Federmann's trail; now, and henceforth, it was all *terra incognita*.

Like a sea, its tall undulating grass being its waves, the *llanos* stretches southward for one thousand miles to the upper reaches of the Amazon; these plains, neither prairie nor desert, yet a little of both, are in flood during the wet season and a flaming dryness in the dry season. It is a flat, almost treeless plain, which stretches from the Aragua river to the Orinoco and beyond, coming up the lower spurs of the Andes.

There are two seasons on the *llanos:* the dry and the wet. In the dry the sun beats down with a daily mean temperature of 90°, and the burnt clay earth, then thinly covered with brittle grass, becomes oven hot. The eastern trade winds as they blow across the *llanos* become heated by this earth heat, and it becomes like a desert sirocco. The rivers dwindle to slow-flowing rills, the creeks dry up like the parched land. Alligators, snakes, lizards and frogs remain buried in the dry mud until the rains come. When it does, life is awakened; the reptiles crawl out of their mud ovens, ravenously hungry, and the plains are transformed into a sea of green high grass. At intervals of every ten or twenty miles larger streams cut through the *llanos,* running from mountains to the Orinoco. When this occurs, there is a swamp, a fringe of trees repeated on either side of the river, then once more the seemingly endless *llanos.* In human terms it was sparsely populated.

By August 1535, half of the army of conquest was incapacitated. These were left to rest under the captaincy of Andreas Gundelfinger, while Esteban Martín, with one hundred and thirty men, tried to scale, to probe again the Andes for a pass which would lead them to the highlands and into the land of the "gold-rich Indians of the Valley of Xerara".

In September, the once pride-filled army of discovery reached the larger Masparro River and the villages of the *llanos*-dwelling Masparro Indians. Malaria, heat, lack of food and pneumonia, for they were always wet in the rainy season, began to take its toll of the living; numerous Indians died, followed by eight soldiers and nine horses. There they rested or, better, existed, while those strong enough to do so foraged for food.

Gundelfinger and the estimable veteran, Esteban Martín, set off to scout the lands for maize and *yuca* which, Philip von Hutten confided to his dairy, "was a food dangerous alike to the ill and the well since they were not accustomed to it". A goodly portion of the half-dead were put upon much-needed horses and sent back to Coro. As they disappeared over the horizon, Hutten with unwonted morosity said: "So it is for this that we will lose the fruits of our long and painful journey".

On 12 March 1536, after covering five hundred miles from Coro in nine months, they came upon an impetuous river in a depopulated region, but with a plague of jaguars, who devoured two horses as well as an Indian in his entirety.

They next reached the Río Ariporo (Hutten wrote it as Lorabo), small as rivers went in that region, and an upper tributary of the great Meta river; it flowed precisely along the 6° latitude. The date was 19 March 1536. Strangely enough, unlike all the others, the people had not abandoned the village. After the usual exchange of food, mostly *yuca* and maize, the conquistadors were shown numbers of small golden ornaments of the purest gold. Closely questioned by Esteban Martín, they said they had got the gold through trade from a people who lived toward the west, high in the cold mountains. The name of the chieftain was "Wakiri". Esteban Martín heard it as *quay-quiri* and this was not far removed in sound from the word that he and Micer Ambrosius Dalfinger had heard before the Valley of Xerira.

The chieftain averred that he had seen the gold with his own eyes during a trading mission and offered himself as guide. Immediately all the physical fevers disappeared. They were replaced by the gold fever.

At once Esteban Martín set off for the mountains with a *quay-quiri* as a guide. For days they struggled up the sides of the lower Andes. The approach became vertical and the second attempt to breach the rock wall of the Andes to find a pass failed; ironically enough they were, without knowing it, only forty miles from Sogomosa, the most eastern village of the Chibcha federation, famed for its temple and veritable depository of gold and emeralds.

On the bleak, elevated plateau, near to that which is now Bogotá, capital of Colombia, lived the Muisca. Since their principal god was called "Chibchachum", this name was apparently confused with the people and so they became in our histories the Chibcha. It is among these that El Dorado, the Golden Man, had its origins.

Even tribal holdings were not large, as such theocracies go; its total length did not exceed 180 miles, its width not much more than 90 miles. The land at this altitude is somewhat uniform. In the protected valleys below eight thousand feet there was a low forest. When the land-height increased the vegetation was scrub, low-lying and gnarled: plants are coarse-leafed and brilliantly flowered. Above ten thousand feet are the high, treeless, grass lands, the *páramo*, dominated by a lofty succulent called the *fraijelón*. Lakes were holy. There were five such lakes; of the five, the one which was to play an important part in their religion was Guatavita, close upon Bogotá.

War and agriculture held primacy. War was politics and politics were war. The Chibcha were sedentary, with fixed habitats, albeit with unfixed frontiers. They were agriculturists – as all tribes, lowland and upland. In this extremely mountainous country their principal food plant, as it was with most Andean dwellers, was maize, large-kernelled corn, having a rainbow hue of colours; of it, there was one annual crop. Next, the potato, ". . . which is like a truffle", wrote Don Pedro de Cieza, "and when cooked is as soft as boiled chestnuts. Like the truffle it had neither skin nor pith and it is also born underground". As potatoes grew in the higher altitudes, there were two crops a year. Next in order, *quinoa*, which – Don Pedro rightly says of it – "has a leaf like a Moorish chard, grows as tall as a man's height, produces some white seeds, some red, which they eat boiled, as we do rice".

Their planting implements were simple: a sharp fire-hardened stick to break and turn the soil; a heavy-handled headed wooden club to break the earth clots (the women's

78

The vegetation on the *páramo*, the cold, bleak plateau of the Colombian cordillera above 9,000 feet. This uninhabitable land had to be crossed by all who wished to move from the intermontane valleys down into the hotlands.

task); and stone axes, which could be made steel-sharp by chipping. With these simple tools they cultivated, beside the base foods, oca, which is a tuber, mealy and watery-sweet, *cubios,* a tuberous nasturtium, and other root crops. Other ground crops were beans (red, kidney and lima), and the sweet potato. Red peppers were planted about their houses, squashes were grown in the maize fields, along with beans which used the cornstalk for support; and tomatoes were planted. Fruit-yielding trees – avocado, *papaya, guava,* and soursop – were cultivated, and pineapples grew plentifully in the lower, warmer valleys.

Yet no matter how much the variety, it did not mean that there was a great surplus of food. While all these plants under cultivation sound impressive, *crop diversity is not equivalent to food abundance.* Most of the Andean tribes lived in a region where crops yielded only one yearly harvest and where rainfall was inconstant, and so were the main aggressors into other tribal lands to obtain food.

There were, if ecology of the lands offers confirmation, not more than 250,000 such *Muiscas,* divided into three sub-tribes, all of similar speech.Physically they were built like all mountain people: short, broad and deep-chested (since their habitat was high-placed they needed large lungs because of the thinness of the air). Their hair was black, thick and cropped, their faces round and eyes jet black. They painted their faces in patterns of red and black when engaged upon some important business, such as war or merrymaking. Upon their heads, when not ornamented with feathers or gold, they wore thick caps, woven from the grey fibres of the *cabuya* plant. As all others, they went barefoot. The nose septum was pierced for disc-shaped pendants, as were the earlobes for golden ear-spools. Above the biceps was a narrow, woven band to restrict the flesh, which was repeated on the leg below the knee; this gave, so they believed, strength to arms and legs.

Since the Chibcha-held lands were generally cold, foggy and wind-swept, all went fully clothed. Men wrapped a skirt around their waists, extending below the knees; another thickly woven cotton piece was tied over one shoulder in the Aztec style.

Chibcha women were naturally less robust; their hair, long, and black and lustrous, was allowed to be braided. Their earlobes were pierced for golden earrings. Their necks were almost always adorned by a stone-bead necklace. Bare feet matched bare heads. They wore the skirt, as did the men, and a patterned woven cotton blanket was draped about their shoulders as a shawl, held together by a golden pin.

The houses that formed Chibcha villages were built of upright wooden posts set directly on the ground, completely devoid of stone. Most were circular in shape, fashioned with a conical roof made of plaited *ichu*-grass, a roofing which lasted for a generation. Other houses, usually communal, were rectangular in shape, with grass-thatched gabled roofs.

There were no buildings, no temples poised on artificial mounds, as among the Aztecs or the Mayas, no stone-laid temples like the Incas. The chieftain's "palace" differed only in its greater size and in having at the entrance massive sheets of beaten gold, held by rope-fibre ropes, which tinkled and clanged in the wind.

The interior of the house was as bare as the exterior. The mud floor was hardened by the treading of feet, and sleeping racks were raised on cane grids over which were thrown the skins of hairy tapirs or of deer, or cotton blankets. Stools, sometimes ornamented with thinly beaten gold, were only for the higher men; lower men squatted on the ground. Food preparation was done around large stones which held clay pots; smoke found its way up and through the interstices of the grass roof. A rack held wooden spoons, stone axes and split bamboo knives. Meat, if there was any, hung over the fire on wooden hooks. An immense clay pot, covered by large leaves, held the maize *chicha* (beer). Illumination, other than from the fires, came from splinters of heavily resined pinewood.

This was the "Golden City" of the Golden Man.

The foundation of the society was the couple. Marriage was at early age and when a young girl became nubile, she was commanded to sit in a darkened corner with her face covered for six days and six nights. After that she was bathed, then there was dancing and drinking. Prospective wives could be purchased or, if a young man prized a girl, he would sit in front of her house several days offering either woven cloth or a goodly portion of maize. Chastity was a matter of indifference to the male, if not a state of actual distrust, yet once union was made, dalliance was not allowed. A male might have two, or even three wives, depending upon his ability to maintain them, in which case the wives had separate quarters (quarters being no more than woven mats fixed on poles to make a square); the polygamous husband fixed himself another. The higher man, like higher men everywhere, was a polygamist.

Although the great lords' life-condition was no better than their subjects', they were carried in ceremonial litters. They were virtually encased in gold – earrings, headgear, armlets, nose septums, spears, shields, and even their chairs were of gold.

The tribe was headed by a Zipa who was carried about in a wooden litter covered with thick golden plate. The lower people, as among the Inca, swept the road before him. The Zipa was, in short, an absolute monarch, but his descent was matri-lineal.

"When they [the chieftains] go to war they all wear rich ornaments of gold, and great crowns on their heads, and thick arm-bands on their wrists, all of gold. They carry before them great banners which they prize highly. I saw one", wrote Cieza,[3] "which they gave as a present to my Captain which weighed three thousand pesos-weight of gold, and a golden goblet of more than two hundred and ninety, and two more loads of this metal in different kinds of jewels. The banner was a long, narrow blanket attached to a pole and covered with small pieces of gold, like stars."

Gold as metal, however, did not exist in the Chibhca lands. It was obtained through extensive trade.

All of the rivers in the valleys of the Cauca beyond them to the west were highly auriferous. It was obtained by placer operations. Since gold is virtually insoluble, its great natural weight tends to make it settle in masses in streams and by compression it becomes ingots; nuggets are known to have reached one hundred and sixty pounds in weight.

"I recall," wrote Don Pedro, "that a soldier by the name of Toribio went out to forage for food and found in a river a rock as large as a man's head, all veined with gold which went through the stone from side to side; when he saw it, he picked it up to carry it back to camp. And as he was going up a hill, he saw one of the Indians' little dogs, and he ran after it to kill it, dropping the stone of gold, which rolled back to the river."

Where *eluvial* gold has flaked off from its auriferous quartz origins, it becomes *alluvial* gold and as it is propelled downstream tends to become small beads. Gold being virtually an indestructible metal, it never tarnishes, no matter how long it is contaminated even with salt or other corrosive elements; buried gold will emerge from centuries of entombment as bright as when originally worked. Since gold is soft – as soft as lead – it is, in its native state, highly malleable.

The Chibchas, as all the rest, knew casting through the lost-wax process. They could weld gold and were even able to make a *tumbaga* in which bronze-cast images were washed with gold, giving it a pale cast of gold, yet serving something of its purpose.

It is curious that, inquisitive as Pedro de Cieza was, he never reported seeing these superb gold pieces being cast, for the Indians had to employ crucibles, charcoal, and – through the use of a primitive bellows – obtain a heat of 1,063° C. in order to liquify gold, in which state it could be poured into clay or stone moulds. It is possible that these barbarian goldsmiths surrounded their operations with magical precautions. Copper which they got from ores by reduction was also used to cast images, then gilded to make it *tumbaga* ("coarse gold," Don Pedro called it). When heated, copper ores became as plastic as potters' clay. At a temperature of 1,083° C. it becomes liquified, and can be poured into a mould cavity. Metallurgy had then to be fairly well advanced, meaning the use of tongs, crucibles, moulds and a good knowledge of metallic reaction to heat. All these techniques were known by these tribes.

There was among the Chibchas, it must be assumed, some social specialization of labour, such as gold-artificers and weavers; since trade was vital for the Chibchas, they had to accumulate surpluses. War was small scale, in any terms, yet *total,* insofar as houses were burned, warriors killed, prisoners taken for either slave labour, sacrifice or food.

For trade items, the Chibchas had salt – a veritable,

inexhaustible mountain of salt – copper, which they cast in bars (for there was an open mine three days' walk from Zipaquirá at Moniquirá, located on the well-used salt trail) and emeralds from their own sources at Somondoco and as well from Muzo in the panchés country. Salt and emeralds – these possessed the virtues of effective trade items: easily transportable, cheap at the source, expensive at the market place.

Nor did the land height permit the growing of cotton or tobacco. These and coca leaves had to be obtained from the lower, warmer lands, as well as trumpet shells from the sea to call down the gods, hardwoods for lances, fish (important for its iodine content and eaten to keep down the incidence of goitre) and much else that their lands did not furnish.

Although they grew no cotton, they were excellent weav-

The Chibcha goldsmiths as envisaged by a sixteenth-century artist, Theodor de Bry. All the misconceptions of El Dorado are here: in the background, gold is merely being scraped off the ground; in the foreground gold is being melted in an earthenware pot, where Chibchas are blowing on a fire. High temperatures to melt gold (1075°F) were obtained by using charcoal and pipeblowers. (From *Americae Pars VIII*, 1599, British Museum)

Pottery rollers for the decoration of cotton cloth. Cotton weaving was one of the Chibcha crafts. Cotton did not grow in Chibcha territory (it was too high and cold), but raw cotton was obtained by barter. Many of the textiles were decorated by such pottery tools. These, however, are not Chibcha but Quimbaya. (From the archaeological collections of the Museo de Bogotá, Colombia)

ers. Their *mantas* were either painted or else decorated by clay stamp rollers which impressed a fret design, usually in red or black. In this moneyless society, the trade ratio for exchange was for one woven *manta* enough raw cotton to weave three. Markets were held every four days where tribesmen offered their personal surpluses in trade. The four largest markets were held at Bogotá; at Zipaquirá, the salt centre (two days' walk or about 30 miles north); then at Turmequé (three days' walk from Bogotá); and finally at Tunja (one day's march – some 20 miles – from Turmequé).

The Chibchas brought up cotton, smoked fish, arrow poison, chonta-wood (used for spears), coca leaves (masticated for the cocaine extract and used by the shamans and

A Cagaba with tobacco plant. The hard headgear is spun from the fibre of the cabuya plant. The garment is coarse cotton.

the very old) from the warm country. To the east, a salt-gold trail led from Tunja, one of the high-placed Chibcha centres. Even though it was over 9,000 feet in altitude, there was a trade route down to the flat tropical plains. Within a day's walk, cargo-carrying Indians would have reached the foothills; within two, the banks of the wide Upia river; within three, the banks of the great Meta riber, which is one of the larger tributaries of the Orinoco. The Chibcha traded salt, in sugar loaf shapes, golden trinkets, copper, stone axes, woven materials.

To the south, the salt-emerald trail led up the upper Magdalena river to the ancient trading centre of what is now Neiva. Lying directly on the 3° latitude in the warmer valley, in direct line with the snow-covered peak of the Nevado de Huila, the great trade centre of Neiva has its

A Cagaba holding a limestick and gourd used in mastication of the coca leaf.

trade lines in all directions. It was here, as we shall see, that Hohermuth and his men were to be directed by the tribes to the East. From Neiva, trade easily reached the tropical *llanos* to the east while other trails moved west into the Cauca valley and yet others south into what is now the territory of Ecuador. Neiva was a six-day journey from Bogotá.

In Ecuador was that area called "Esmeraldas" ever since the conquest of Francisco Pizarro. The territory was so highly auriferous and gold was so plentiful that they made fish hooks of it. Gold from this "Esmeraldas" was traded from tribe to tribe to Neiva, where they in turn by the same process acquired emeralds, which could only have come from Chibcha territory since there is no geological formation in this area that produced emeralds.

In February 1531, when Francisco Pizarro was on his way to make his conquest of Perú, marching through Coaque, they found the natives rich with gold and emeralds ["most abundant"]. One emerald that fell into the hands of Pizarro himself was as large as a pigeon's egg. The province that was named Esmeraldas produced none.

The Chibcha realm was formed, politically, into three unequal suzerainties. The Zipa ruled over six political districts from Bacatá (Bogotá) to the north; the Zaque from Tunja to the south; and a smaller tribe, although of similar speech and customs, was ruled by an *Iracá,* over the extreme south-eastern portion at Sogomoso (anciently Sugamuxi), famous for its Temple of the Sun.

As most who lived in area where the sun appeared infrequently, religion centred about a sun cult. Wherever there were lakes, caves, hilltops, there were shrines to the Sun God, but lakes were the sacred places. Idols of stone or wood were placed at their edge and became a place of pilgrimage for the people who placed their offerings of golden figurines, called *tunjos,* and emeralds. Human sacrifice was performed on prisoners for the Sun God and extraordinary sacrifices with children, who were bartered for, as we shall see, from the eastern tribes on the *llanos,* the flat lands. These were reared as temple servants, then ritually sacrificed. The rituals toward the sun cult were not designed to secure holiness, purity or peace with god; what they wanted was to conjure the Sun God to give the withheld gift of rain for good crops, or an infertile mother to bear children.

The gods, as all gods must, had to be appeased. The Sun God had to be fed to keep up his strength. Young girls were sacrificed to Bachúe the earth mother, who was offered burning incense; another, goddess of the rainbow, who aided women in childbearing, was offered emeralds. Those who followed the weaving craft gave a toast of *chicha* to their patron goddess.

What diverse ideals under which man has existed! He has adored ferocious gods always under the threat of despair, death or annihilation, yet everywhere, despite all this, man remains a normal human being.

Their galaxy of gods is believed by many to exhibit religious parallels with those of Central America. Foremost of these was Bochica, a cultural folk hero who, like Quetzalcoatl, was white. Many of the elements of the American theocracy were repeated in the Chibcha solid political pattern. "The most arresting parallels," writes Gerardo Reichel-Dolmatoff, "are: emphasis on 'dawn' in creation myths; multiple creation of the universe and mankind; the concept of several stratified worlds difficult of access; association of colours, death and life forces, and beings with the four world quarters; special abode for those dying in childbirth or by drowning; reptilian origin or deities; masked dancers impersonating the deity; nine as a ritual number; illness attributed to sin; symbolism of 'broom' and 'sweeping' for forgiveness of sin; confession; divination."

Near to Bacatá or Bogotá is Lake Guatavita. Fashioned round like a cup so as to catch the first and last rays of the sun, Guatavita was a sacred lake lying in the frigid desolation of the altiplano. It held high place for the Chibcha. In its watery depths lived a powerful deity who must be propitiated. Each time a Zipa was confirmed as chieftain, he had to have his office consecrated by the underwater deity. It was so spectacular a ceremony that those who had come from afar to trade "and to do other business", and perchance witnessed it, carried the impression back to their own tribal lands. While the Indians encircled the high rim of the lake, each holding a golden offering in his hand, the chieftain had himself anointed with a sap tapped from a tree and known as *el varniz de Pasto*. On this was blown gold dust, until his whole figure, from head to foot, was a golden gilded image of the Sun God. Then propelled into the centre of the lake – there is an extant Chibcha-made golden piece that depicts just this to verify its history – he submerged himself in the frigid water and stayed there until the golden particles had been washed off, descending like so many golden flakes to the turgid lake bottom. Then, on reaching the shore, his people confirmed him as their chieftain and rained the golden trinkets into the lake.

This was El Dorado, the Golden Man.

The Chibcha, to compound the confusion, was presumed to be the kingdom of gold whereas all the gold that it possessed had been the accumulation from trade.

Unaware of this confusion in Spanish and German minds, the Zipa went about performing his golden ablutions only dimly sensible that something was happening "out there" and wholly unaware that three armies, in three directions of the compass, all three in ignorance of the other, were moving in his direction.

For Philip von Hutten and Esteban Martín the months of April, May, and June were a repetition of all other months: *llanos,* thick-jungled rivers, perilous crossings, attacks by Indians and death omnipresent. Philip von Hutten seemed then not in the least discouraged; he was still animated by that "strange desire"; he carefully noted each tribe and river they crossed, the names of tribes, and their chieftains. So, in this manner, they came to the villages of the Amos tribe in the Valley of the Upia river, which was a roaring, cascading tributary pouring into the larger Meta river. It was the rainy season. The force of the water was such that they could not ford the boiling river. They were forced to remain there, and about, for eight months.

On 24 December 1536, they brought in prisoners who had beautifully cast gold and silver pieces. Again, when Esteban Martín questioned them, they said it came from the people in the highlands. At that moment they stood without knowing at the very door of the Golden Man. Not

The Golden Man (El Dorado): reality and unreality. The Grand Zipa of the Chibchas being anointed with resin, while another assistant blows gold dust over him (possibly true). In the background, Indians drinking corn-chicha from golden goblets (which was a reality). The actual attire of the Chibchas was a long, heavy cotton poncho. Engraving by Theodor de Bry, Frankfurt, 1590. (British Museum)

too very far away there was a horrifying hiatus to pass, the Valley of the Upia. This was the trade route of the plain-dwelling people with the Chibchas, almost 70 miles west-ward from where they stood on the Mesa de San Pedro, close upon the canyons of the Upia river, although of sheer vertical ascent to some 10,500 feet.

December 1536, after crossing several large rivers, for they travelled along the skirts of the mountains, they crossed the raging Guatiquia river at 4° latitude. They were on a direct line with Bogotá. Today, a paved road runs up from the *llanos* through the city of Villacencio through mountain passes, as high as about 11,000 feet on the way to Bogotá. Then, in 1536, their tortuous path was only paved with death. Yet once more, upon seeing the *llanos*-based Indians in possession of gold and silver ornaments, Esteban Martín set off "with fifty Christians to explore the mountains and seek out the pass". They had, of course, no way of knowing they were then in a direct line with the lagoon of Guatavita which held the secret of the Golden Man. In the higher land, nearly 5,000 feet ["or thereabouts," said Philip von Hutten], they were fiercely attacked by Indians using spears and darts and who protected themselves with shields made of the thick hide of the mountain hairy tapir ["like those used by the Bohemians," wrote Hutten to offer a comparison].

A three-day march and almost 70 miles away was the city of Tunja, the second capital of the Chibchas. Again, Este-ban Martín volunteered to lead fifty mounted men in search of this "Wakiri" and the people rich with gold and again Martín was frustrated by the precipitous mountains. They were attacked by Indians, lost men and horses, and so returned.

For eight months they lived among the Guahibo. They were generally nomadic, rarely spending more than two or three days in their palm-thatched houses. A hunting and food-gathering tribe, their principal food-gathering was the guapo root, also sought and eaten by the herds of wild pigs and deer. Wild pineapple when found was eaten with avid pleasure. The palm of life was the fruit of the *becirri*. During April and June they went from tree grove to tree grove, eating as much as their stomachs would hold. This was the happiest time of the Guahibo year. It was not the happiest year for the Europeans who rested among them.

"The 19th of January 1537," Philip von Hutten marked down in his Diary, they found on the *llanos* which they called "San Juan" between two rivers, a large area which suggested that there had been a "great population of Indians". They found maize and *yuca* in abundance and from it they prepared a banquet. Georg Hohermuth ordered that they set up a cross and, that being done, the settlement was dedicated to *Nuestra Señora* – our Lady. It became later a colonial outpost and is still known as San Juan de Llanos. This was one of the large trading centres for the Chibcha tribes who came down, bringing their trade goods of salt, gold, silver, copper, painted woven cotton cloth and other trade goods. In turn they carried away, among other things, a more precious trade item – children. Since the Chibchas were not expected to immolate their own children for divine sacrifice, they traded gold for children of the Guahibos. This was the importance of this Indian centre. It is fully possible that the Chibchas erected at some time or other a temple of some size, for the tradition of "gold on the River Meta" was well known.

Once more the march southward. This time they kept close to an isolated mountain area (now known as the Cordillera Macerana), which thrusts itself deep into the flat plains. Within about 70 miles of painful march, they reached the Río Guaybero (Hutten called it *Bermejo*, which was close enough). The land gave no direct indication of it; there was the same sea of grass, the same plains, but they had passed over an unseen divide. The rivers they had been passing flowed into the Orinoco. Now they travelled through lands where the rivers all flowed into the Amazon.

It was not until some of Georg Hohermuth's men had

sickened and died from eating manioc that they were made to realize they had passed a line, ecologically then undetermined, between the sweet (that is, the non-poisonous) and the bitter (the poisonous) manioc-eaters. The presence of one or the other of these two manioc determined the whole cultural life-pattern. The poisonous manioc looked like the sweet variety; the plant had the same slender grey stems which supported compound leaves and grew head high. When the plant was pulled up there were large tuberous brown roots, with a bark-like integument, a single tuber, weighing as much as two pounds, attached to the stem.

If non-poisonous, the peel of the manioc need only be stripped, then placed in an earthen jar with water and steamed, but when it was poisonous, an entirely different, more complex method, had to be used. Between the bark peel, permeating into its fibres, was a high percentage of prussic acid. This was partly got rid of by washing and grating. The damp, soggy, grated manioc (or cassava) was

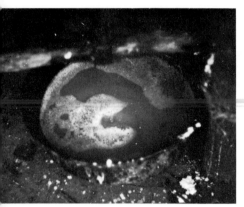

Poison (prussic acid) being extracted from the root of the bitter manioc or cassava.

Cassava bread roasting on a cumal-like pottery grill.

Cassava cakes drying in the sun on a Kofanes rooftop.

put into a basketwork cylinder – six feet long and three in diameter – whose fibres were woven so that its diameter diminished when it was pressed downward. The basketwork cylinders filled with grated cassava were hung up, a pole inserted in a loop in the lower part acting as a lever; when it is pressed, the poison juice filters out through the grating of the wicker-work. The manioc-cassava flour is then baked on a wide flat ceramic *cumal* which makes the flour adhere into a gargantuan pancake. These, dried in the sun, became rock hard.

This cassava is the staff of life for forty per cent of the Indians of South America; it was certainly the stuff of life of the conquistadors. It could be dipped into stews, it could be powdered into water, forming a thick gruel, or converted into beer. The women would chew the manioc bread, by which process the saliva converted the enzymes of starch into sugar; then they boiled it and allowed it to ferment in one of their huge earthen jars. Within two days it was

converted into a thick maltish beer and, if consumed in sufficient heroic quantities, it could intoxicate.

"We were told," wrote Philip von Hutten in his diary, "at the village near to the Guaviare that four years ago [that is, 1533] there had appeared a group of Christians." The information that the Indians gave Hutten concerned Alonso de Herrera who, leading an expedition, had died from the effects of a poisoned arrow. Many others had been killed, and the expedition dispersed.

This information was startling enough to Georg Hohermuth and gave a needed stimulation. They feared that others might forestall their discoveries.

At this point, Georg Hohermuth, on the Río Guaviare, decided to fix their position. Aided by Diego de Montes, who had been a navigator, they took out their astrolabe which somehow had survived battle, and continued immersion and flight. For centuries the simple astrolabe had been used to determine latitude. It consisted of a disk of wood with a circumference marked off in degrees. Suspended by an attached string, it had a movable pointer and by this means the angular distances could be determined in degrees. Hohermuth took this reading of the sun. "And we became aware of the fact," wrote Philip von Hutten, "that our position was 2° 45 minutes away from the equator." Considering the primitive instruments and their ravenous position, Georg Hohermuth had made an error of only five minutes by modern calculations.

They were now among the formidable Huitotos who defended themselves against all that the men of Coro could mount, but, in the mêlée, they captured an Indian who told them that if "we took a direction more to the right (this is due west) we would come to a very rich province". The walking distance was "twenty or thirty days" and the area would have been the well-known trading centre of Neiva, situated on the Upper Magdalena river and within range of twenty or thirty walking days; that is, about 80 miles. Hohermuth followed this clue and advanced for two days, where they came upon a large village at the River Papamena. The Indians here confirmed that what they had heard was true. On a trading mission they had brought back "sheep" [that is, *llamas*] and gold, but had been ambushed and murdered by their enemies, the *Istockas.*

The information about the presence of *llamas* ("sheep of Peru") was correct for the most northern outposts of the Incas had extended into the area defined by their informants.

It was here that the word "fighting women," which they translated as "Amazon," first enters the literature of the Golden Man. They were told that on a larger river, far down, which could be reached by descending the Caquetá, was a kingdom of women who lived without men and fought like men.

"Wherever they got this nonsense," said Philip von Hutten when this had been explained to him through translation, "it is impossible to say."

The rainy season had caught them on the edge of the Caquetá river, one of the great tributaries of the Amazon. Had Georg Hohermuth again used his astrolabe, he would have found himself at precisely 1° north of the equator. They had covered about 1,200 miles across jungles, *llanos,* mountains and had reached the most northern reach of the Inca Empire. Since they could not cross the four hundred-foot river, the Governor asked Esteban Martín to make one last try to find the pass, for again they had information about "sheep of Peru" and "a people rich with gold". It was to be Esteban Martín's last journey. With forty selected men and two guides, Martín led his men in torrential rains up and into the forested montaña. On the second day, the two Indian guides deserted. The next day they were attacked. Two soldiers were killed. All were wounded. "It was really a miracle that anyone escaped the slaughter." It was Esteban Martín's time: he was shot so full of arrows that he resembled a hedgehog and it was only his natural tenacity which kept him alive for a few days. Martín's death

97

Llamas, the "sheep of Peru", described by a contemporary of Hohermuth's as "the size of a donkey with long legs and broad bellies, their body and neck resemble a camel . . .". They had something of the quality of a myth, like the Amazons and other strange tribes reported in those parts.

"terrified the whole camp. He had been the Governor's closest officer, and the best of us all to know how to speak and deal with the Indians".

"We had *the* fortune within our reach," said Hutten, but now, with hunger, the terrible rains, belligerent Indians, everyone in one voice demanded that Georg Hohermuth turn back to Coro.

Georg Hohermuth calculated that they were five hundred and fifty leagues, or one thousand five hundred miles, from the port of Coro. The long voyage through the same terrain offered no new hope unless Nicolaus Federmann had received their message and would bring them fresh horses and food. The return journey began over two years since leaving Coro, on 13 August 1537.

"Many of us were without our swords, we had no more crossbows to defend ourselves. When we had started out we had more than sixty crossbows and twenty blunderbusses, now they were lost or unserviceable." The long voyage to Coro, over the same terrain, offered little hope. All the Indian villages were burnt or deserted. Horses sickened and died or were slaughtered for food while still alive. Men, when they dropped, were often left there, most being too weak to dig a grave, raise a cross, or say an Ave Maria.

On Christmas Day 1537, they again reached the River Upia.

They passed the graves they had set up years before and in early January 1538 they reached the Ariari river, having covered two and a half degrees, one hundred and sixty-five miles, in five months. Here they made peace with the tribes, obtained fish and maize, but most of the horses succumbed for lack of salt.

Near the Apure river they heard from the Indians that white men in large numbers had recently passed that way. From the Indians' description of the large German with a red beard and matching red hair, it could only have been Nicolaus Federmann who must have come out, as requested, to give them aid and reinforcements. Philip von

Hutten was ordered to ride out with the twenty serviceable horses to find him, but after coming to swollen rivers and hearing that it was "months" since Federmann had passed by, Hutten returned to share the last misery of his companions.

"Only God and ourselves," Hutten wrote to his father, "know the privations, the misery, the hunger, the thirst which we suffered in these three years. I am full of admiration for the human spirit that it could withstand for so great a length of time these fearful exertions. We were forced to eat insects, snakes, frogs, lizards, worms, herbs, roots, as well as devour human flesh, which is contrary to natural law . . . We were so reduced at one time that we boiled and ate the deer-hides which the Indios used for their shields."

On 27 May 1538, three years to a day since they had set off to find El Dorado, what was left of the expedition stumbled into Coro. Captain Gundelfinger brought in forty-nine walking skeletons. Hohermuth, with Hutten, headed a long line of eighty-five half-clothed men, covered with festering veld-sores (*harapos*). "We were not clothed more than the naked Indians," Hutten wrote to his father.

Hohermuth had lost three hundred dead for less than a handful of gold. He was taken in delirium to the islands of Santo Domingo.

It *had been* the expeditious group of Nicolaus Federmann which had crossed the path of his Governor, but he was not coming to his aid. Federmann was going on towards his own objective: the Golden Man.

Nicolaus Federmann returned from his expedition from Guajiro beyond the Lake of Maracaibo, in high Swabian umbrage over the loss of precious time. He had followed his Governor's command, penetrated that neck of land on the Santa Marta, built a small fort at Río Hacha, and founded a city. He was then set upon by Pedro Fernández de Lugo, Governor of Santa Marta, who with his title

100

deeds in one hand and a sword in the other, with an armed multitude behind him, declared that this land did not belong to the Bélzares (the Welser), but to his governación. So, being outweighed militarily and legally, Nicolaus Federmann retired to Coro, bringing back all his malcontents and cursing loss of time which he could have used searching for El Dorado.

It was then December 1536. Having heard rumours – for who could have escaped all the activity of ship-building going on in Santa Marta – that Gonzalo Jiménez de Quesada was about to mount a huge expedition to search out the golden source, over which he, Nicolaus Federmann, as he believed, had an indisputable priority, he wished to start forward.

At the end of the year of 1537, having heard nothing from Georg Hohermuth, and presuming that he was dead, Federmann set off with his small force and marched toward the *llanos* to find the "Valley of Xerira". At first Federmann followed the same route he had taken in 1535. There was, too, the unmistakable spoor of Hohermuth: graves, burnt villages, bits of equipment rusting in the jungle.

Federmann's men pushed on to the banks of the Valley de Tocuyo. There he was amazed to find himself looking at pitiful survivors of an expedition of Diego de Ordaz – the white men of which the Indians had spoken to Hohermuth. They were, as most who explored the lands, hungry, desperate and half-dead.

Federmann learned that they had joined Diego de Ordaz, the famous conquistador of the Aztecs, who, being discontented with Mexico after the arrival of the first Viceroy, had fitted out ships and caravels in Spain at his own expense and left Seville with four hundred and fifty men on 20 October 1531.

Now that one such as Diego de Ordaz, who had taken part in one of the most cruel and audacious of conquests, which was of Mexico, should have been seduced to follow the illusory golden trail, suggests how deeply the gold fever

101

gripped all those in Europe who had heard of it. Was Ordaz ever aware that the Island of Maruja, at the mouth of the Amazon, was 2,500 miles distant from Bogotá? And not merely distance, for every mile of it was fraught with death in all of its most bizarre forms. Yet he was ready to give full ear to the lure of gold which in the passage of time had metamorphosed into a golden city.

"This whole Spanish realm," wrote one of the chroniclers, "is so desirous of novelties that whatsoever they be called, with a peep only, of soft voice, to anything arising above water, they speedily prepare themselves to fly and forsake all certainties. . . ."

Somewhere above the lower Amazon, although he kept its precise place secret, Diego de Ordaz said he captured a canoe in which an Indian had an emerald "the size of his fist". As he ascended he heard the one thing the Indians repeated over and over again – *gold came from the River Meta.* The Meta was a tributary of the Orinoco whose headwaters rose in the *páramo* just east of Bogotá. Now the usual things happened.

It was there that the treasurer of the expedition, Gerónimo Dortal, took over the aspirations of the dead Diego de Ordaz. He was confirmed in the concessions of Ordaz and at the end of October 1534, he prepared to ascend the Orinoco with two hundred men and "find that province of Meta of which he had learned through the Indios that it was a land of great wealth".

The search was pure lunacy, a form of madness. Dortal, believing himself wise in the ways of expeditions, first sent up his captain, Alonso de Herrera, with one hundred picked men and nine boats; the while he, Dortal, would wait for reinforcements. Now Alonso de Herrera, of whom it was said that he "knew better how to kill Indios than to govern them", did advance as far as the River Meta. This meant overland portage of the boats, or winching them against the current. They came to the confluence of the Rivers Orinoco and the Apure and took the south branch of the river. In forty days of struggle against water, sky, insects, and Indians, and seemingly the very world itself, they reached the confluence of the Meta. Herrera took his position with an astrolabe and found they were at 6° north latitude. "I do not believe," said Oviedo, the contemporary Spanish historian, when he read the report, "that any of those who took part in this expedition would have taken so much trouble to get into the paradise."

As many feel that failure is not caused by the *thing in itself* but the lack of proper approach, so the treasurer Gerónimo Dortal believed that he himself must lead an expedition to the golden lands. At the end of 1535, he led a similar expedition up the same river, passing through the same horrors. This time, he turned north instead of south, and went up to the Río Apure. In time, had he followed it, it would have taken him into the heartlands of the Welser holdings. However, despair and hunger caused dissension. The soldiers fell on the poor treasurer, trussed him up like a cocoon, and one group sailed with him down to Paria to be delivered up for "justice". Another group set off toward Coro: and so in this manner they met up with "Capitán Barba Roja", no less than Nicolaus Federmann himself.

Nicolaus Federmann now found himself with a triad of forces: his men from Coro, those of Santa Marta who had joined after him at the fracaso of Guarjibo, and now the "men of Diego Ordaz". There was no common interest or camaraderie, except to find unparalleled riches, so with that as an adhesive they set off together, in April 1538, to find the Golden Man. Although Federmann would have preferred, as his second-in-command, the redoubtable Esteban Martín, he was fortunate to have Pedro Limpias in his stead.

Pedro Limpias was one of the oldest veterans in Coro. He had been there before the Welser had arrived and deeply resented their presence, but even greater than his faith in God and Spain was his belief in the existence of El Dorado. "It was he, Pedro Limpias," said a contemporary historian, "who brought back from the Lake of Maracaibo the idea of the El Dorado to the colony of Coro." Such was Limpias. He will reappear.

Pedro Limpias, one of the "new men", a native of Estremadura, that bare and wasted land in Spain which had given so many hard bitten conquistadors to the Americas, had once been charged with wholesale cruelty to the Indians. He was the sort of man of whom his contemporary Pedro de Cieza de León complained, "If they wanted one pig, they killed twenty; if four Indians were wanted, they took a dozen . . . Were one ordered to renumerate the great evils, injuries, robberies, oppression and ill-treatment inflicted on the Indios during these operations, there would be no end of it. . . ."

Limpias was such a one. Federmann had earlier brought a charge against him, characterizing Limpias "as a man of sordid fortune, who in my name killed and robbed the Indios". How they were reconciled no one knows; perhaps it was because Federmann had need of one of his experience. Anyway, he buried the past, but Limpias never buried it; the sequel was to dye the skeins of this tapestry in blood red.

As he had been once before in 1530, Federmann was to be his own historian of this, his last search for the "Valley of Xerira and the people rich with gold".

Federmann himself kept the notes on paper parchment or animal skin which, in time, he made into a letter-report to his old friend Francisco Avila, living in Santo Domingo. From this it can be learned that he first followed the spoor of Hohermuth, and it is known from Philip von Hutten that they almost met. Yet Federmann had no intention of being merely a relief column, he was determined now to find this *fata morgana* himself, so he avoided contact with Hohermuth by taking a higher route, all of which he had to make anew.

All through the remaining months of 1538, Federmann

led his motley army of three hundred foot soldiers and horses across the now familiar landscape. All along the way, they kept probing for a pass to the heights; they had then no idea geographically that the *cordilleras* was a continuous mountain barrier from Colombia to the Straits of Magellan; they thought of the Andes as being an isolated peak, such as was the snow-covered Sierra Nevada that overlooked Santa Marta, and that they could get around it; nor did they know that the Upia river, a tributary of the Meta at 5° N. latitude, led to the pass, one of the entrances to the land of El Dorado.

By February 1539, with familiar death eating into their ranks, they had marched to the Ariari river, one of the westernmost headwaters of the Guaviare, the same river whereat Georg Hohermuth with extraordinary skill had plotted that he was then 2° N. latitude.

It was doubtlessly founded where two years previously Hohermuth had found Nuestra Señora (San Juan de Llanos). Federmann named it "La Fragua", the "forge", which suggests that he had a smithy set up to cast and then re-shoe his horses for the climb that lay ahead.

Not every Andean river is necessarily a pass, and this, the Ariari, went uncompromisingly upward. It had to be followed, meaning a climb from five hundred feet to twelve thousand. The river, by then, was thundering and cascading, leaving only a perilous path; this brought them up to *páramo* of the Suma Paz.

They had found the passage!

After all these years of advance and retreat, Federmann had gained the heights. Now only the *páramo* had to be crossed. Only the *páramo!* The intense cold killed most of the Indian carriers and the earth was so deeply frozen that they had to leave their dead unburied; twenty horses were lost on the first day. In his letter to Avila, Federmann, who thought that he had been through every form of climate and condition that nature could devise, was unable to find the proper words to describe the desolation of the *páramo*

105

and the deathbite of its winds. They had done that which even a dog could not do. They, those that lived, crossed over by the pass which even to this day (although the orthography is incorrect, the sentiment is well placed) is called "Fredreman".

Those who lived followed Federmann, passing westward along the river bank of the Suma Paz into Pandi, and over the now famous natural bridge of Icononzo, an immense natural cleavage under which a river poured. Chibcha villages began to appear, there was food and there was some gold.

It was 1539. It had taken them two years to reach the margins of the Land of the Golden Man. And there, waiting for them, was one who had anticipated Nicolaus Federmann by one year, the lawyer-turned-conquistador from Granada, Capitán-General Gonzalo Jiménez de Quesada.

This time, on one of the most fascinating moments of exploration, there was to be no historian, no scrivener, royal or private, who would be there to describe the famous meeting of the "three" discoverers of El Dorado. There is only the acrimonious letter of Nicolaus Federmann to a friend to describe the state of soul of one who had spent ten heroic years in search of an *ignis fatuus,* only to see it dissolve into myth again just as he was about to embrace it.

[1] The Codex Köler, British Museum Add. MS. 15, 217. A collection of memoirs, biographical notes, written by different members of the Kölers of Nuremberg. There is a portrait of J. Köler, the conquistador, and his horoscope and coat of arms. His notes on a *Journey to South America* occupy about 40 pp. of MS.

[2] Zeitung aus India Junker Phillips von Hutten Aus seiner zum Theil unleserlich geworden Handschrift in Meusels Hist. Litt. Magazin 1785 1. Jahresbericht der Geogr. Gesellsch. in München für 1880. This appears here in English translation for the first time.

[3] From Pedro de Cieza de León, Parte Primera de la

Spanish and German conquistadors climbing the Andes aided by
Indians who, as usual, were the cargo-bearers.
(Theodor de Bry, 1599.)

Chrónica del Perú . . . (Seville, 1553) Translated as *The Incas of Pedro de Cieza de León* by Harriet de Onís, edited by Victor W. von Hagen (University of Oklahoma Press, 1959). This part of Cieza on Colombia was not used in the above titled translation. It appears here in this translation for the first time.

PART 2

THE
MEETiNG

ROUTES OF
━━━━ Nicolaus Federmann 1537-1539
•••• Gonzao Jiménez de Quesada 1536-1539
▬ ▬ ▬ Sebastían de Belalcázar 1536-1539

SANTA MARTA
Sierra Nevada
CARTAGENA
Sierra de Perija
CORO
Tocuyo
Lake Maracaibo
BARQUISIMETO
Tamalameque
Cauca
VENEZUE
Orinoco
MEDELLIN
Sogamoso
Meta
Tunja
Zipaquira
Ibagué
BOGOTA
CALI
San Juan de Arma
Guaviare
Neiva
Popayán
San Augustín
Vaupés
PASTO
Mocoa
COLOMBIA
Quito

ECUADOR

CHAPTER VI

The Lawyer of El Dorado

*First by the prowess of my weapons, Finest
in all chivalry, And then later, in my
fashion, by A heroic account of my deeds,
For I am a man of letters; My quill-pen, I
wield like a sword.*

Gonzalo Jiménez de Quesada had been trained for
the law – that profession which, avowed Philip II,
makes disputes whereof none existed before. Even
while he practised, the *sueños dorados*, those golden dreams, came over him. He had reached an age – he
was then thirty-six – when most men begin to think of
annuities and the comfort of the hearth; instead, he was
day-dreaming of the manner in which he would lead an
army "all ravenous for discoveries" through the lands that
would lead to the Golden Kingdom.

Fourteen hundred and ninety-nine, the year of Quesada's
birth, was not particularly notable. Christopher Columbus
had returned in 1499 from his third voyage in chains, in

reprisal, it is said, for his fatal mismanagement of those islands he called a terrestrial paradise. Amerigo Vespucci, a Medici man who had been victualler for ships bound for the newfound lands, had himself sailed in that same year and had come upon the lands he called Venezuela, Little Venice.

So the future conqueror of the Chibchas and discoverer of El Dorado did not burst into the seething Spanish world with anything resembling panache.

The records state that his mother, Isabel, was the daughter of a cloth-dyer, but a wealthy cloth-dyer; his father, Gonzalo Jiménez, the son of a linen-weaver. The notarial records, all very neatly penned in a clear script and arranged and tied into a parchment folder, are still extant and record that Gonzalo, the father, rose above his base lineage, studied and then practised law, earning the legal title of *licenciado*.

Granada has been Gonzalo Jiménez de Quesada's birthplace. He was an issue from unquestionable antecedents "that", it is said, "there was not a better-planted family tree in the whole genealogical forest". The founders of the family Jiménez were pure Goths, who interbred with the Moors of Toledo, even while retaining their Christian prerogatives, and thus were "enriched by the finest fertilizer known, the blood of the Moors." So while they could not qualify as *caballeros de los cuatro costados* (gentlemen on all four sides), since Moorish blood was present in the blood stream, Don Gonzalo Jiménez, when he had sired seven children, of whom the eldest was named Gonzalo, could make claims to be, as he in fact was, a person of some distinction. For Gonzalo II, it was singled out in the marriage contract that his grandfather, on his mother's side, would be obliged to pay for all the costs attending his legal studies at the University of Salamanca.

The university, founded in 1230 by Alfonso (some say "the Wise"), was founded on a city which had been Celtic, Carthaginian, Roman: Salamanca's institution then rivalled those of Bologna, Paris, Oxford, and as throughout the Renaissance, it was the centre of Spanish learning. Hernán Cortés attended it briefly as a boy of fourteen and to it went Gonzalo Jiménez.

Gonzalo Jiménez de Quesada was a student at the University of Salamanca when Charles V arrived from Flanders in 1517 to take over his inheritance as King of Spain, and may doubtless have been one of those students who took part in the popular riots that attended the arrival of the Hapsburg who would be king.

There was a tremendous vigour to Spanish life then. There were in Spain eight functioning universities. Salananca had been founded in the thirteenth century, and gained in a century an excellent reputation, attracting many foreign students, "as though to a fair of letters", said one who remembered it, "and of all virtues." It was open to everyone, higher or lower. Salamanca had many advantages even though bound by strict Spanish conservatism; anatomists were allowed to dissect cadavers, and it was at Salamanca that Christopher Columbus had revealed the first secrets of the lands he had found. Salamanca welcomed with enthusiasm the flood tide of the Renaissance, for Spain's printing presses turned out no fewer than seven hundred and twenty books, printed in twenty-five different towns, before the end of the fifteenth century. All of which, since Quesada was part of it, became his intellectual inheritance.

Having "become consummate in grammar and law" he had come down, as the Spaniards had it, from Salamanca when the civil war of the *comuneros* broke out. Then it turned out to be a struggle of the people of the *común* against the nobility, and uprisings took place all over northern Spain. The royal storehouses at Medina del Campo were set afire, the factories holding goods for the great fair were sacked and, as a revolution, it spread to the south toward Valencia.

Quesada, together with many other notable sons, did

113

not find that a civil war, as some held, was one of the greatest blessings that can happen to a nation. When the revolt had been put down, commerce resumed on a greater scale than ever, and Charles V found his power increased. The lesser nobility took over all the municipal offices, for these lower public offices had once been closed to them. However, the *hidalgo* class (equated with the squirearchy of Tudor England) had, outside of public office, no gain from the general prosperity. It was a matter of pride and tradition than an *hidalgo,* a contraction of *hijo de algo* ("son-of-somebody"), was a gentleman and could not demean himself by taking any part in industry or commerce (unless it was large scale).

The Council of the Indies itself in 1530 expressly disallowed any of their officials to trade on a small scale, since to do such would cause a gentleman to lose caste. Thus many such lived in poverty, if not actual want, in order to save enough so that he might give, even if for one day, the impression of grandeur. "The poor *hidalgo*", wrote one in contemporary satire, "goes up the street with such a comely gesture and countenance, who did not know him, would have taken him for a near kinsman of a Count or at least his chief chamberlain." Often he lived a life of semi-starvation, inhabiting a house of indescribable poverty and squalor. Yet, day by day, he "braved it out" in the streets, with his cloak and sword, speaking grandly of his honour and of "his estates".

Although there are no fulsome records of it, there is no doubt that Gonzalo Jiménez, now styled "de Quesada", after a battle in the city of the same name against the Moors, in which his family played a good part, did practise the law in and about Cordoba. One who knew him personally states that "he began to practise in the same courts as his father for several years".

As has been stated and yet cannot be emphasized too strongly, the year 1534 was the moment when the dream of the golden cities was transmogrified from myth into reality

114

when the galleon *Santa María del Campo* unloaded at Seville its enormous pile of golden and silver ingots, melted down from the hoards taken by Francisco Pizarro from the Inca at a place called Cajamarca. Jiménez de Quesada was no longer able to resist the call of conquest. Nor, in point of history, could Pedro Fernández de Lugo.

The high-placed Lugo family held the governorship "in perpetuity" of the strategically placed Islas Canarias, a considerable distance out into the Atlantic in direct line with the Spanish Sahara. The native population, the Guanches, who had put up a stout resistance, were in time overcome, and effective Spanish occupation began in 1479. The Canarias remained from the very beginning the starting point of all west-bound voyages and usually its terminus. For a family as the Lugos to hold so important a post "in perpetuity", bespoke its closeness to both king and government. So when the great news of Francisco Pizarro's first gold ship came to Pedro Fernández de Lugo's ears, he petitioned and was granted by the Crown, rights to the governación de Santa Marta territory which lay thirty miles from the mount of the Río Grande de Magdalena river and to the east it had a frontier with the Welser holdings on an ill-defined border. It was on a more direct route, so it was believed, to the land where *el hombre dorado,* the Golden Man, had his kingdom.

Pedro Fernández de Lugo, after an inspection of his new fief, had returned to Spain to recruit men and money. His smooth-tongued subordinates, holding out the chance of a 200 per cent return on money, enticed many to give their private holdings over to his enterprise. Preceded by a roll of drums, a sergeant, hand on hip, strutted up and down in the *plaza.* Youths looked on open-mouthed as Indians, painted and feathered, moved about. "Young men, as you have no doubt heard tell of the land of the Golden City, it is to the Americas you must go to find this Land of Fortune. Do you wish for gold, pearls, diamonds? The savages will pick them up for you. The roads are paved with them.

The chief is carried on a sedan-chair lined with gold, golden diadems encrusted with emeralds hanging from his lips, his ears."

By this year 1535, Gonzalo Jiménez de Quesada had heard (and who had not, for town criers conveyed the news everywhere) of one Francisco Pizarro, who first discovered the ramparts in 1527 of what he called the "Kingdom of Gold" and had made his way back to Spain in the summer of 1528, bringing some Indians taken from a place called Tumpiz or Tumbes, and enough gold and silver ornaments to give his astonishing "first contact" a metallic reality.

As for himself, Gonzalo Jiménez de Quesada faced the prospect of genteel poverty and this poverty would be like rain, dripping ceaselessly, disintegrating his finer tissues and his delicate adjustment, leaving him nothing but a bleak and gaunt framework. Bit by bit poverty would destroy his human instincts, his elegant desires and all else, starved away by the stress of impoverishment. If he was to die, he decided he would die not *of* something but *for* something. And now, Pedro Fernández de Lugo was here to aid him in dying *for* something – in the search for the Golden Lands.

Quesada sold his remaining equities along, if we may believe it, with some that were not his, for the poet has him say, on quitting his native and beloved Granada:

> . . . my faithful mistress,
> Weeping, said farewell to me
> When I had to leave Granada
> For *some* miscreant deed of mine.

How "miscreant" it is not precisely known; only this: that he, Jiménez de Quesada, "offered his services" and was made second-in-command.

"For when", wrote one of the historians, "Jiménez de Quesada offered his services to Pedro Fernández de Lugo, it was as a man who, though trained in letters and the

116

peace of study, had vigour and an excellence of mind. Good fortune led him to embark on this difficult and hazardous adventure, and to take into his own hands the journey to and discovery of the sources of the Great River of the Magdalena."

CHAPTER VII

The Men of Santa Marta

S anta Marta lay facing the blue, pellucid Caribbean Sea (then called the "North") on the edge of an immense crescent-shaped peninsula. Behind it lay a lush, enfolding tropical landscape which spread about immense *ciénegas,* swamp-marshes, which were possessed by flamingoes, egrets and roseate spoon-bills and fringed with water lilies and tall grass in which crocodiles, iguanas, and manati held sway. In the hinterland rose the verdured mountains of Santa Marta, culminating in the snow-covered peak of Sierra Nevada.

Despite its paradisical surroundings, the colony had continued in ill-fortune since its founding in 1501. At the time of the arrival of the new galleons and Pedro Fernández de Lugo, the residents were even more "bestial" in appearance than the Indians, reduced to rags and animal skins. The miserable fortification, built on sun-dried brick, was in a state of collapse. The church was unroofed, the hospital without beds, so that before the Governor undertook expeditions he had first to rebuild the city, set up docks, at

118

which new ships had to be constructed, and finally to set about "pacifying" – that is, killing, the Tairona Indians who, during the decline of the colony of Santa Marta, were regaining their lost territories.

In the low-lying mountains not much above a thousand feet were the villages of the Taironas, one of the most cultivated tribes of Colombia. Living in federated villages, united under the control of a single chieftain, the Tairona built their villages on the steep sides of the inclining mountains. "To reach them," wrote a Spaniard, "one has to climb stairs of well-dressed and placed stone . . . the villages are near streams with their streets well traced and orderly and strong, well-built houses."

House foundations were of stone, the buildings of wood and grass thatch. Agriculture was advanced and orderly with "plants grown in irrigated fields and terraces . . . done in the same way as those in Lombardy". There was an active trade between the Taironas and the people of the mountains in Central Colombia, doubtlessly the Chibcha, in exchange for the fish, gold and cotton from the coast. The Taironas brought back well-woven mantas and emeralds.

"There is much gold and copper in Santa Marta", said López de Gómara, who was the chaplain of the redoubtable Hernán Cortés, "and chalcedony, emeralds, and pearls; the land is fertile, and irrigated; corn, *yuca,* and yams flourish there. The Tairona pride themselves on having their houses well furnished with dyed or painted mats of palm or rush, and cotton hangings set with gold and baroque pearls, at which our Spaniards marvelled greatly; on the corners of the bed, they hang strings of sea-snail shells so that they may make a pleasant sound. These sea-snails are big and of many kinds, more shining and finer than mother of pearl.

"The women wear aprons about their waists, and wear their hair dressed in great plumes. They look very well in these, and taller than they are, and therefore are said to be comely and beautiful. The men go about naked, although some of them cover their privacies with pipes of gold."

119

If there was so much gold about that men could use it to cover their privacies, the Governor ordered his men, now that they were full and glorious and just fresh from Spain, to attack the Tairona villages. This would have been just one more thrust for gold had it not been for the discovery of Marcobaré; the only thing that gave the sound of improbability in the whole mad search for gold. As they struggled up the sides of the stone stairways and terraces, the soldiers were startled to hear a donkey bray. Now mules and donkeys were long part of the Spanish scene, and as the besieging Spaniards knew that the animal was not indigenous to America, an Italian among them, Edmundo Malatesta by name, with a touch of the humanities (one wonders what such a one was doing in such a galley) thought it might be the ass Silenus of classic times. After the battle the town was duly burned. With dead Indians about them, with a few pesos-weight of gold, they had the braying donkey in hand. How had he come hence? A Spanish ship had been wrecked, the donkey swam ashore, was captured by the Indians who, since they had never seen such an animal before, had slung him by a pole and so, in relays, carried him up the mountain. Having baptized him Marcobaré, after the chieftain of the Taironas, down he came the same way.

Marcobaré was put in the charge of Sargento Mayor Salinas and so brayed itself through the conquest.

On 6 April 1536, with six newly-built galleons prepared to sail up the Río Grande and the army of conquest arranged in its eight companies, the whole gallant company of over a thousand men were assembled in the *plaza* of Santa Marta. To a fanfare of trumpets and snare roll of drums, the moment of Jiménez de Quesada had come.

"I, Don Pedro Fernández de Lugo, Legate of the Canary

Cagaba Indians of the Sierra Nevada in front of a Men's Lodge (with curious roof comb). They are descendants of the Tairona tribe who had an advanced culture and traded with the Chibchas. They may be said to resemble the Chibcha-Muiscas, and have maintained many features of their original culture.

121

The landscape of the dwellings of the Cagabas, outside a village on the arid lower slopes of the Sierra Nevada.

Islands and Perpetual Governor of Santa Marta and its provinces, for his Majesty, name as my Lieutenant-General the Lawyer, Jiménez de Quesada. I name him General both of the Infantry and of the Cavalry of the Army, that is ready to set out on the discovery of the great Río Grande de Magdalena."

There was no mention of finding out the way to the golden kingdoms, for obvious reasons. The Crown – that is, Charles V – had a passionate interest to find a fluvial way to the South Sea in order to reach spiceries. He had aided and financed the voyage of Fernão de Magalhães (that is, Ferdinand Magellan) and the ship *Victoria* had returned with a king's ransom of spices; but the way to the "Spiceries" lay around the Cape of Good Hope, which was Portuguese territory. Spain, for both wealth and prestige, wanted her own "way to the Spiceries". The route about Cape Horn, called euphemistically by the Germans the Magellan-strasse, was a "street" with omnipresent death and destruction. Since Nuñez de Balboa had found in 1513 "the other Sea" by going across the Isthmus, and Magellan by sailing around Cape Horn, and more recently Francisco Pizarro had sailed "the other Sea" to the Incas, first of the gold kingdoms, then a strait must be found. No matter how much gold, it was spices that were uppermost in the Spanish quest. For spices had begun it.

Charles V of Spain was well informed. Letters of discovery were personally addressed to him and it is obvious that he read many of them, and so when it was strongly hinted by a conquistador-turned-geographer that they believed the Río Grande de Magdalena flowed parallel with the South Sea – that is, the Pacific – and might lead to Peru, a reply said: "I have your memorial addressed to us . . ." and the Crown insisted that they would be well-served if their Governors would find the sources of the Río Grande. Now although it was not yet determined, the Magdalena did flow southward, one thousand miles or more, to 2° S. latitude, only one degree from the city of Pasto,

124

which was the most northern extension of the Inca Empire. It was, as they were to find, navigable only half of this distance. So this royal interest in the Strait "to the other Sea" caused Pedro Fernández de Lugo to accept the Crown's instruction. Yet to obey did not mean to the Spaniard the same as submit. *Obedezco pero no cumplo* was the Spanish phrase ("I obey but I do not comply"). That, as we shall see, is precisely what will occur.

Now on paper the strategy appeared sound enough. The expedition to search out the lair of the Golden Cities would be divided into two parts: Quesada would go overland with six hundred men and horses; and four captains, overseeing six caravels and two hundred men, would sail in the fleet of low-draft brigantines they had built in Santa Marta, and would make their way with the rest of the army, supplies, and horses up the Yuma (Magdalena) river. This river being only about 35 miles from Santa Marta, they would then proceed up the river two hundred miles to the known trading centre of Tamalamaque, which had been discovered by Ambrose Dalfinger in 1531 and since then was known to "the men of Santa Marta". As the distance to it was almost the same by land, both parties should arrive at thee appointed rendezvous at the same time.

The army – for it was the largest body of men ever to arrive on America's shores – looked very well on parade, with the knights in their elegant armour and plumed Perpignan hats. In contrast, the old settlers, dressed in home-spun cotton and hemp sandals, cut strangely forlorn figures. The newly arrived would soon learn the lessons. They would adopt padded cotton armour, which, when soaked in brine, can stop an arrow. As for that steel armour, the tropical sun would bake them in it and the tropical rains would rust the hinges.

With metal about the saddles jingling and clattering, the cavalry were protected in quilted armour – "a surcoat of sacking filled with cotton to the thickness of three fingers". A mounted man comparisoned in such fashion made him a frightening figure. It is as well that the cavalry gave ear to the older and more experienced colonists about its protection. One captain emerged from battle with two hundred arrows sticking in the quilted armour.

They left on 5 April 1536. The small fleet of ships unfurled the gay departure bunting and the flags of Castile and León waved in the Caribbean breeze. The Captain-General, Gonzalo Jiménez de Quesada, mounted, as befitted his position as the Vice-Governor, led out his six hundred and twenty foot soldiers and eighty-five horsemen. There were accompanying monks and priests to see to the Indians' welfare; Royal notaries to read the *Requirement*; a Royal treasurer to see that the King's fifth, the royalty of 20 per cent of the gold and silver recovered, would be put aside for the Crown; and two or more Royal scriveners to put down all that would occur. And, of course, two hundred or more Indians to carry the impedimenta of the conquest. And with the cavalry went the celebrated Marcobaré, loaded as the rest, and braying all the way.

Not all of this army were, as the colonists thought, *chapetones* – that is, tenderfeet. Many were hard, callous soldiers who had seen wars in Italy, Hungary and France. Some had even fought the Turks, as had Juan de Junco, one of the captains. He had been trained and had fought

The Toledo blade, finest then in Europe and the weapon of the Spanish tercio. (Mary Evans Picture Library)

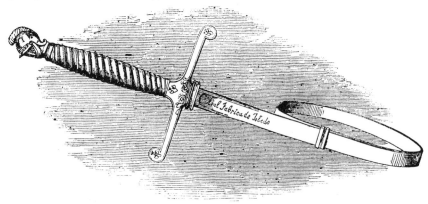

under the great captain, Gonzalo de Córdoba, and was a Spanish *tercio,* one of the finest soldiery in Europe and the best swordsmen, who used long pikes, javelins, and the famous Toledo sword, marked with its motto of a dog, and also arquebuses – that deadly silent crossbow, with its six-inch iron-tipped bolt. They were truly invincible. As had been shown everywhere in the New World, their boast was true; these men would take not more notice of a host of Indians who greatly outnumbered them than they would a "handful of flies".

The northern-born Spaniards were accustomed to the extremes of heat and cold, as in Burgos, where there were nine months of winter and three months of hell, or, to retain the Spanish pun, *nueve meses de invierno y tres meses de infierno.* The Spanish *tercio* had immense endurance, a dogged tenacity of purpose. In addition to all this, those who followed Quesada had before them, like the vision of the Holy Grail, the golden apparition of El Dorado. Captain Juan San Martín, who moved in front of the *machateros* – those who cut the vegetation to make a passage for the cavalry – was, like all the rest, an accomplished horseman. He was also an accomplished observer. He kept a journal, wielding a pen as well as a lance, since much detailed information about the progress of the expedition is due to his *Información de Servicios.* Lázaro Fonte, a *pícaro* of high degree, obtained his captaincy by the appeal he made to the men. Ambitious, active, energetic, he was still young; sturdily built, his face tanned a deep rich brown from the sun, his legs a little bowed from long days in the saddle. Of his deeds and misdeeds, we shall say more.

The whole procedure of leading this army into lands completely unknown to him is more remarkable in the person of Gonzalo Jiménez de Quesada. He was trained as a lawyer, not as a soldier. Now at thirty-seven, in the full confidence of the Governor, which speaks much for his personal magnetism, the fate of the lives of his men were in his hands.

Now the easiest way to reach the Río Grande de Magdalena and the rendezvous with the galleons would have been to go directly south from Santa Marta. This meant, however, crossing an endless skein of rivers, marshes and lagoons. The other which was longer was to follow the coastline eastward from Santa Marta, sand-filled with dry scrub and cactus, for about one hundred miles. Then, upon reaching a small perennial river, called by them the "Ranchería", and with an assurance of fresh water, follow its fluvial path inward and southward. All of which Quesada did. At that place called the Questa del Soldado – the hill of the soldier, doubtless in memory of their crossing – the army mounted it and crossed barren foothills and then came down on the other side upon the first rills that marked the César river. Named after Capitán Francisco César who had discovered the river in 1534 and whose decaying body lay buried under one of the great ceiba trees, it was the river of conquest. Micer Ambrosius Dalfinger had first passed this way in 1530. The Chimili tribe were naturally hostile. The earth was marked by the earlier thrust by ambulant Christians, and Quesada soon found himself riding through a veritable purgatory of nature, a purgatory made by man, who, in his folly, fashioned for nature and himself so many purgatories.

Progress, territories, Indios, death, all was duly marked in Quesada's own *cuaderno de la Jornada* (literally "The Book of Journeys"). Most of those days were little journeys in hell. The direction they took toward the Río Grande for the rendezvous at Tamalameque – still very prominent on modern maps – was down through the swamps, bogs and *ciénegas,* through which the César river flowed.

It was April 1536. In April torrential rain fell. The path they took, as direct as possible, followed the lower spurs of the Sierra Nevada. For every mile there were rills to be crossed, and about every five miles rivers, marshes and swamps. There were snakes, like the *cuelbra X,* its back marked by a hooked cross, whose bite could bring lingering death. Crocodiles were also rife, for this was their paradise, and their jaws could crush a leg in a single snap. The pack animals sank up to their bellies in the swamp. and this meant long and painful extraction, loading and unloading – almost always in fierce downpour. Night camps had to be made on dank earth. Fires were difficult to start. Fevers began. Malaria, given by the night-kiss of female anopheles, fevered the blood, alternately chilling and heating; exhaustion brought death.

At first the Indians met the encroaching army head on, but when tactical lessons were painfully learned, they hung on at the tail end dispatching stragglers. All such were destined for the stew-pot. The halt and wounded were placed on the horses, the fit walked, and the Indians carried. In days their loads grew lighter for the consumption of food by 822 weary men each day soon reduced the supplies. And when they did come across Indian settlements, they fell on the stored maize, *yuca,* and beans like a devouring swarm of locusts. It took them three months to cover some 70 miles. Shallow graves marked the way like milestones along Roman roads. The priests, for this was one of their functions, gave perfunctory last rites, then the grave was opened and shut in great haste. "Sometimes", the scrivener said, "a hand clenched in its last agony was unable to be flexed and remained above the ground, seemingly to wave farewell to those who went in search of that accursed gold."

The horsemen moved ahead to reconnoitre, to search out food supplies. The army followed. They came now into open savannah country, followed the verdured river, crossed the bogs of swollen rivers. Now the thought of the gold was supplanted by the thought of food, and they hurried on to reach the river and the meeting with the flotilla that was coming up with supplies and fresh men.

By following this route, they had to move through the César river and into country of the hostile Chiriguanas. They had no aid from these Indios, for they had already experienced white men when, five years before, Micer Ambrosio had passed by. But there was food, for the land was widely cultivated with maize, now in the ripening season of July, and there were *yuca,* ground nuts and varieties of beans. Food-wants were somewhat lessened now, for a head count revealed that for every mile that he had covered Jiménez had lost one man; and they had covered two hundred miles from Santa Marta. While they rested in what must have seemed an earthly paradise, Captain San Martín was sent with an advance group to see if the vessels had arrived, and after many weeks he reported that they were coming slowly toward Tamalameque.

So the army made its way around the same swamp of Zapatosa, that had hindered Ambrosius Dalfinger's men five years before, trod on the same crocodiles and frightened the same flocks of ghostly egrets, spoon-bills and flamingoes.

By 28 July 1536, four months out of Santa Marta, they reached the trading village of Tamalameque. This time, the Indios did not choose to play host as they had in the past. The trading centre and village was a half-island protected by water on three sides, and accessible only by a wooden causeway. Now the *tercios* were in their element and as always they won. The native houses were full of supplies, especially of large amounts of white salt in ceramic trays. They waited here. They nursed their wounds, buried their dead and waited . . . waited impatiently for the arrival of the fleet. After months of waiting, while the graves multiplied and time and fever had elimiated half of his men, the "fleet" came into view.

There was no fleet – only two battered vessels which were able to keep the tryst; the other four vessels had either sunk or deserted. There was, however, some bread (hard as a rock and mouldy), a few barrels of Castilian wine, linen from which bandages could be made for their wounds, but no food in quantity. Instead of succour, two hundred other hungry mouths were added to Quesada's forces.

"O por Diós! That men of flesh and blood", wrote the

historian, "should have had only their hands for breaking two hundred leagues across a most dense and difficult mountain, a mountain so craggy and lowering that all of them together could have broken only a league or two a day, had they been equipped with good iron tools. How much sickness racked bodies which had been delicately reared in a mostly kindly religion? How many pestilential fevers and other diseases?"

The great river was not an orderly one like the Teutonic Rhine. In full flood it broke its banks, creating subsidiary streams and flooding the land deep inland, to form lagoons far back from the river. This compelled the land force to go further inland, so that the plan to trek beside the galleons, winching the heavy ships against the river's flood tide, was manifestly impossible.

Most of the men asked to be returned to Santa Marta. Of this, Quesada's speech has been recorded: "The natural grief I feel, gentlemen, at the loss and death of so many friends, does not drive *me* to despair. Grief is part of our nature . . . Those who set out for wars and conquest put themselves into close touch with death . . . It would be ignoble to return with nothing done".

The moment was now at hand in which, as has been revealed, Quesada was going to obey but not comply. He no longer intended to search for the source of the Río Grande de Magdalena; he was going to turn inland and follow "the salt trail", for he too had heard that "where the salt comes from, there are people rich with gold".

A crisis was at hand and the legally-trained Quesada met it; all those who wished to return should embark on the brigantines and sail back to Santa Marta, while those who, like himself, wished to continue, went in search of the Golden Lands. This left less than two hundred to do battle.

Yet ill-fortune cannot always be present. Captain San Martín, going ahead with his mounted troops as was his wont, found a well-used trail twenty-five miles away which led up the River Opón to the high *cordilleras*. Here, there was a well-inhabited fertile plain and all along the way they found houses which contained those peculiar salt baskets.

This being conveyed to Quesada, he lost no time organizing the expedition to follow the salt trail. The armourers saw to their weapons; the crossbowmen restrung their arquebuses and new bolts were made; lances were sharpened; the horses were re-shod. Of the large army that left Santa Marta, close to one thousand in all, there were left two hundred, twenty-seven of whom were mounted. When all had been counted and the information penned into *The Books of Journeys,* Quesada said: "I intend that we start on the morrow, as soon as it is light."

After Mass on 28 December 1537, at the smile of dawn – as the Spaniards say – the sun rose slowly, dispersing the mist that wrapped the thick forests, setting all the feathery tops afloat as a great silent sea. Then the sun, having won its perpetual victory, lifted the veil that overhung the forests and the small army began its trek upwards.

At first it was just another river – and nameless. It came down from the mist-shrouded heights, curving, twisting, flowing through marsh into the Magdalena. It was easier to have everything punted up in canoes than attempt to go around the quagmires of marsh and bog. Captain San Martín, picking his way between one jungle-rimmed stream from another, was poled ahead, and the main body under Quesada followed. Later the river took on an individual character and then it acquired a name.

This brawling stream led upward toward a village ruled by a chieftain called Opón. So the stream became the Río Opón. It was a name to be remembered. Juan San Martín in writing his *Información de Servicios* – for it was the custom that a man had to prove to King and Council that one's services were worthy to claim a reward – wrote that on the first trip of exploration he had come across a canoe poled by three Indians, who, on their appearance, dived into the water. In the canoe, San Martín found finely woven cloth dyed a purple colour, and, packed in leaves,

132

loaves of fine salt. This salt that Europeans saw came from the salt mines of Zipaquirá. They did not then know where the salt came from, and were only aware that, as the Indios had repeated as in a refrain, "where the salt comes from, there are people rich in gold". The sight of that dazzling white salt sealed the fate of the Chibchas.

San Martín now left his canoes where the lower foothills are (and which are still called *Cerro del Indio*) and followed a well-beaten track upward to a plain. Quesada and the main body followed. After forty miles – with the salt trail visible all the way – they came in sight of a village. In the grass-thatched houses they found again woven cotton *mantas* and salt. The natives attacked, men were wounded, but, as usual, in the end the Indians were routed. However, in the mêlée, San Martín seized one by the wrist. They called him "Pericón" and he eventuated into one who was, said San Martín, "intelligent and agile", which, one must hold in this tale, is a curious combination, "for the two qualities seldom go together, just as honour and profit are seldom found in the same bag".

When shown golden plates, Pericón, by sign and voice, affirmed that, where the salt comes from, there is metal such as that held before him. San Martín was jubilant. Pericón went through the same pantomime with Quesada and his one hundred and sixty-seven men, and it is written, although mayhap with hindsight, that the men burst into rude verse upon hearing this which, losing much in translation and rhyme, would be:

> Tierra buena, Tierra buena,
> Good Earth, which marks the end of our pain,
> Gold-filled earth, a place to always live,
> A land of abundant food,
> A land of large cities and even larger tribes,
> A land where people go dressed,
> A land possessed of hope and serenity,
> A land which marks the end of our sufferings.[1]

Thus they arrived at Opón (which is still marked on the modern maps as such). At the highest point of the river stood a large village governed by Opón, the chieftain whose name was given to the place and river. It was relatively high country (2,297 feet), cool and forested. Orchids clung to thick-branched trees, and giant tree ferns, standing stark and bare, looking like little palms, made their appearance. Toucans, large-beaked and gaudy, were about. The chattering of flocking macaws opened the day and closed it. Rain fell. The going was all uphill, and the poor horsemen had to constantly mount and dismount and urge on their mounts, while burdened with iron harness, which rubbed raw their unprotected skin and made them feel, at the day's end, such as Don Quixote had felt ["molido y quebrantado" – that is, all broken up], as though they had passed through a grinding mill. Night after night, they slept the sleep of the just or the unjust, for both are equal in sleep, under the Southern Cross, which hung, so it seemed, immediately above their heads. The morrow was a repetition of the day before. The night dew was so heavy it dropped off the forest leaves like rain. Yet always, and at each village, were the well-woven baskets, sugar loaves of salt, and now, and more frequently, gold in sheets, or cut in bizarre ornaments.

Opón, the chieftain, now joined the agile Pericón and the braying, conquering ass, Marcobaré. Opón said that he would show the Spaniards the way to other villages, filled with more of what they had seen in his, and he came along as their *cicerone*. Not precisely freely: around his neck was a stout leather collar and to it a rope, held tightly by a horseman; so, faithfully, Opón guided them through the hills.

At Chipata (it is still there and on the map close upon the larger city of Vélez), an Indian village settlement in the valley around which hills towered to about 7,000 feet, Pericón admitted that he no longer knew the language.

Quesada had reached on 11 March 1537 (he marked it

most carefully in his *Book of Journeys*) the most southern edge of Chibcha territory "where the language changes". Here they also found their first emeralds. The treasure had also been swollen by 1,173 pesos-weight of gold. Here they also found something that gave them that which gold could not: a delectable food. These were potatoes. Since it resembled and grew underground like a truffle (*turmas*) they called it the "Valley of the Turmas". Now Pedro de Cieza had already described how tasteful it was, and Quesada, since it gave his soldiers' palates something, and as he knew that "an army travels on its stomach", called here for a halt.

Pericón, who had served briefly as interpreter-guide, was now to make his last appearance. The ragged army of Quesada was in the lands of the Chibcha. Villages appeared more frequently, as did amounts of gold, woven clothes and the ubiquitous salt. Before they moved forward again, it was the moment of the *Requirement*. Two of the monks who survived among the one hundred and sixty-seven assembled

The toucan, gaudy inhabitant of the cooler forests surrounding Opón, where Quesada and his men followed the salt trail.

all the Indians that could be found, with a pressure of outward force. Pericón took his place beside them and the peroration, now so familiar, was given out, all of which Pericón, who understood nothing, tried to interpret. The Spaniards had come for their betterment: temporal and spiritual. If they resisted neither their King nor their God, then blessings, not precisely detailed, would fall upon them. How it would be beneficial to them was not made plain to them or to us.

Quesada now made his speech, for all had to be recorded in the *Book of Journeys* to show that he had complied with the instructions of the Council of the Indies, the Church and the Crown.

"We are now", said Jiménez de Quesada, in his best legal manner, "in a settled and well-populated country. Let no one show violence to any man. We must have confidence in God and carry out matters with a *light hand.*"

A light hand! Jiménez de Quesada knew that he and his men were here primarily for gold (although the founding and population of cities was also an official principle). Gold was not going to be taken with a light hand. It may well be, as was said, that speeches acted as anodyne to the conscience, for Quesada did seem to feel that the natives had an inherent right to their land and he seemed to be able to hold his men, revenous for the sight of gold, to strict accountability.

In following the route along the valley carved out by the Suárez river past the larger lake of Fúgene and the smaller one of Suesca (more or less the route of a present-day railway), they came, after brushing aside Indian attacks with a "light hand", to the large settlement of Nemoncón. There, from wooden platforms painted red, hung large sheets of beaten gold.

After that golden harvest, and still following a well-worn trail, they came upon Zipaquirá. Everywhere about were shafts that entered the hills between pockets of black coal, and all about them Indians were leaching salt. Salt baskets, filled with the finest salt, were so plentiful that the place was immediately called the "Valley of the Villages of Salt".

The lawyer from Granada, the last to enter the field to search for the land abounding in gold, had, by a happy mixture of fortune and perception, followed the trail that proved that "where the salt comes from, there are people rich with gold". Actually the source of salt and the process which produced it impressed the Spaniards almost as much as the source of gold. Salt had always been in short supply in Europe. In Latin countries it has always been and still is a State monopoly. "The Heavens know", wrote Pliny, the Roman encyclopedist, "a civilized life without salt is impossible and is so necessary as a basic substance that its very name 'salt' is given metaphorically even to intense pleasures, such as *sales* which is wit." It had its place in law. It was also money, since *salary* derives from it. Many were its uses, civil and military as well as religious, since "no sacrifice is carried out without the *mola salsa* – which is salted meal".

All grain-eaters had to have salt, for as condiment, preservative, tonic, ritual, this sodium chloride had a primeval necessity in the earliest of societies. Men laid roads to get to the sweetness of salt: the movement of salt has been one of the great life lines; of all tastes – salt.

In the Americas, tribal wars were fought over the sources of salt. For the Aztecs it was an article of tribute and it so appears in Moctezuma's tribute books. They also controlled the salt-leaching ponds in the saline lakes that lay about Tenochtitlán (the seventh month of the Aztec calendar was marked by a fête to the salt workers).

About Yucatán's Caribbean shore, the Mayas had a province where their chieftains were called "Lords of the Sea". A bishop writing of Yucatán, in the sixteenth century, averred that the Mayan fisheries were on a very large scale. They also had salt in great quantity, and that taken from Eban was "very white and highly concentrated; it was a great trade commodity".

At Zipaquirá, Jiménez de Quesada and his men came upon infinite quantities of pure salt, so closely associated in their minds with the gold which eluded them. Salt was the single most valuable trade item in the Chibcha lands, packed into recognizable baskets or ceramic containers which must have changed little since then.

In Colombia, the tribes who lived within reach of the sea were obviously well provided with salt, but most of the interior tribes in both Andean and jungle areas lacked it. And so it was stolen, traded, swapped and passed from hand to hand, often over great stretches of space.

Pietro Martire d'Anghiera (born in 1468), the Italian humanist attached to the Court of Spain – and known to us as "Peter Martyr" – was an insatiable letter-writer and inquirer of what was found in the New World. He asked one Peralonso Nino about the habits of natives of the Antilles and the coast, and learned that salt in the form of salt bricks was a great trade item. "They hold fairs to which each brings the products of his region . . . Salt bricks were traded into the interior for which they got 'little birds and many other small animals beautifully made of gold of the fineness of a German gold florin'." The Chibchas did not distil salt from springs, for they controlled the principal salt sources of all Colombia, in reality an inexhaustible mountain of salt at Zipaquirá.

When the Andes were formed, there had been a geological upthrust from the sea carrying to a high altitude an immense deposit of pure salt of vast proportions. The Chibchan salt workers (who must have had their guild and cult as did salt workers everywhere) purified the salt, shaped it into sugar loaves and packed it in ceramic dishes, easily identified by all tribes who traded to pass through various tribal lands to reach Zipaquirá. It was the principal source of Chibchan trade wealth, and the many paths were salt trails. This was what other tribes, living far from them, when questioned by the Spaniards, meant when they said *"in the land of salt where the bowels of the mountains are white with salt – there is the Golden Man"*. It was by following the salt trail that the conquistadors at last understood the meaning. It led Quesada to his glory and the Chibchas to their doom.

The great Zipa was less a gold king than a salt king. For the Chibchas as we have seen, had in reality an inexhaustible mountain of salt at Zipaquirá, forty miles or two days' walk from Bogotá (the capital of Colombia).

In the end – but then who could have foretold it? – the salt mines of Zipaquirá would be of greater and lasting wealth than the gold. The mines at Zipaquirá which have furnished salt since the time of Quesada are now worked a half mile under the ground. The galleries are so vast that the salt workers have cut out of pure salt a cathedral as long and as tall as Notre Dame in Paris. Walls, the Stations of the Cross, are all sculptured out of solid rock salt.

There Quesada rested and counted the heads and horses. Only one hundred and sixty-six men had survived (one having been garroted for theft) of his original eight hundred. Two hundred horses had been killed, died or been eaten. This left him with only forty effective horsemen.

At first, the Chibchas took them for a new and strange form of anthropophagi. They deserted their houses, leaving food and a goodly portion of worked gold and emeralds. At Guacheta, the people fled and left an old man tied to a stake offered as food. The Spaniards released him, while the Chibchas watched; considering perhaps that the anthropophagi found the old man too tough to be eaten, they sent down children. When the white men disdained these, they sent down a man and a woman and a recently killed deer. The Spaniards kept and ate the deer, but sent back the Indians. Seeing they were not man-eaters, the whole village surrendered.

The army advanced on a large village called Chía. The grand Zipa, arrayed in gold with lip pendants, nose rods, ear bangles, brassards and calf bands, all in gold, entered battle carried in a golden litter. The mummy of a former Zipa, also arrayed in gold, was carried along as a talisman. As this was not precisely the type of arms to use against skilled horsemen, his warriors were slaughtered. The Zipa fled. This was neither Mexico nor Peru. The Chibchas were less numerous; moreover, they sent their warriors piecemeal into battle and they were rapidly destroyed.

140

Quesada now bent to his task with his Chibcha informers to find out something about the people. It seems that just before their arrival, an outbreak of hostilities had occurred between the Zipa to the south and the Zaque to the north, so this tribal friction aided the Spaniards and they did not lack Indian spies. It happened here, as it happened all over the Americas during its conquest, that tribes traditionally at war (since all Indians were enemies of each other) never united long enough to combine against the white man. They did not regard the white man as *the* enemy. There was no general word for *Indian,* nor a similar word to designate people of similar colour, culture or language. When the Spaniards gave them a verbal unity by calling them "Indians" it was a racial unity which they had never possessed.

They certainly were not wanting in bravery. At one moment in battle a solitary Indian advanced on to a plain and by gesture challenged any one Spaniard to single combat. Man to man combat was well known between Moor and Spaniard. Lázaro Fonte, in persistent readiness for fight, leaped on to his saddleless horse, lance in hand, and charged the Indian. For one who had never faced such a centaur-like combination, he waited bravely for the assault. Lázaro Fonte, too, had a chivalrous streak. He threw away his lance to deprive himself of a great advantage, dextrously manoeuvred his horse out of the way of a thrust, seized the Indian by his long hair lock and so led him back to camp.

The "King" Bocotá (from whose name Bogotá became the name-place of the new Vice-royalty) escaped his pursuers but within his fiefdom, and still using the *light hand,* the Spaniards invaded and made it yield the first treasure – six hundred pesos-weight of gold and one hundred and forty-five emeralds.

Emeralds, after the ruby the most precious and costly stone ($20,000 the carat), set the soldiers ravenous. Emeralds had first been offered to Colombus on his second voyage, and they had been seen in Santa Marta in 1514

141

when the Spaniards, after burning a village, found "jewels of gold and emeralds". Diego de Ordaz, the same who had followed Cortés in the conquest of Mexico and was the first white man to scale the smoking volcano Popocatapetl, when performing his search in the lower Amazon river for the Golden Man, found among the Indians one "as large as his fist". Emeralds reached by trade as far north as Florida, where Cabeza de Vaca was given "beads of coral, turquoises and four or five emeralds".

The Chibchas controlled, in addition to salt, the only source of emeralds throughout the Americas. Every emerald, wherever found, in grave or shrine, or mummy, whether found in Mexico, Central America, "Esmeraldas", in Ecuador or Peru, came from the realm of the Golden Man.

Hernán Cortés found the Aztecs with emeralds, which they called *quetzal-itzli,* since it had the vivid green of the tail feather of the quetzal bird. "The kings of Mexico", wrote José de Acosta, "did much esteem them, some did use to pierce their nostrils and hang them therein: also they put them on the visages of their idols". As soon as Moctezuma was elected chief speaker of the Aztecs, the first thing that he did to celebrate was "to pierce the gristle of his nostrils, hanging thereat a rich emerald".

One mummy of the Zipa was found buried with emeralds for eyes; others were placed in the ears, nose, mouth, navel. The Zipa litter was encrusted with emeralds and many – there is no way to divine how many – were cast into the lakes during the Golden Man ceremonies.

An emerald is a bright green variety of beryl (*zummurrud* in Arabic, *smaradgus* in Greek) and had many virtues ascribed to it. It was a preventive against epilepsy, it aided in childbirth, if held close to the stomach, it prevented dysentry in the wearer, and it helped to preserve a maiden's chastity; chemically, the stone offers nothing but its beauty. An emerald is actually an aquamarine with the inclusion of beryl, which has been crystallized in some remote period of

142

geological heat, its brilliant green colour caused by the chromium within it.

The region of Muzo in Colombia, where the fine emeralds come from, lies in the cool rain forest, five days' walk from Bogotá, two days' hard travel from the salt mines of Zipaquirá, within an isolated area of jungle between the *cordillera* and the Magdalena, a low range of heavily forested mountains and rivers alive with iridescent butterflies. Here are veins of quartz shot with emeralds, for under a crust of mountains formed of black shale and bituminous limestone it is veined with quartz and iron pyrites, and this is where emeralds are found. By shearing off the precipitous face, veins of white stone calcite are exposed, calcite which crystallized to form carbonate of lime. Emeralds are often found in these lime cavities and prising out from the bituminous shale and white quartz is the way emeralds are recovered.

When Francisco Pizarro was making his way down the

The Muzo emerald occurs in nests of calcite deposited in a black bituminous limestone associated with quartz. Often the quartz is shot through with bubbles of beryl, which may lead to a large head in which are clustered, in the matrix, the emeralds.

Pacific toward the Incas for his second, and final visit in 1531, his ships put into Bahia de Sardinas off the coast of Cayapas in Ecuador. "Here was a fair river of emeralds so called from the quantities of the beautiful gem found on its borders, but which was not visited owing to the superstitions of the people who said the mine was enchanted." In January 1531, the three ships of Francisco Pizarro anchored in the Bay of Manta "in the rich province of Coaque", and his cousin, Pedro Pizarro, wrote of seeing "quantities of gold and emeralds". The most famous was the emerald kept in the Temple of Manta, which was cut in the image of the god *Umina*: "as large as an ostrich egg", wrote "The Inca", Garcilaso de la Vega, who heard of it from his conquistador father. Those emeralds that fell into the hands of Pizarro's soldiery were large, uncut and round "like pigeon eggs". The Dominican Fray Reginaldo de Pedraza, who accompanied the expedition, told the men that the only way to gauge the genuine from glass is to crack them with a hammer, since a real emerald would resist "all such blows". He then made a considerable fortune by selling the broken emeralds in Panama.

Emeralds were traded, directly and indirectly, for gold. There was no gold to be had in the immediate Chibcha territory, but it was obtainable in quantity along the Cauca river, and in even greater quantities from what is now Esmeraldas, the northern coastal province of Ecuador, bordering Colombia. By one of those *non sequiturs* of history, the Chibchas were called the Golden Kingdom although they produced none, while Esmeraldas was called such, although there were no emeralds except those got by indirect trade from the Chibchas.

Now having learned that at Somondoco there were emerald mines, that was where Gonzalo Jiménez de Quesada wished to go. A condor's flight to Somondoco from where they stood in the ruins of the village of the grand Zipa, Bocotá, could be done within ten minutes, for on a straight line it would be forty miles. However, since the Spaniards were land-tied and the Andes fold and unfold with towering sierras and deep barrancas, one must needs follow the river valleys. They moved north following the Bogotá river, still so named, and reached in two days' journey the large Chibcha settlement of Turmeque.

When attacked, Quesada had ordered the trumpeter to sound the call to the horsemen, who then rallied, made their usual spirited charge, and routed the attackers. Writing down all this on 2 June 1537, Quesada called it the Valley of the Trumpets but which – in the names over the land – became Turmeque after (as usual) the name of the local leader. He promptly yielded up gold and emeralds and he also, under torture, revealed the way to the source of the emeralds.

The conquistador, certain now of being able to hold the territory with his scant number of men, dispatched one of his six captains, Pedro Valenzuela, to search out the emeralds at Somondoco. Eastward from Turmeque the land height falls rapidly from out of the frigid uplands into the montaña, where tagua nut palms grow and tree limbs are orchid-covered; here was the Somondoco river and there the emerald "mines".

The "mines", Captain Valenzuela soon grasped, were not mines at all, for one does not mine emeralds as one mines gold. Crush a vein of gold-bearing quartz and there is gold, but emeralds, which, chemically, are beryllium with the right mixture of chromium (the more chromium in the mixture the deeper green and more valuable), are found in bituminous black shale, buried with white quartz, which is shot with greenish emerald bubbles. Within this black mass, with only the simplest of tools, a rich pocket can be found often not larger than an Indian's blanket manta. In this pocket are found emeralds, the most concentrated wealth known to man.[2]

It is natural that under these circumstances Captain Valenzuela and his men found few emeralds. The Chibchas did not mine them, but exposed the emerald pockets by painfully cutting and chipping at the earth. In the main, however, the heavy rainfall caused the black friable shale, containing emeralds, to tumble into the rills, streams and rivers, and there they were found.

Within a fortnight – that is, on 14 June – they had returned somewhat dispirited because the gold and emeralds recovered were of such smallness. However, they did report to Quesada from their viewpoint at Somondoco that they had seen, between the interstices of clouds, great grassy plains stretching out like the sea.

Capitán San Martín, ravenous as ever for new discoveries for His Majesty, as he wrote in his *Information,* set out to the east. His orders were not to expend more than ten days in the search. The Chibcha guide brought them over a pass to a raging torrent, which had gouged out a valley, and they followed the river – the Lengupá (it still retains the name) – one of the tributaries of the larger one, the Upia, which flows into the gargantuan Meta river, and so is part of the Orinocan fluvial system. They soon found themselves in a montaña which had already defied the many assaults made on it by the German contingent, even then, in 1537, making their fatal passage across the bare, anaemic *llanos.* Rain was constant, Indians few, food but little. The horses swam in mud, the soldiers were reduced to eating grubs and roots; and there was no Golden City. They endured. The only light moment that their historian could recall was that in one of the tribes that lay on the boundaries of the Chibcha realm, they took among others an Indian girl "so beautiful and modest and so well-behaved that she would have competed with Spanish women, who were adorned with these qualities".

The ten-day time limit being up, San Martín ordered the return over the same disordered route. Since, after God, the Spanish owed their victories to their horses, and as San Martín had a squadron of them, which were of such value, Quesada sent out a search party, and finding themselves lost in a marsh, promptly named "ciénega", for such is a

One of the many forms of El Dorado, the Golden Man, the fecund myth of earth-riches.

Ancient Mexican feather-fan, brought to
Europe in 1524. (Museum für Völkerkunde, Vier

Colombian gold birds, standing on sockets, evidently for the insertion of
wooden shafts. Bernal Díaz referred to "twenty golden ducks, of fine
workmanship" which he saw among the treasure from Mexico, brought back by
Columbus in 1519. The knowledge that such objects existed spread gold fever
among the Welser and the Fugger, and led to the Search for El Dorado.
(Dumbarton Oaks, Washington: Robert Woods Bliss Collection)

marsh in Spanish, and night falling on them, they hid in the foliage. At midnight, they were awakened by the braying of an ass, a sobbing fearful sound that only the conquering ass could give out. It was the sound of Marcobaré. He was offering a safe conduct. Even more, the conquering ass caused the men, when joined to San Martín's group, to look further afield and there they heard of a great and populated place, called "Hunsa".

An Indian revealed it. The place, only ten miles from where Quesada was encamped, was the principal village of the second highest chieftain among the Chibchas, his title was "Zaque", and his name, which no one used since he was soon to die, was "Quemenchatocha". Fifty selected horsemen and his best captains, including, of course, the redoubtable Lázaro Fonte, were chosen for the surprise assault.

For the record, Jiménez de Quesada went over all the old laws about pillage,, and the "light hand" and the crime of plundering. Yet one must face reality. In our account there are many moral inconsistencies just as there are many emeralds. Although ostensibly commissioned to find the source of the great river, Quesada had abandoned the enterprise when it became obvious that it could not be done with the few men and worn ships at his disposal. His patron, Don Pedro Fernández de Lugo, Governor in perpetuity of Santa Marta, had outfitted, at enormous expense, an army of one thousand, now reduced by God's will to one hundred and sixty-seven. He did not expect to be repaid for all this magnificent outlay by a continuous record of barbarian souls which had been brought into God's habitat. Nor the King. It was set down that he was to have the fifth – that is 20 per cent – of all wealth found and, please God or no, he would not want his royal fifth filled alone with men's souls.

Finally, Quesada's men had not lost their teeth, health and conscience only to make a harvest of souls to enlarge the spiritual largesse of God. Gold or its surrogate, silver or green fiery emeralds, fabulous enough to be the talisman of Charlemagne – this was the heady stuff of conquest. Quesada had to make the speech about pillage for the record, which he did, but in his lawyer's heart, he knew that whatever feelings he had about justice and humanity would vanish in collision with actuality. "Such is the usual fate," he mourned, "of theories in this vale of tears, and possibly is the best reason why *it* deserves that name."

Now Tunja, anciently Hunsa, is the city that Hohermuth had heard of but never reached, lies on a high, treeless plain, at 9,250 feet altitude, mid-distant between the low-lying *llanos* plains and the deep valleys of the Río Grande de Magdalena. The air is hard and sharp as a diamond. The world is open and in the clear light everything is sharply etched and definite, and unsoftened by vegetation. In what way fifty heavy-armed cavalry, unable to soften the noise and rattle of metal, were able to approach the large settlement, without detection, even though for five long months war had been waged all over the land, must have been, as said the soldier-historian, "that of God's will".

They saw houses lining streets at right angles, built of wood or wicker work, and artfully thatched with ichu grass tufts, surrounded by a high, wooden palisade.

Men walked the streets in woven cotton mantles, tied at the shoulder, and in sandled feet. Hair was worn long, or gathered in nets. All had the nose septum pierced through in which golden ornaments were placed. Ear lobes were pierced for other gold earrings.

In the centre was the "palace", the construction of which, like all else, being of painted wood, but larger and more imposing. In it lived one of the triumvirate rulers of the Chibcha realm, the Zaque.

In the last rays of the fast-sinking sun – for here, near to the equatorial line, there is no lingering sunset – "a wondrous spectacle broke before the Spanish eyes". From nearly every house hung thin golden plates, thin sheets of gold beaten to foolscap thinness swinging lightly in the night breeze, and giving out tinkling sounds like an aeolian harp. The golden plates reflected and gave back the sun.

148

Fifty men against ten thousand! There were, it was remembered, many Indians, "innumerable, *como hormigas*" – like ants. And like ants, they swarmed about Quesada. A nod to his lieutenant and they dismounted, took out their Toledo blades, and ordering the others to wait his call, Quesada boldly burst through them "taking no more notice of the pressing Indians, than he would a handful of flies".

Within minutes, Jiménez de Quesada had gone through the door of the wooden palace and faced the Zaque. Aged and corpulent, dressed like all the rest but with more gold, his sandled feet resting on a woven mat, he sat on a wooden stool decorated with gold plate and emeralds. He was as composed as anyone could be to see strange men drop from outer space: "seeing so unexpected an arrival of bearded men in form and countenance and from a part of the world so distant . . . mounted upon great and unknown monsters".

Now the *Requirement* required that before any violent action, the leader must state why he was here, his mission and his purpose. Since time was at a premium, Quesada made short shrift of it. He was a vassal of a mighty king, who had sent him to help the Indians and to ensure them their possession of their lands. It must have seemed madness to the Zaque, if these words were translated correctly, that he was to be assured of his lands, when no one threatened to take them from them except Quesada and his men.

"Still", one of the historians avowed, "the speech did not strike him badly," so the chieftain asked that Quesada withdraw while he consult with his council. This was precisely what Quesada would not allow; they unsheathed their weapons, advanced, and brushing off the guard, seized the Zaque. At that moment, they were only two. No such daring was exhibited by those other famed conquistadors, Cortés and Pizarro, who were surrounded by men, cavalry, even small cannon. Here the two were alone. They raised the cry "Santiago and at them". The force of the cavalry

149

brought down the stockade and so into the mêlée went the men of Santa Marta forgetting, momentarily, all about "the light hand". Through it all, Quesada never let go his grip on the Zaque and either through age or acceptance of the greater force, he stood resignedly. In a moment, so it seemed, it was all over. Stupefied by the suddenness of it all, terrified by the horses, whose hooves cut them as badly as the Spanish swords, the warriors did nothing more than cower.

Then Quesada's men went berserk. They cut down the golden plates. With lighted torches, they rushed about gathering gold, emeralds, a mummy of some chieftain whose eye sockets, navel and palms were filled with emeralds. They found woven cloth bags, full of emeralds, and gold dust waiting to be smelted. There were many of the great trumpet shells from the ocean sea, rimmed with gold, used to "call down the gods". Each roof, ornamented with furled wings of an eagle or condor, was pulled down, and thus the loot was gathered.

"We have found another Peru, Sir General, we have found another Peru," one shouted as gold plate piled on gold plate.

But had they? It seemed so when they discovered yet another treasure trove at the trading centre of Sogomosa, two days' distance from Tunja on the high heights from which, on a clear day, one could see the flat *llanos,* stretching out endlessly eastward, like a wayward sea. The temple, of wood like all else in the realm of the Chibchas, had within a row of mummies, all properly decorated with artificial eyes of emeralds, head-dresses of parrot feathers and burdened with golden ornaments. Whether by design or purpose, the tinders of the torch-bearing myrmidons set the whole structure ablaze, and the old priest, strangely enough white-bearded (for beards were a rarity among them) fought them off from the venerated mummies. Then he himself perished in the flames. The booty was gathered: gold, beads, gold-spangled mantles, gold-plated chairs, litters, and all matter of golden things, "of such a heap," said San Martín, who helped to make the pile, "that Quesada, when mounted, was all but hidden in the golden loot".

They now turned their full attention to the apparition of the Golden Man, going off in search of that which had already launched many an expedition and would continue to do so for another two hundred years – the Golden Man about whom they had heard so much.

Now where was this Golden Man?

They were led up to a bare land, high above the village of Guatavita and there lay a lake, in a savage and desolate region, round and symmetrical, and more than 10,000 feet above the sea. It had a circuit of over three miles, a diameter of about three-quarters of a mile. At the edge was a large round thatched building built in their style; from the edge, steps led down to the water's edge. This, they were told, was the lake of Guatavita. It was here that the legend of El Dorado had its origin.

It was said that many years before, an enormous meteorite had fallen on the *páramo* of Guatavita and buried itself in this lonely place. It had formed an immense hole and, in time, a lake. Folk memory retained the occurrence, how its burning mass had dropped down from the sky, and shaken the ground like an earth tremor. They believed that a golden god had descended from the sky and that he now lived in the bottom of the lake. That is why, when a new leader of the tribe was elected, he covered himself with gold dust and made his ablutions in the lake, so as to acquire some of that god-power for his people.

An old man of Guatavita remembered the ceremony and described it. After 1470, as the Spaniards counted it, the whole ceremony had been stopped by the Zipa, who had deprived Guatavita of its independence. Other old men, happy to talk of the past, gave the Golden Man an anthropomorphic twist of it. ["In olden times . . . the Zipa impaled his wife's lover and forced her to eat his flesh while listening to songs made for this occasion. Then the Zipa forgave

151

her. But she, upset by the needless cruelty, ran from him with her girl-child and threw herself into the lagoon of Guatavita. Below, she took up a new life with the 'Snake Dragon'."]

This was disputed by another.

At every new installation of a chieftain of Guatavita, the ceremony of the Golden Man was repeated. The men smeared their bodies with red achiote, a blood symbol, and walked in a long line toward the lake of Guatavita. Others, adorned in feathers and golden ornaments, were also bejewelled with emeralds. Some blew on bamboo pan-pipes, four-note flutes, while others puffed on huge conch shells "calling down the gods". The priests were next in line, wearing black cotton robes marked with white crosses. Meanwhile the Zipa's body had been greased and blown over with fine gold dust. He appeared solidly gold, as the Golden Man. Having arrived at the rim of Guatavita, he was led down the steps to the lake's edge, and there took his place in the centre of a balsa raft and was propelled to the lake's centre.

Under torture, the informant shouted that this *was the only Golden Man,* for there was neither Golden City nor gold sources in their land; all their gold came by barter from elsewhere. The Spaniards peered into this lake, which only reflected the sky in its varying moods, and remained unbelieving.

The historian Oviedo, his entire sonorous name being Gonzalo Fernández de Oviedo y Valdés, (who has entered history and remained as Oviedo), made an early inquiry as to the nature of El Dorado, this Golden Man "from those Spaniards who had been there". Oviedo had arrived in the New World as early as 1514, and settled in the Isle of Española – Santo Domingo – where he was appointed his-toriographer of the Indies. He had a strong interest in natural history, a remarkable inquisitive mind, and an edi-tor's ability to ask pertinent questions of those *tercios,* who were making new history while destroying the old. He was able to ferret out the plausible. The result of these inquiries was a well-known and invaluable work: *Historia Natural y General de Las Indias.*

"So I made an inquiry of those Spaniards who had been there, why this prince, chief or king, was called *dorado.*[3] They answered that, according to what had been heard from the Indians concerning that great lord or prince, he went about constantly covered with fine powdered gold, because he considered that kind of covering more beautiful and noble than any ornaments of beaten or pressed gold. The other princes and chiefs were accustomed to adorn themselves with the same, but their decoration seemed to him to be more common and meaner than that of the other, who put his on fresh every morning and washed it off in the evening . . . The Indians further represent that this *cacique,* or king, is very rich and a great prince, and anoints himself every morning with a gum of fragrant liquid, on which the powdered gold is sprinkled and fixed, so that he resembles from foot to head a brilliant piece of artfully fashioned gold."

Therefore El Dorado was no more than the Chibchas said he was. There was no Golden City. If gold which had escaped their eyes lay anywhere, it lay below, around the edge of the lake of Guatavita, or had been carried down by its weight – for the specific gravity of gold is as heavy as a melted iron ingot – deep into the mud bottom of the crater lake of Guatavita. The only one among them who then took the folk tale as true was Captain Lázaro Fonte. Unobserved, he went down the stone-laid stairway, walked the grass-lined lake shore, searched among the small fringe of shore line and there discovered an emerald set in gold. Pocketing it, he kept his own counsel.

Now the restlessness among the soldiers, the muttering of uneasiness over the undivided treasure, galvanized Quesada into action. He had the Royal Treasurer, who had somehow survived the march and the battles, select a commission to deal "fairly" with the booty. It is not known nor has it been

Tunjos – crudely-cast anthropomorphic figures, used as golden offerings and cast into Andean lakes.

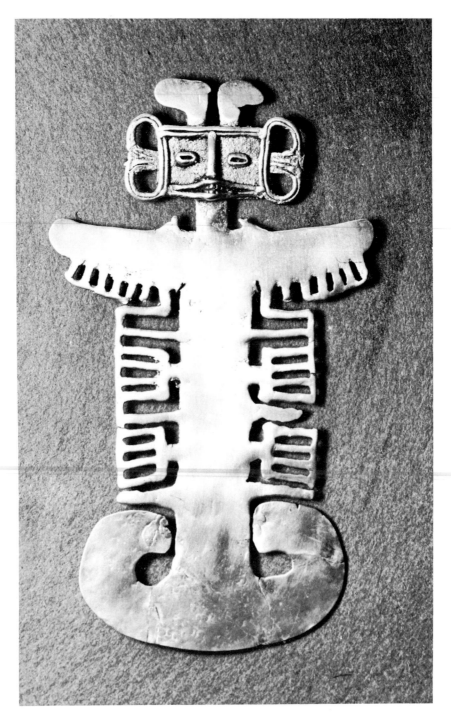

Cast gold talisman from the belligerent Pijaos tribe, enemies of the Chibchas.

Quimbaya gold chest pendants, showing the use of nose ornament and ear spools.

Examples of gold flasks, vases, bottles and other ceremonial objects found in graves of the Quimbayas on the Cauca river. These tribes were neighbours of the Chibchas. (Museo de las Américas, Madrid)

Details of the head-piece of a golden *tupu*, showing the excellence of the casting of small figures. (Cleveland Museum, Ohio)

Highly stylized cast gold instruments. Use unknown, but possibly for inhaling snuff.

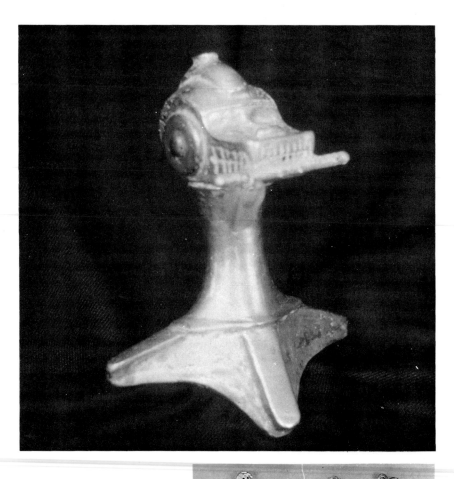
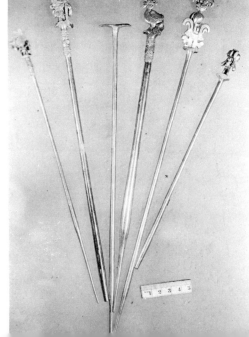

recorded, the manner of reaching an equitable distribution. In Peru, Pizarro melted the ransom of the Lord-Inca, Atahualpa, into ingots, which then could be equitably distributed.

The conquistadors soon found, however, that all that glisters is not gold. Much of that found was made into *tunjos,* which were basically copper, crudely made anthropomorphic idol figures, with limbs and features. The illusion of three dimensions was done by the application of thin, gold wire, which became the limbs, eyes, mouth and head-dress. These were *tunjos.* They were cast from copper and given only a thin surface of gold, a process, called *tumbaga,* which, if not invented by the Chibchas, at least was developed by them. There was an open copper deposit at Moniquirá, on the salt road between Bogotá and Vélez, and since they had no gold, they adopted this technique by which the piece looked like gold, but was not. By heating the casting and soaking it in acid, the immediate copper surface was removed, leaving a thin skin of gold. Since the gods, to whom *tunjos* were offered, did not know the tumbaga process and, further, as it looked like dull gold, the *tunjo* bothered no one; that is, until the Spaniards arrived.

The fact that the Chibchas worked a copper mine which was in their realm and did have alluvial gold in rivers should have explained to the conquistadors that they were not lying. The *tumbaga* process was widely used because of the shortage of gold.

Pure gold to the Spaniards was that which had fourteen or more carats. This gold the Chibcha craftsmen hammered into sheets; designs from it were cut, shaped, and joined by heat and hammering. Gold pieces were developed by pounding a thin gold sheet over a design, carved in bas relief stone or hard wood; the hammered golden sheets

A free-standing golden receptacle from the Cauca valley.

Ornamented golden *tupus,* used for holding women's shawls together. (Chibcha and Quimbaya)

161

were often of gossamer thinness, so that the stone design became embossed on the gold.

They also cast golden bells, bracelets, and beads, hollow and solid; there were golden *tupu*-pins, which held together a woman's shawl, topped with exquisitely cast figures of animals, birds and frogs. They plucked excess hair from their faces with golden tweezers, they cast or hammered golden masks for their mummies and crescent-shaped ornaments to be put in the the nose septum.

As the conquest of their realms prevented the continuance of the extensive trading missions, in which salt, cotton weavings and emeralds were traded for gold, the Spaniards did not see it arriving from other lands nor witness the goldsmith at his task. One who had seen it elsewhere explained how: ". . . they have their forges and anvils and hammers, which are made of hard stone. The hammers are the size of eggs, or smaller, and the anvils are as big as a Mallorcan cheese, made of other hard rock; the bellows are as thick as two fingers or more, and as long as two palms. They have delicate scales with which to weigh, and these are made of a white bone which looks smooth like ivory; also there are some of a black wood, like ebony".

In the raid on Tunja they found 136,500 pesos of fine gold, 14,000 pesos of *oro bajo* and 230 emeralds. The value of all this loot cannot be estimated in modern terms. Still it was immense in any terms, and in any epoch. The royal fifth amounted to 40,000 pesos-weight of gold. Each foot soldier received 520 pesos-weight of gold, every horseman one thousand. After the royal fifth, the lawyer of Granada, with a fine legal hand, dealt seven parts of the whole to himself and reserved nine parts for his patron, Pedro Fernández de Lugo, who so notably combined inexperience with self-assurance, but whose kindness and generosity in times of trial earned him the title of "the Good".

After that, came the division of the emeralds. It had been a most worthy five months. Not a Spanish life was lost, but the Chibcha culture was totally destroyed because it possessed in itself no permanence. Although they were supposed to have lived in large towns, the buildings were of wood; all disappeared. There were no large, well-developed roads, like the Incas', and no stone-built buildings. They had neither rebus writing like the Aztecs nor hieroglyphic as the Maya: even the Indians of the North American plains, as regards their own tribal history, had a form of pictorial writing. The Chibchas had none. Chibcha pottery ["although competent and technologically well-made," so noted Dr. Gerardo Reichel-Dolmatoff,] was far less elaborate than most pottery from the lowland cultures. The many small, stone objects, in the shape of frogs, humans, or birds, which were well-made and highly polished, served only as moulds on which the Chibcha gold-workers beat out their golden images. The most common artifice used in the ceremonies involving the Golden Man was a human figure of elongated triangular shape, with wire-like features, eyes, arms, hands and headpiece, made in wire-like technique. And these, much to the conquistadors' discomfiture, proved to be *tumbaga* – that is, bronze castings with a thin gold wash.

Relief stones such as this, embossed with frogs, birds or human beings, were used by the Chibcha goldsmiths. Thin sheets of gold, placed over the stones and beaten, took on the embossed shapes.

Triangular-shaped *tunjos* cast with filigree to give a third dimension. Chibcha.

Engraving of the Chibcha-Muisca "calendar" which led to the belief that the culture of these tribes was as advanced as the Aztec, Maya or Inca. The original drawing was made by Alexander von Humboldt on the basis of Padre Duquesse's *Disertación sobre el Kalendario de los Muyscas, Indios naturales del Nuevo Reyno de Granada*. The symbols were interpreted as referring to lunar months. In fact the object was merely a relief stone for embossing gold leaf.

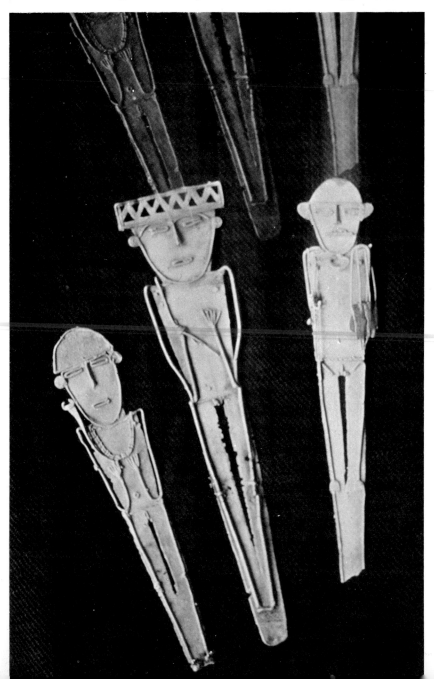

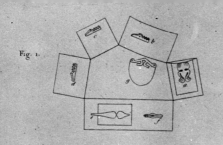

Fig. 1.

Fig. 2

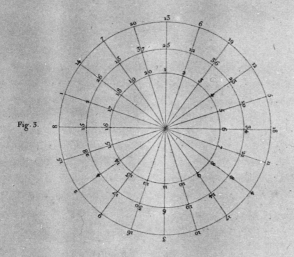

Fig. 3.

Fig. 4.

	1. Ata
	2. Bosa
	3. Mica
	4. Muihica
	5. Hisca
	6. Ta
	7. Cuhupqua
	8. Suhuza
	9. Aca
	10. Ubchihica
	20. Gueta

Calendrier Lunaire des Muiscas

Anciens Habitans du plateau de Bogota

Dessiné p[ar] J. D. Duquesne 1801   Gravé par Beaugé

The *evidence* of archaeology is that the Chibcha was not of high culture. Their memorized history was only of limited span and, unlike the Inca, uncounted in great detail. They had no calendar as did most advanced tribes. The one carved stone which Padre José Domingo Duquesse, a parish priest of Bogotá, claimed was a Chibcha calendar was in fact only a small relief, a carved stone, with various animals and abstract carvings, used for embossing gold. This, put into the great Alexander von Humboldt's hands, when he visited Bogotá in 1801, he inadvertently and incorrectly (using the archaeological daydreams of Padre Duquesse) elaborated as a Chibcha calendar and under the great authority of his book, the illusion was created and still will not die, that the Chibcha could be classified culturally as advanced as Aztec, Maya, and Inca.

"The legend of El Dorado," concludes Reichel-Dolmatoff, "combined with the wealth in natural resources and manpower of the rising kingdom of New Granada, contributed to the myth of Chibcha 'civilization', a myth which has persisted down the centuries, but which lacks the evidence of archaeological fact."

Still the "men of Santa Marta" continued to believe the myth of the Golden Man and a City of Gold. It must have been some deeply ingrained mediaeval belief in a golden Utopia that time had now transmogrified into a golden city in South America. It had been so long in their collective social consciousness that they refused to discard their belief.

However, an entire people, the Chibcha, had been destroyed. Within five months, thousands had been dispatched by one hundred and sixty-seven determined, ruthless, not unique soldiers for those times except for their daring.

It should not be believed that this destruction was countenanced by Crown or Council. The captains, as it will be seen, were to be called to account by the King. "So many cities razed, so many nations exterminated, so many millions of people put to the sword", grieved the essayist, Michel de Montaigne, writing at the time, "and the richest

166

and most beautiful part of the world turned upside down for the traffic in pearls, gold and pepper! Base and mechanical victories! Never did ambition, never did public enmities drive men against one another, to such horrible hostilities and miserable calamities."

Thus did Michel de Montaigne confide to himself and to the world in his essays. Born in 1533 in Bordeaux, of which he was at one time Lord Mayor, his *Essays* was one of the most enduring and popular books of the time. It was the only book that we know to have been in William Shakespeare's library, for his signature is on the title page of the first English edition. "Their gold", continues Montaigne, writing in high umbrage, "was found, all collected together, being of no other use than for show and parade, preserved from father to son . . . for statues and for adornment of self, and palaces and temples, whereas our gold is all in our circulation and in trade. We cut it up in small and change it into a thousand forms, we scatter and disperse it."

As for the conquistadors themselves: "We have from them their own narrations, for they not only admit these conquests, but boast of them and preach of their depredations. Could it be a testimonial to their justice, or their zeal for religion?"

Quite rightly so. The lawyer from Granada confided the event in his journal. He penned it with emphasis in his lost *Historical Compendium* that when the fabulous treasures had been "satisfactorily distributed", the Friar Domingo de las Casas, who had gone through all these little hells, riding the while on the back of the braying, conquering ass, Marcobaré, now came forward and asked for general contributions to found a chapel to say perpetual masses for the souls of those who had perished – that is, the Spanish soldiers – before they had conquered Bocotá and the Chibcha kingdom. The soldiers, it is recorded, subscribed most willingly.

Naturally, all of these events, as the time-distance factor was immense, were unkown in Santa Marta, as they had been unheard of since the two brigantes had come back with the halt and the dead. It was now that the legal training of the conqueror of the Chibcha was put to use. It became his plan to assume the *de facto* governorship over all the land would call "New Granada", after the land of his birth. He would go to Spain, seek out the King, and ask, as in the manner of Pizarro and Cortés, for his titles and bequests.

François Rabelais, who was just about then preparing, at Lyons, his first edition of *Gargantua,* gave his free, open, laughing testimony of his natural detestation of "hypocrites and the wiles of lawyers. How could fools hope to understand the laws . . . records, bills, plaintiffs, answer demurrers, and other such devilries." It was simple, therefore, for Jiménez de Quesada to convince his rabble laity soldiers that they knew nothing of legal procedure. In the words of Rabelais "their brains had been philogrobalized". The lawyer-conquistador made out a power of attorney to his brother, Hernán, naming him his surrogate whilst he ordered a brigantine built on the Great River so as to make his way to Spain to claim the governorship.

Not surprisingly in this account of golden-spangled follies, events then took a curious twist.

Capitán Lázaro Fonte had been overheard, saying that the manner and methods of their General were not correct and that he, Lázaro Fonte, may God be his witness, would, when he reached Cartagena, the rival city of Santa Marta, near to the Magdalena river, denounce their General for concealing the most valuable emeralds which he did not account for before the Royal Treasurer.

Now Jiménez de Quesada gave himself pride for his absolute integrity over the divisions of spoils. Fonte was brought before him and was himself accused of having obtained emeralds (which he had, on the narrow waterline of the fabulous lake of Guatavita) and was charged for conspiring to defraud the King. He was sentenced to death.

For the first time, Quesada faced full and complete rebellion. Lázaro Fonte, a great captain known for his prowess of horsemanship and his bravery, and who had often saved lives, should not be so "served". Rarely can a lawyer be moved by mere humanity, especially when the "Majesty of Law" is touched. So the captains who pleaded for Fonte left the realm of the "Majesty of the Law" and turned to practical considerations: "Let not your sense of justice", said a spokesman, "be overclouded . . . We are far from Spain and cannot get new recruits and Capitán Fonte is one of our best soldiers. General, spare him."

Spare him he reluctantly did. He was to be banished to the "pacified" Chibcha village of Pasca, 22 miles south-east of Bogotá, in high country, at the edge of the great *páramo* of Suma Paz. Lázaro Fonte was to be exiled to a still hostile area without fighting weapons of any kind. It seemed certain death.

The soldiery made silent protest. On the morrow, twenty horsemen accompanied Lázaro Fonte, who went by foot to Pasca, and into what must have been presumed to be his death place.

That unpleasantry having been resolved and the carpenters among them having reported that the brigantine which they had built of green timber on the River Magdalena four days' journey hence, or sixty miles westward and downward from Bogotá, was in readiness, then at that moment a horseman rode up to inform Quesada that a large Spanish army was advancing on their territory.

The Commander was the redoubtable conquistador, Sebastián de Belalcázar.

[1] *Elegías de Varones Ilustres de Indios* (Madrid 1748). Juan de Castellanos was the author. He was born in Seville in 1523, left Spain, served as a soldier throughout the Antilles and lived in Santa Marta after 1550. At forty, he became a priest and was transferred in 1561 to Tunja – famed for its gold and emerald hoard – where he lived for forty years. The *Elegías* (elegies on famous men of the

American Indies) were written in his old age (he died at 84, for the manuscript is dated 1606) and were based on his gatherings of the notable events of the conquest and search for El Dorado from many of the old and wound-marked conquistadors who still lived. The fourth part of the *Elegías* concerns the conquest of the lawyer of Quesada. He wished to write a new *Cid,* and desired to "out-glow" Alonso de Ericilla's famous epic of the conquest of Chile. He wanted his epic to be for ears "enamoured of the sweetness of this and wished those conquests of the north to be sung in the same measure". They are not. Yet through the rhythmic verbiage, an occasional line carries something of historicity which is, when said and done, all that can be asked of vibrant, violent action being set in the straitjacket of a pedestrian rhyme scheme, wherein truth and fantasy must necessarily scan.

[2] Emeralds, when relatively flawless, since most have pyrite flaws, are worth $20,000 the carat. Five cc weight is a gram; thirty grams, one ounce. One ounce of the best grade emerald is worth over two million dollars.

[3] Spanish *el hombre dorado,* shortened to *El Dorado.*

CHAPTER VIII

The Meeting

Also among those golden things
Was a certain king, who
Went aboard a raft so as to make
Ablutions of his golden self in
The lake.

I F his life, as some said, was like a waking dream, a fairy tale, it must have been more like a nightmare – a *quita sueño*, as the Spaniards call it – for there was much blood spilling in his life. Then, if as others say that two-thirds of Sebastián de Belalcázar's life was a question mark, it is only that the pertinent records were not properly sought and properly read. The date of his birth, it is true, is not fully certain – 1499 or thereabouts – but the form and date of his death is no longer open to question. As for his arrival in America, it is well documented: Bernal Díaz de Castillo, the companion of Cortés in the conquest of Mexico, and that earthly historian of it who vowed he would not twist facts "this way of that", stated that on his

171

voyage "out" in 1514 to Panama among his companions was
Sebastián de Belalcázar. Not that that was his original
name. "Throughout the whole conquest", wrote Germán
Arciniegas (who himself has a wonderful disregard for cor-
rectness) "one never knows who is who. Names are always
being changed about. One never knows where men were
born, who their parents were, or what their original names
were."

Sebastián de Belalcázar could have been named Moyana,
in all likelihood, since he was then illiterate and could at
first not even scrawl his name; those whose duty it was to
keep the records recorded that he was born in the Moorish-
Spanish city of Belalcázar in Estremadura, that nursery of
conquistadors.

So he became Sebastián from Belalcázar and the name
remained. Now simplicity does not mean simpleminded-
ness, nor does illiteracy equate with stupidity, so for all of
his fourteen years young Sebastián showed early his worth
to those pioneers who were trying to open up the Panama
Isthmus and reach "the other sea". By the year 1527, he
had already been listed as one of the founders of the city of
León, in Nicaragua. At the age of twenty-seven, he was
serving as alcalde – that is, mayor of the young colony. In
1530, he received an invitation from Francisco Pizarro, who
knew him from their "Panama days", to join them in the
conquest of Peru. Belalcázar went with horses and men,
was given the title of Capitán, and so on 1531 joined the
Pizarro brothers in the rape of the Sun.

Feared, loved and respected, a formidable triad of virtues, Belalcázar was "courteous to everyone" and – which
seems strange enough in this all-hating world – he was
"disinterested in money matters". Small as were his blue
eyes in an expressive face, which revealed its Moorish
blood, those eyes were ablaze when he felt himself crossed.

He would round three score years and ten before he
yielded to death. He was stronger than Rumiñaui, the
Lord-Inca's best general; he feared neither Indians, jungles,

disease nor hunger; he vanquished all his rivals; he had, it was long thought, even conquered time. That which would defeat him, in the end, would be – a woman.

So, in the year 1533, Belalcázar was "disembowelling Incas with considerable delight" and was rewarded a Capitán's share of the distribution of Atahualpa's ransom, with 407 marcos of silver and 9,909 pesos-weight – that is 9,000 pounds of gold: a sizable fortune. Yet he seemed to give no thought of a squirearchy, or living on or improving his estates in Nicaragua. He pursued his ambitions. When Runiñaui, the one-eyed general of Atahualpa (called "Stony-eyed") evaded capture and fled with the remnants of his army, falling back upon Quito, Sebastian of Belalcázar followed them fifteen hundred miles from Cajamarca to Quito. There in that city close upon the equatorial line, he defeated the last of the Atahualpa's forces and founded, in 1534, the city of Quito.

The sounds of El Dorado came to him in the year 1536. His Indians were pacified, the town council was functioning, a priest had brought wheat grains to high-placed Quito, which took root and grew well. Belalcázar sent out scouting parties northward to see what lands lay ahead. It being reported that it was empty of men – that is, Spaniards (since Indians then were not counted as people) – he was gearing himself to proceed leisurely when an Indian from the town of Llactacunga, who traded north, at a place called Neiva above the waters of Río Magdalena, told him of the land of the Golden Man.

> And gave speech to Belalcázar
> Telling him of
> Things of his country, rich in
> Emeralds and gold.
> Also among those golden things
> Was a certain king, who
> Went aboard a raft so as to make
> Ablutions of his golden self in the lake.

173

On his regal form (as he had seen)
A fragrant resin was laid
And upon it a coat of powdered gold
Golden from foot to the highest brow,
So that there he was, as resplendent
As the beaming sun.

It was, says the historian of this conquest,[1] this Sebastián de Belalcázar, who, "then light of heart", called this Gilded Man "El Dorado".

The royal road of the Incas, twenty feet wide, paved in humid areas, spanned with stone cantilever bridges over small streams, hanging bridges made of plaited rope hawsers over deep canyons, went as far north as Rumichaca. The cultural influence of the Incas, however, spread far beyond that point, for llamas, which were originally developed from the wild guanaco stock, were used beyond the Inca realm, being known to those tribes of the montaña east of Pasco – that is, the provinces of Sibundoy and Macao, which the expeditions of the Welser had reached. Doubtlessly, the Inca state was known at the large Indian trading centre of Neiva.

Without so much as a "by your leave", nor informing Francisco Pizarro, Belalcázar left a lieutenant in his place and started off in 1536 in a leisurely fashion to find this man he had dubbed "El Dorado".

Since he intended to found cities, cut out of the nothingness he believed existed, and form an imperium of his own, Belalcázar took along giant mastiff dogs, cattle, horses, hosts of Indians and a huge herd of swine and pregnant sows. Progress was thus pig-paced.

Early in his career he had been called "the donkey boy",

An ingenious bridge constructed by the Cagabas (San Miguel culture). Bridges were pre-conquest. Pedro de Cieza de León observed in 1547 that, "Over the rivers they build bridges of certain thick strong lianas which grow on the trees . . . fastening and joining them with strong cross-braces". In the bridge pictured here, only vines, bejucos and lianas with sapling lengths are used in the construction.

175

for when in his native Estremadura a donkey that he had been leading having got itself inextricably mired in mud and would do nothing to get out, Sebastián struck and killed it. So faced with choice of punishment or flight, he flew to the port of Cadiz. After clearing with the *Casa de Contratación* (that he was not on the wanted list), he took ship to the New World. Since he was semi-literate (he could not even remember the date of his birth, nor his precise last name), the ship's articles listed him as Sebastián from Belalcázar, the village wherein he was born.

By following the route of the Upper Cauca valley, with a river ever a source of water and fish, he brushed aside such opposition as appeared. In 1537, he founded Popayán, then by marching along the same southern route along the Cauca river and valley, he founded Cali, also in the year 1537, "which in the process of time", said the voice of Pedro de Cieza, "will be one of the richest countries".

In July 1538, recorded his treasurer de la Peña, the Capitán Belalcázar left Popayán to inquire they way to what he called "El Dorado". He went with two hundred men, doubled southward around the gigantic Sierra Nevada de Huila, eternally snow-covered by reason of its altitude of about 15,000 feet. By so doing, he passed over the divide, and discovered the sources of the upper Río Magdalena. So down this valley for eight months he moved, passing many villages. The march, complained one soldier, was filled with "sierras nevadas y unas montañas del malos caminos y males indios" (bad mountains, bad roads and bad Indians). They were travelling through the country of the Pijáo, fearsome warriors; Belalcázar lost twenty of his troops at one time to attacks by poison arrows. Pedro de Cieza recalls the episode. "It must not be thought that the wounds from these arrows were very great, but with the poison on the arrows it was only necessary to make a skin prick and bring out a drop of blood when quickly the poison (*curare*) reached the heart. The victim overcome by nausea bites his own hands and begs quickly for death. So fierce

176

is the flame of this poison that it consumes the entrails."

The one of the twenty who survived was Diego López. He told Pedro de Cieza that, being wounded in the calf while crossing a river, he had his friend cut into the poisoned flesh unmercifully. This prevented the poison from entering the blood stream. So now Belalcázar's forces were reduced to one hundred and eighty-nine men.

They reached the Chibcha trading centre of Neiva, where tribes from the *llanos* to the east, and the gold-rich lands of the Ecuadorian coast to the south-west, and those with salted fish from Cauca, met. There they bartered. Located on the right – that is, the east side, of the Upper Magdalena river – Neiva was (and is) on the 3° N. latitude, in direct line, in truth, with snow-crowned Huila, fifty miles westward.

Having already been warned now that "certain Spaniards were about", as was his wont in these circumstances, they travelled cautiously. For by then the report reached Quesada that Belalcázar "was coming from Peru, a very rich and prosperous country, wearing rich clothes of silk and fine cloaks, silver ornaments, coats of mail and with many Indian servants . . . and a great quantity of pigs to sustain them". He sent out Hernán de Quesada, his brother and second in command, with a small band to acquire an estimation of the situation. Coming suddenly upon those whom they had dubbed *Peruleros* (or men from Peru), horses scented other horses, the alarm was raised and the cavalry of each force faced each other. Then, aware of the irony of the moment, a Capitán of Belalcázar advanced, welcomed Hernán de Quesada with outstretched hands. Amidst "great courtesies", they entered Belalcázar's camp. The contrast between the two forces was glaring. Two years in battle and terrifying travels had reduced Quesada's men to appear as mounted gypsies. Belalcázar, who had travelled leisurely, still maintained certain pomp, with armour, plumed helmets, well-equipped crossbowmen, litter upon litter of pigs, and sows. There was a feast, for

177

The massive monolithic remains of the San Agustín culture, a mysterious tribe which lived between 555 BC and 1200 AD in the extreme upper reaches of the Magdalena river valley, 5,000 feet above sea level. They were discovered only in the late eighteenth century, and excavations have revealed that these early people cultivated root-crops and maize. They had bronze implements and worked gold. They obtained bark cloth by trade from hotlands. It is uncertain whether they traded with the Chibcha tribes.

Magnificent Quimbaya armband of beaten gold.

The chirimoya, delicious tropical fruit from the hotlands.

Kofanes country: Llanos being burned to fertilize the soil.

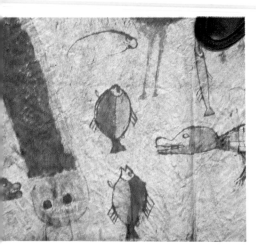

Paintings on bark cloth by a Macaguajes indian, showing animals seen on his journeys.

Monolith of the San Agustín culture representing actual or ceremonial cannibalism which played so prominent a part among the tribes at the time of the conquistadors' arrival.

Stone figure of a snake hawk with its prey. The oil of this bird was believed to be an antidote to snake bites.

Quesada's men had not tasted bacon, or pig, for years and from this Belalcázar learned that he had been forestalled in finding the Man of El Dorado and his lake. What he did not know was that the number of men Quesada had at his disposal was now reduced to one hundred and sixty-six, nor that they no longer had powder for the arquebuses, or that the crossbowmen lacked bolts for their weapons, that many lances were unserviceable. But Hernán de Quesada quickly discovered that Sebastián de Belalcázar had precisely the same number of men, one hundred and sixty-six.

Belalcázar believed and so stated that these lands lay in his patent and jurisdiction. Hernán de Quesada took the position that the lands were those under the royal patent for Pedro Fernández de Lugo of Santa Marta, whose general, his brother, had conquered and effectively occupied them. But his legal point was to be allowed to be discussed between the two leaders. Don Sebastián, with his men and his pigs, was invited to visit the lawyer of Granada: and so he did, riding slowly up the Andes from the hot valley of the Magdalena river to the temperate zones. There, in 1539, the two conquistadors met at Tibacuy, a village south-east of Bogotá.

What neither Belalcázar nor Hernán de Quesada then knew was that meanwhile a third element had been intro-duced into the geometry of forces. Nicolaus Federmann had gained the heights and was on the way to the lake of Guatavita. As we saw before, the Indian guides had told Federmann that if he would like to find people rich with gold on the "otra banda de la Sierra" – that is, on the other side – he must follow the paths to the east. Avoiding Hohermuth, Federmann and his band had painfully climbed from the flat *llanos,* almost at sea level, up through the rain-drenched montaña which was heavy with vegeta-tion, and crossed the Sierra de Suma Paz and the bare *páramo* at over 12,000 feet above sea level. They took forty days to go from the hot plains to the area of permafrost:

181

San Agustín culture: stone fountain of Lavapatas, probably used for ceremonial purposes. The entire exposed rock surface has been carved with swirling animals, lizards and zoomorphic figures.

"twenty-two days", he wrote, "going through a *páramo*, an unpopulated, frigid land". At the place which is still called "Federmann" in his geographical honour, "I lost", he wrote, "many people; and horses: of the three hundred which I left with, only ninety survived, in the march there died seventy men."

They were guided to Pasca, the same Chibcha village twenty-five miles south-east of Bogotá, where Lázaro Fonte had been banished by Quesada and still survived. While out hunting for deer or tapir, he had come across a band of Spaniards with dogs and horses, dressed in animal skins. Of the two avenues of conduct open to him, Lázaro Fonte chose the one of reconciliation to his general. On a piece of polished deer skin, writing with ink made from the red dye of achiote seeds, he wrote a warning which he dispatched by an Indian runner from Pasca. It was delivered to Jiménez de Quesada six days after he had the first report as to the number of Belalcázar's forces.

"My Lord. I have had certain news that a band of Spaniards are at hand. They are coming up from the *llanos*. They are close by and will arrive here (at Pasca) tomorrow. Let your Excellency determine quickly what measures to take." Neither Federmann nor Quesada had heard of each other's presence. Belalcázar had been aware of neither, yet all had heard of the Golden Man, all journeyed from different parts of the continent, and all met at the same time. It was like a tale out of *Amadís*, that famous Romance of Chivalry.

Not, however, to Quesada. He took along his best capitáns, mounted they rode to Pasca, where there was a warm scene of reconciliation with Lázaro Fonte. He was then armed and given back his horse.

Ahead of Federmann's skin-clad band, a lone figure on a worn horse, hair and beard, blending into the animal skins that covered him, rode out of the mist. He stopped, looked upon this apparition of mounted Spaniards, saluted and gave his name – "Pedro Limpias, an old conquistador from Venezuela".

It was the same Pedro Limpias who had made the first excursion in 1530 with Micer Ambrosius Dalfinger to Lake Maracaibo, the same Limpias who, by straining truth here and there, brought back to the Welser colony at Coro the first notices of the people rich with gold. He was very much, as he said, "an old conquistador of Venezuela".

When the rest came up, they were alike ill-fed, fever-stricken, their doublets made of animal skins, hair long and loose falling over the shoulders "after the Indian style". The horses were lean, the ribs showing through the blankets, and they limped from being unshod. Amid them was Federmann, undistinguished from the rest, except for his red hair and matching red beard. The bitterness that he felt, although then unexpressed, he later poured out in a letter to his friend, Francisco Dávila, citizen and alderman of the isle of Santo Domingo: "He had", he wrote (for his letter seems to be the only record of this march) "broke his group into three parts or divisions, so that each section might look for food and not descend in their hundreds upon one village of *llanos*-dwellers." It would be tedious and overlong to repeat the report of a trek which in no wise differed from the others except that in the midst of their extreme hunger, when they would eat horse, saddle and skin, Federmann would not allow them to kill nor eat the chickens. Even when pushed to starvation as they were, it speaks much for the character of Federmann and the discipline that they arrived with hens and roosters, which were to be ancestors of the domesticated fowls of Bogotá.

If Quesada's men had been abashed by the splendour of Belalcázar's forces with their shining armour, silks and cloth from Perpignan, they felt in the presence of the "men of Coro" well presented in their Chibcha woven cotton garments, as compared with the skin-clad skeletons before them. Quesada naturally offered them food, turned over cotton garments to clothe their skeletons, and then he sat down in pure wonderment.

Has there ever been in the chronicles of conquest a

185

situation like this? Three armies all bent on the capture of the Golden Man, marching from three directions; Federmann from the east, one thousand miles through jungles and *llanos;* Belalcázar from the north, eight hundred miles from Quito; and curving in from the south Jiménez de Quesada, nine hundred miles from Santa Marta – all three unaware of each other's presence, all three believing that El Dorado lay under their jurisdiction, all three meeting at the same time with the same number of combatants. There they faced each other, each of the three groups taking positions that formed a triangle with each side holding a front eighteen miles long; it was the plane geometry of equilateral military forces.

However, even though one of Quesada's capitáns, under oath, stated that Federmann had arrived into Chibcha territory with one hundred and sixty men and seventy horses, Federmann in his official account averred that he arrived with two hundred and thirty men and ninety horses. Also he admitted that when he had notice of the arrival of Belalcázar, this very much affected his decision to quickly make terms with the conquistador of the Chibcha.

First, Quesada would turn over to Federmann 4,000 pesos-weight of gold and a number of emeralds. Federmann would allow such of his men who were willing to do so to be incorporated in Quesada's forces. The legal dispute over whose jurisdiction the land of the Chibcha lay would be decided by higher authorities. That done, Quesada, now having a superior force, turned to Belalcázar.

It seemed hardly possible that in this highly charged atmosphere with so much at stake mere reason would find a place in the *dramatis personae.* All were, in a sense, desperate men. Each one of them had disobeyed his superior, and his life could be made forfeit. Federmann had gone off to find El Dorado when he was supposed to have aided the Welserian Governor Hohermuth. Quesada was planning to assume command over his superior in Santa Marta.

Belalcázar had in effect deserted his governorship of Quito without even informing Francisco Pizarro. Only success would justify each and every one's rebellion against authority. Still, reason prevailed.

Quesada, the principal conqueror of the Chibchas, had not studied law at Salamanca merely to cajole the bumpkins in local taverns. He set to work with legal pen. Now many a struggle gained on the battlefield has been lost by the shuffling of words in legal abracadabra. And so it did at El Dorado. The lawyer-conquistador on 17 March drew up a temporary agreement. All three captains agreed to return to Spain together, and at the same time lay their respective positions before the Council of the Indies. Since Jiménez de Quesada was not really certain that El Dorado lay in his jurisdiction (for who knew where anything was in this perplexed geography?), he awarded the Welser 4,000 pesos-weight in gold and emeralds, although Federmann averred that the payment was less, only 15,000 ducats of gold. The result would be that this nemesis of the Golden Man would draw up his accounts in prison. Sebastián de Belalcázar was similarly pacified, and so the three proceeded on the next business – that is, to found and settle a town, as ordered in their *capitulación* (their Contract).

On 29 April 1539, one of those rare sunlit unmisted days on the plain of Bogotá, Quesada, Federmann and Belalcázar became the three founders of the city. The lawyer of Granada went through the ritual of founding the city. First he tore up a tuft of grass. Then placing his foot in the hole from where the grass had been torn, he said: "I take possession of this land in the name of Most Serene Emperor, Charles V of Spain." Then he mounted his horse, drew his sword and challenged anyone either on horseback or on foot to deny his right to found the city. There was, of course, no challenge. Next, the notary drew up the deed of confirmation. Names were signed. Then Quesada marked out with his drawn sword the sites of twelve grass huts to be erected; he left space for the church, a cabilde, erected a cross, and near to it a gibbet. So was founded Santa Fé de Bogotá, in time to be the capital of the Vice-royalty of New Granada and in further time the capital of the Republic of Colombia. The same ceremony was repeated at Vélez, which had priority over all the first-founded cities, since it was near the first Chibcha village discovered at Chipata, and finally Tunja, north-east of Bogotá, where they had reaped the most extensive booty of gold and emeralds, and which was the "other capital" of the Chibchas.

After which the three conquistadors, with an equal number of retainers, descended into the valley of the Magdalena, where a ship had been built on the river's edge at Guataquí. They reached the sea-washed fortress of Cartagena de las Indias by 20 June 1539. Their arrival at Cartagena was obviously a sensation. No one had ever heard of Bogotá. Quesada had been swallowed up for three years and no one knew whether he lived or died. There, too, he learned that the Governor, Pedro Fernández de Lugo, was dead, having died in 1536, and his son, Alonso, departed for Spain. The news of Quesada, the Chibchas, the gold and the emeralds was not long reaching Santa Marta, only a half-day's sail from Cartagena, the acting Governor demanding Quesada's presence and an accounting. The conquistador refused. The Governor was dead. He would give no account except to the Emperor.

On 8 July 1539, the three conquistadors left on the same ship, since Quesada wanted to avoid landing at Santa Marta, and Federmann wished for the same reasons not to go into Coro, and as Belalcázar had no wish one way or another, the ship was directed to Cuba. The ship touched at Jamaica. That their next destination was Cuba is known from an official letter. The Governor of Cuba, Gonzalo de Guzmán, wrote to the Emperor: "On the 24th of August arrived a ship on its way from Jamaica, with people from Cartagena . . . Lic Ximénes (de Quesada), Belalcázar and Federmann. They had sailed from Cartagena on 8th of July, 1539."

Federmann wrote to Francisco Dávila, citizen and regider (alderman) of Santo Domingo, to whom he was under obligation for an indebtedness, and from this source Federmann's personal narrative was preserved. "Iba a *Castilla*" (I am going to Spain), wrote Federmann to his friend, "to lay before his Imperial Majesty all these matters and to ask that proper justice be done to the province of Alcázares (Bogotá-El Dorado)." Federmann betrayed his bitterness, charging the dead Ambrosius Dalfinger and the living Georg Hohermuth with incapacity and want of courage, since "they might otherwise, the one in eight years, the other in three, have secured the wealth of El Dorado which now the 'men of Santa Marta' have taken and carried away in sacks".[2]

Federmann had little moment to lay anything before anyone, least of all the Emperor. He was arrested in Ghent by an agent of the Welser on the charge of defrauding them of gold and emeralds. Only after he had stayed several long months in jail was he transferred as a prisoner to Spain and the case was laid before the proper Spanish authorities.

Gonzalo Jiménez de Quesada stopped off at Lisbon late in 1539, and there met Hernando Pizarro, one of the four Pizarro brothers, who had brought yet another treasure from the Incas to the Spanish Court, and was on his way back to Peru, where a civil war was in progress. The two old conquistadors met, talked, and it is reported, gambled. Both were jailed by the night watch for gambling after hours. Meanwhile, Alonso Fernández de Lugo, son of the dead governor and inheritor of his titles, contracts and claims – one of which was the new empire and its gold and emeralds recently found – was laying his legal snares for the lawyer of Granada.

For the moment the search for El Dorado had lost some of its charm, except, as we shall see, for Philip von Hutten.

Belalcázar also had an immediate successor. A year after Belalcázar's return to the Old World, Gonzalo Pizarro was in Quito in Peru to search out the land of cinnamon and the golden realm.

Of the four Pizarro brothers, Gonzalo (born in 1506) was the most personable. Although his origin was as obscure as all the others, all having been sired in bastardy of different mothers by one founding father, Gonzalo had a bold and commanding appearance, approaching all his adventures with a contagious enthusiasm with which he infected his followers. But Gonzalo also had a singular naïveté, accepting all that was told him without proper examination – bravado, brutality, lust and *real* piety all found synthesis in the person of Gonzalo Pizarro. He had been at the siege of Cuzco and had taken part in almost all of the well-known episodes of the defeat of the Incas. So he had come to Quito to fill the void left by the departure of Sebastián Belalcázar. Yet no sooner had Gonzalo arrived and taken over the governorship of Quito than he announced that he was raising an expedition.

In 1540 east of Quito in the Upper Amazon on the Río Napo, a Spaniard, Pineda by name, had made an armed sortie while looking for "buried" Inca treasure. In so doing, he had found in the tropical montaña what he thought to be a cinnamon tree, a botanical error, of course, since the odour of this cinnamon came from the buds of the blossoms, whereas the real cinnamon comes from the bark of the tree. He also learned from the tribes there "of a people further down who go around adorned with gold". Hearing this, Gonzalo Pizarro, without making any other independent inquiry, declared that he would go off to find this "land of cinnamon". The search for the strait that would lead to the South Sea, and thus to the spiceries, had been a primary requisite demanded of all conquerors who sought the seal of conquest from the King and Council.

Francisco Orellana was to be second in command; the same who was destined to discover the greatest river in the world and sail its entire length. He was a conquistador of property, a founder of the city-port of Guayaquil, and a

190

conqueror of other lands. He had been born in 1511 at Trujillo, Spain (the birthplace also of the Pizarros), came out to the Americas as a page to a conquistador and had early in the game lost his left eye to an Indian arrow. He was twenty-nine when he set off for the "land of cinnamon".

Pizarro gathered two hundred and ten Spaniards, many horses, pigs, dogs and llamas, and, as the land was not yet depopulated, four thousand Indians. They moved in the direction of a snow-covered height called Suru-Urcu, and crossed the bitterly cold *páramo* of Papa-llacta. As if the ice-laden winds on these frigid heights were not quite enough, the volcano Cayambe erupted, and the Spaniards remembered how the earth had opened, swallowing a whole village in a Mephistophelean vapour of sulphurous smoke.

The down-going was so heavily verdured that the jungle seemed less a land than an element. The forest was so vast, so titanic, the trees so thickly massed, that the sun never penetrated the lower part, and so constant in temperature, so exuberant in growth that the Spaniards on their first acquaintance with it had to be re-orientated to size. What were mere grasses in Spain were here bamboos sixty feet high, the milkworts and periwinkles of Europe here were the size of trees, and the lowly violet here became a plant the size of an apple tree.

Into this verdured hell passed the long defiles of Gonzalo Pizarro's army. Within seventy days and after covering one hundred and fifty miles people died at the rate of four to the mile, and when they arrived at the land of cinnamon "we found", Gonzalo Pizarro wrote to his king, "the trees that were said to produce cinnamon . . . but it is a land and a commodity in which Your Majesty cannot be benefitted".

So "finding ourselves on the banks of the Río Coca we came to the conclusion that the best plan would be to build a boat . . . and on it float down to some region of plenty". On the banks of the Coca, the most western tributary of the Napo, which in turn flows into the greater Amazon, they

built a small brigantine, large enough to transport the weaker as well as all of the heavier cargo. There was no problem of obtaining wood. Nails were made by converting the iron of the horseshoes of the dead horses into spikes, chicle sap extracted from trees when boiled became their pitch, and the tattered clothes of those who looked for "the land of cinnamon" became the oakum for caulking.

In the two months they launched the *San Pedro,* the first European ship to sail the inland sea of the Amazon. Orellana captained it, while Gonzalo Pizarro led his men through the riverine forest. At night the two, river and land groups, bivouacked together. All that could be eaten was eaten: horses, pigs, cattle and even, when need was great, the Indians ate Indians. Food-gathering in the jungles, as all knew who had followed the path to the Golden Man, is laborious and unrewarding, so that Pizarro, having heard that just below where the Río Napo swelled with the concourse of many rivers was a "rich land and populous", ordered Orellana to sail there, procure provisions, and then bring the *San Pedro* back to where they waited. It was his singular naïveté again and it would be his doom. He never considered that a river current of 10 miles an hour cannot be gone against by sail; still Orellana obeyed. The ship was propelled into midstream and disappeared. It was then that Francisco de Orellana made his famous remark: "After boiling our boots in herbs we set off for the kingdom of gold." The *San Pedro* would not return.

On New Year's Day, 1542, the fifty-seven men on the *San Pedro* were aware that all of the larger rivers they had travelled were only a fluvial prelude to the great one they had entered. They were now in the main stream of the greatest river in the world, which they called "Orellana" after their captain.

The illusion of the nearness of the Golden City was heightened by the fact that the villages of the Machipara

Giant plants in jungle areas such as those encountered by Gonzalo Pizarro and his men.

193

Indians had houses "glimmering white". They were attacked by Indians "in a great many canoes . . . gaily coloured". This gave them all the outward trappings, in their minds, of the Golden City. Later on, when they passed these other villages which lay back of the river, on the flat *llanos* that lay between river and river, he observed that: "There were many roads here that entered into the interior . . . very fine highways."

Since we know that by now transmogrification of Golden Man to Golden City was complete, the Golden Man had vanished, but in another shape, as the Golden City, it was transferred to the lower Orinoco, then into the Amazon. The myth, protean as myths should be, was now an Amazon city with fine highways, and the small lake of Guatavita had moved fifteen hundred miles from its original site.

Then came the Amazons. Orellana came upon "the excellent land and dominion of the Amazonas". It was here that the myth of the Golden Man coalesced with the Amazons. They were attacked by fighting women. "These women were very white and tall, and wear their hair very long and braided and wound about the head, and they are very robust and go about naked, except their privy parts which are covered. With their bows and arrows in their hands, they do as much fighting as ten men, and indeed there was one woman among these who shot an arrow a span deep into one of the brigantines; others did the same until our brigantines looked like porcupines.

"The Indians said that their houses were of stone and with regular doors, and that from one village to another went roads . . . with guards stationed at intervals along them so that no one might enter without paying duty. The

Gonzalo Pizarro and Francisco de Orellana, finding themselves on the banks of the río Coco, built a boat to float down the Amazon to "some region of plenty". This contemporary woodcut of ship-building in America (by Theodor de Bry, 1594) gives a good idea of the carpenters' tools in use at the time. Orellana obtained nails by converting the iron of the un-needed horseshoes; tattered clothes were used for caulking. (British Museum)

Captain asked if these women bore children; the Indian answered that they did. He asked him how, not being married, and there being no man residing among them, they became pregnant; he replied that these Indian women consorted with Indian men at times, when desire came over them. They also assembled a great horde of warriors and went off to make war on a very great chieftain whose residence is not far from the land of these women, and so by force they brought them to their own country and kept them with them for the time that suited their caprice, and after they found themselves pregnant they sent them back to their country without doing them any harm. Afterwards, when the time came for them to have children, if they gave birth to male children they killed them or sent them to their fathers, and if females, they raised them with great care and instructed them in the arts of war. He said, furthermore, that among all these women there was one ruling woman; she had the name Conori.

"He said that there was in their possession a very great wealth of gold and silver, and that in the case of all women of rank and distinction their eating utensils were nothing but gold or silver, while the other women, belonging to the plebeian class, used a service of wooden vessels and clay. He said that in the capital and principal city in which the ruling mistress resided, there were five very large buildings, which were places of worship, and houses dedicated to the Sun, which they called *caranain,* and that inside, from half of man's height above the ground up, these buildings were lined with heavy wooden ceilings covered with paint of various colours, and that in these buildings they had many gold and silver idols in the form of women, and many vessels of gold and silver for the service of the Sun."[3]

The *San Pedro* and its sister ship, *Victoria,* newly-built, emerged at the mouth of the Amazon and sailed on to Santo Domingo.

There Francisco Orellana made his report, and took, as usual, the sea-way to Spain, where he was confirmed in his discoveries. His "Amazons" raised public curiosity and funds, and he sailed out again with five hundred men to become the "Governor of the Amazons", and to search for the Golden City. Still embracing the delusive phantom, he died on shipboard in sight of the Amazon river.

[1] Fray Pedro Simón, *Prima parte de las noticias historiales de Tierra Firma* (English trans.), Hakluyt Society Publications, London, 1861.

[2] The original letter is lost, but part of it was preserved in Oviedo's *Historia General y Natural de los Indias.* Lib XXV Cap. XVLL, pp. 317–320.

[3] Friar Gaspar de Carvajal of the Order of Santo Domingo kept the journal of this epic voyage. Born in 1504, he was thirty-seven when he wrote it (1541). He was one of the very few who lived to enjoy his reputation. As Vicar-general and "Protector of the Indians", he survived "a thousand little hells", dying in Lima at the age of eighty.

"I have chosen to take upon myself this little task and recount the progress and outcome of our journey and navigation, not only in order to tell about it and make known the truth in the whole matter, but also in order to remove the temptation from many persons who may wish to relate this peregrination of ours or publish just the opposite of what we have experienced and soon; and what I have written and related is the truth throughout: and because profuseness engenders distaste, so I have related sketchily and summarily all that has happened to Captain Francisco de Orellana and to us companions of his who went off after separating from the expeditionary of Gonzalo Pizarro" . . . The writing was done under considerable handicap, for during one battle he was struck in the eye with an arrow. "They hit no one but me", he wrote, "they planted an arrow shot right in one of my eyes, in such a way that the arrow went through to the other side, from which wound I lost my eye."

CHAPTER IX

Philip von Hutten's Strange Desires

As God is my witness it is not that I am motivated only by the vision of riches, rather, the trip which I am about to make is to fulfil my strange desires, which I have for long had. I could not have tranquilly died until I had visited the New World – Philip von Hutten (writing to his brother in 1535)

HE marvellous element in a myth is that it is not bound in time or space or credulity. Since it lies in the realm of the supernatural, it does not have to obey the laws of logic or enter the realms of antithesis. So it was with El Dorado.

In itself, the Golden Man was not wholly mythical. An Indian chieftain was ceremonially smeared with resin and dipped in gold dust, this strange custom being enacted where the salt and emeralds came from. All Indian informants in the beginning had said no more. The Spaniards

199

were led to the salt and to the place where the emeralds came from; they had talked to Indians at Guatavita who had seen the ceremony and they had been taken to the lagoon and shown the place of the golden ablutions.

The fact that the tribe of Indians around Guatavita, who acquired with so much difficulty gold from the without, should do anything so eminently impractical as to throw countless golden images into the lake surprised even those tribes with the most outlandish customs. So it happened that, since intertribal trade was widespread and talk is the life of man, the Golden Man became known to many.

"When I asked", wrote Oviedo, one of the first historians, "why they call this prince the Gilded King, the Spaniards, who have been in Quito or have come to Santo Domingo (and there are at present [1540] more than ten of them in this city), make reply that from what they hear respecting this from the Indians, this great lord or prince goes about continually covered with gold as finely pulverised as fine salt. For it seemeth to him that to wear any other kind of apparel is less beautiful, and that to put on pieces or arms of gold stamped or fashioned by a hammer or otherwise is to use something plain or common, like that which is worn by other rich lords and princes when they wish; but that to powder oneself with gold is something strange, unusual, and new and more costly, because that which one puts on in the morning is removed and washed off in the evening and falls to the ground and is lost. And this he does every day in the year. While walking clothed and covered in this manner his movements are unimpeded, and the graceful proportions of his person, of which he greatly prides himself, are seen in beauty unadorned. I would rather have the chamber besom of this prince than the large gold smelters in Peru or in any other part of the world. Thus it is that the Indians say that this cacique or king is very rich and a great lord, and anoints himself every morning with a very fragrant gum or liquor and over this ointment he sprinkles powdered gold of the requisite fineness, and his entire

200

person from the sole of his foot to his head remains covered with gold, and as resplendent as a piece of gold polished by the hand of a great artificer. And I believe, if this cacique uses this, that he must have very rich mines of a similar quality of gold, because I have seen much of it in tierra firma, that is, on the mainland . . .

"They were ready to give full credence to even greater fictions than the Golden Fleece or the Apples of the Hesperides, and would not have been surprised to find Ophir or Tarshish in the valleys of the Orinoco or the Amazon. The spirit of adventure and romance dominated everyone not only in the Indies but in the mother country as well.

"For all this Spanish nation", continued the chronicler Oviedo, "is so desirous of novelties that whenever they be called with a beck or soft whispering voice, to anything arising above water, they speedily prepare themselves to fly and forsake certainties, under hope of an higher degree, to follow in a 'golden path'."

How often does man act like an intellectual maniac? How often does he unravel everything in theory and tangle up everything in fact? So the dream of El Dorado should have died where it originated, in the destruction of the Chibcha realm, except for a remark made by Nicolaus Federmann, in his letter to Francisco Dávila: "The stories about the Meta river being rich with gold are not wholly false. For that river does rise in the mountains that border the plain: and the House of Meta which was sought for so long is the Temple of Sogamosa, the holy [golden] objects in which the 'men of Santa Marta' carried away in sack fulls."

This, coming from one who had spent ten years in search of El Dorado, provided the myth with new dimensions. It was no longer associated wholly with the Chibchas. It lay somewhere in the vastness of the Amazon. The golden man was transmogrified into a golden city, and it was to that Golden City lying out somewhere in the *llanos* where Philip von Hutten wished to go to fulfil his "strange desires".

After returning with Georg Hohermuth to Coro on 27 May 1538, Philip von Hutten kept himself busy by writing to his family while he waited for Hohermuth to recover from the ravages that came from their first trek across the *llanos* in search of the golden cities.

"As God is my witness it is not", he wrote to his father on 31 March 1539, "that I am motivated only by the vision of riches, rather, the trip which I am about to make is to fulfil my strange desires, which I have for long had. I could not have tranquilly died until I had visited the New World." He knew the sorrow that his absence caused his mother and how it distressed his brothers and sisters. "But I hope that you and my brothers, who are fully aware of a nobleman's honour and his obligations, will understand, and that you must all understand my motivations."

In January 1540, the following year, on his return from the interior where he was already setting up depots for the next search, he learned through his brother Moritz, Bishop of Eychstätt (that is Eichstadt near München), that his father had died: "I learn with great distress of heart of the death of our dear father." He was being pressured to return and take over family duties. He was aware, as he wrote, that his brother, the Bishop, was highly critical of his remaining there. "Take into account, my dear brother, the figure I would cut if I now return home. Nothing but debts. What then if I would return and everyone finds great wealth. I would have spent five years in this country just when honour and wealth is being distributed . . . Therefore, I ask you to reconsider my reasons and do not prithee believe I wish to continue out of disobedience or frivolity. I would so much desire to bring back to Germany honour to our name and family. All through my life (he was then only twenty-nine years), I have searched for fortune and happiness . . . so I will try once more. Then I think my heart will be at peace with itself."

Hutten related all the news about the civil wars in Peru between the Pizarro and Almagre factions, how others from

Cartagena had been killed and eaten, about the voyage of the fleet of ships up the Río de la Plata in Argentina, where only a few returned alive. He wrote of how Cortés had found riches, honour and a title in his conquest of Mexico, everywhere else people were finding kingdoms of gold – "the only ones who have had bad luck are we in Venezuela. Faustus, the philosopher, was right to say that 1538 would be a bad year, and unlucky".

Philip von Hutten was naturally excited by the news of Federmann. "If I had reached him, when his trail crossed ours, I would now be with Federmann in Germany, or Spain, with 20,000 pesos-weight of gold, only for a winter's work. The details of Federmann's journey you can learn from the Herrn Welser – I have no doubt that they will send him abroad again."

Of this there was serious doubt. Federmann was now jailed by the Welser in Flanders. They declared he had defrauded them of gold and emeralds, and there he was still sitting in jail. In May 1540, in Antwerp, while his petition was read by Charles V, Federmann asked that he be personally examined by the Emperor. It is to the great credit of Spain, distracted as it was, that Charles personally intervened. The case was transferred to Spain where Federmann went, having given a heavy bond, arriving at Madrid on 2 February 1541. Already the Welser were feeling the royal animosity. For Charles V had had his fill fighting against the *Luteranos,* and more than one of the Welser company had openly embraced the new faith of Martin Luther. Still the Welser kept up the pressure, perhaps because it was their sight of the gold and emeralds they had been so long promised, and for which so much Welser gold had been expended. Federmann, weakened by his sojourn seeking out the Golden Man, then two years' imprisonment, was already far advanced along the road to death when he appeared before the court.

Meanwhile, he had made out his testament and had put into German his *Indianische Historia: A Beautiful, Agreeable*

Account – and entrusted it to his sister Elizabeth to be published.[1] Then he died. The secretary of the Court read to the presiding judge that "Nicolaus Federmann, German, native of the city of Ulm, which is in Germany, died in his present life – *falleció de esta presente vida* – in this court of Valladolid, Spain, two or three days ago, that is between the 21st and 22nd of February."

Federmann had expired in the arms of the Golden Man.

Philip von Hutten could not have known this. Obviously not, for he was writing: "I am prepared to travel on the new expedition with our Hohermuth, although I would prefer to wait for Federmann."

Then Georg Hohermuth, who had long been ill in the isle of Santo Domingo, died on 11 June 1540, and on 10 March 1541, a letter arrived from Spain from Charles V conferring on Philip von Hutten the title of Capitán-General, and acting Governor of the Welser Colony of Coro. He was then 29 years of age.

In informing his brother, now the Bishop of the Cathedral of Warzburg, of this new honour, he asked him to try to influence the Welser to also make him the new Governor of Coro. "Once this honour will be conferred on me, which is in keeping with our family honour, I will leave for Germany. Whatever agreement you will reach with the Welser, I shall accept it."

Philip von Hutten now worried over the delays: "Our journey is being postponed longer than I expected. We have much news from the other provinces that all our neighbours have started on journeys, but we hope to get there first."

In the summer of 1541, Philip von Hutten began to assemble "two hundred men and one hundred and fifty horses, making ready to conquer rich lands in the name of our Emperor Charles V and the Herrn Welser". On this last search, he was to have an important guest participant: "Some days ago the son of Bartholomäs Welser arrived here: a very clever fellow and we were very pleased to see him. I have no doubt that the Herrn Welser intend to make him Governor."

By this time the House of Welser in Augsburg had fully succumbed to the gold fever, about which the poet had said: "Everything hangs . . ." (Nach Golde drängt / Am Golde hängt / Doch Alles.)

The most variegated of people were affected by the gold fever. "They thirsted mightily for gold," remembered a historian, "they wished to stuff themselves with it, they starved for it, lusted for it as pigs do for acorns". The spirit of gold-search turned into different channels; some set out for the Fountain of Youth, which now became located in the New World, others for the "seven enchanted cities of Cibola", which, it was said, must be in the New World since they were founded by seven Portuguese bishops who had fled before an Arab invasion of Spanish Iberia in the eighth century. And what of St. Ursula and her eleven thousand virgins – did they not vanish also to the New World? And there were the Amazons and Federmann's pigmies. "America as Fantasy" seemed to hold power over all. The European mind was voluntarily hallucinated by it all, they cultivated the myths, extended them until they ramified into the most remote of places.

They were awed by the marvellous. The most thoughtful believed it without believing in it, but did not love it less because of it. What else could they not believe after the Lord-Inca Atahualpa had filled a huge room twice with silver and once with gold, which caused a river of bullion to flow into Europe to circulate as ducats, sovereigns, gulden? And this followed by the hoard of the Chibchas which included over eighteen hundred emeralds. Now even the possible was not enough; people wanted the impossible, which became only the impossible because it was never realized.

Such a one was Bartholomäs Welser, head of the House of Welser. Bartholomäs Welser, sometimes called the Fifth to distinguish him from the others of the same name, succeeded his father, Anton, on his death in 1518. His eyes had first opened in Memmingen, a Reichsstadt, on 25 June 1484. At the age of four he was brought to Augsburg and there reached his majority in the head office of the firm. He, who made a profession of not being astonished at anything, could no longer suppress the excitement that the search for the Golden City created in his banker's soul. It was now thought so important that the head of the Welser group must send his eldest son, heir and namesake, Bartholomäs Welser, to take part in this expedition.

During the fourteen years since the Welser had held the fief of Venezuela it had been a continuous financial drain with scarcely any financial return. Yet the contract that was drawn up had made their position clear. They conformed to the laws of Spain and the ordinances of the *Casa de Contratación* in respect to the founding of cities, the erection of forts, the baptism of Indians, even though this was not their primary objective. Venezuela had not been given to them; it was rather a leasehold, a security for the 141,000 ducats loaned by the Welser to Charles V. Therefore, the *object* of the Welser presence in Venezuela was to recover revenues as quickly as possible in any form. So, in 1541, even though the search for El Dorado had strewn the void with corpses of men and beast, old Bartholomäs Welser now so believed in the reality of it, he was willing to risk the life of his son and heir to further its discovery.

In his own world – that is, the world of the patricians of Augsburg that formed his milieu – Bartholomäs Welser, the sixth of that name and line, was a pleasant, well-informed young man. And for this position, a humanist. He was born and reared in Augsburg and, though there is no portrait of him, he is said to have looked remarkably like his father: the firm Welser jaw, the rather humped Roman nose, sharply highlighted brown eyes, with a bold cavalier moustache and short beard. He came out to this raw, undisciplined New World without any experience for what would lie ahead of him. He was rich. He was heir to the Welser fortune, his father had been ennobled, a Reichsfreiherr, and his aunt, Phillipina, married to the Archduke Ferdinand, so it would have been inhuman if he had not allowed these prerogatives to be betrayed in discussions or arguments with any other who was of debased birth.

On 1 August 1541, after the usual formalities, the Capitán-General Philip von Hutten, aged 29, was ready to "fulfil his strange desires": all of his one hundred men were mounted, including the accompanying padre Frutos de Tudela, all riding unkept, of course, the usual cargo bearer Indians.

Pedro Limpias was appointed principal capitán of the expedition, being the most experienced of all. As we have seen, he had accompanied Nicolaus Federmann in his entrance to Bogotá and had been the first who had brought to Coro the notice of a people dwelling in the high sierra who traded in salt and who had gold. Oviedo, the historian whose job it was to ferret out mere truth from mere surmise, knew this Pedro Limpias personally and found him "a man who possessed much optimism and would be useful in this new march to conquest because he knew the native languages and had practical knowledge of the land . . .". A man of ill-fortune, Pedro Limpias was very "americano" and fully aware of the immense difficulties that lay before them.

Since they were all mounted, and travelling over well-known paths, they reached the River Casanare in four months. Following the first trail they had made on the Hohermuth expedition in 1535, they moved quickly enough, reaching the Opia river by August 1542, in half the time it took them before. There they found the Guaypés tribe, who were purveyors of salt, which came from the salt mines of Zipaquirá. They were only a three-day walk to one of the ancient Chibcha markets at Turmeque, which meant although the Chibcha had already been virtually destroyed the salt trade was still in movement. So were the gold and jewels.

Beyond this they came across the spoor of other groups, who had preceded them. There were the usual burned

Indian houses, horses partially consumed by jaguars and vultures, parts of helmets, broken weapons and, of course, grave upon grave.

They followed on. In the second year out of Coro, Pedro Limpias, with twenty-eight selected veterans, marched to the upper reaches of the Caguán river, a tributary of the great Caquetá (which in turn flowed into the Amazon) and came across at its headwaters on the plains a large settlement of Indians – probably Kofanes. In one of the mêlées that occurred, Pedro Limpias captured a chieftain named "Capta". As his ransom, he offered a crown of fine gold, which he said came from the warrior women who lived far below on the "big" river.

The Amazons – warrior women – was a recurring theme, tall female Indians, full of guile, of great strength, and with many stone-built houses. They followed the course of the Caguán downward, found other Indians who gave some small emeralds and called the place "Esmeralda", which name it still bears.

Then Philip von Hutten, at a date marked 8 May 1543, as inscribed in the journal, ordered a march in the direction as given by the chief called Capta, south-east toward and then along a river which they called the "Vaupés" after the tribe (Gauyaupés) who lived around and about it.

In the three hundred and sixty-mile march, they followed the sparsely populated *llanos,* then mesa tablelands, and several higher areas – as much as 2,400 feet in altitude. Where the upper Vaupés was a mere trickle, a lake was formed during the rainy season, which either in hope or jest was called "El Dorado" (the name still is retained). So as the Vaupés gathered more streams into its riverine body, it became a tumbling river with jungles on its banks.

The jungles were tenanted by jaguars, anteaters, pig-sized capybaras, deer, wild pigs, tapirs, monkeys and sloths. In the trees dwelt a paradise of birds: the snow-crested bellbird whose startled cry is like the melodious sound of a clapped bell, toucans long of beak, brilliant

The route across the treeless plains, from a nineteenth-century engraving. Macabre remains of previous expeditions were always present, reminding those in search of El Dorado how many had failed to find anything but death. (Mary Evans Picture Library)

orange-plumed cock-of-the-rocks, umbrella birds, oilbirds, ghostly egrets, herons, trogons, trumpeter birds, and the bringer of a feathered terror, the harpy eagle. The streams teemed with aquatic life: fish, turtles, dolphins, crocodiles, and cannibalistic piranha, and in stagnant pools, electric eels. But insects were the dominant element. Insects were the masters of the dank earth: army ants, *tumecas,* an inch long with dreaded sting as well as bite, attacking anything that moved. There were other ants which defoliated and carried leaf fragments down into the earth to fertilize fungus gardens on which they lived. Termites moved cryptobiotically inside trees, gnawing ceaselessly into heartwood until trees became as hollowed out as a conduit pipe. There were mosquitoes bringing the tertain fever, flies, stingless bees always in search of exudate, terribly armed wasps, and the minute fly *jejenes.* Insects were a plague night and day; there was no point of rest.

By this time, the death toll because of the lack of salt began for horse and man alike.

The Guayaupés, who received them without contest, gave them food in exchange for trade goods. However, they urged them not to go into the Territory of Omaguas ("flat-heads", as they called them, from their practice of skull deformation) since the white men were too few and they were so many. Hutten ignored that advice and on Christmas Day 1544, between these two jungle-verdured rivers, on a higher *meseta,* they found extended grass *llanos.* The expedition, all mounted, took this road, Philip von Hutten, Pedro Limpias, and forty picked men trying to reach "that other kingdom which is called Homaga [or Omagua]".

The giant ant-eater. Although an eater of ants, it has fierce combative claws which it unhinges when attacked.

A green tree frog, inoffensive, nocturnal and noisy, and quite edible.

The harpy eagle, ruler of the treetops, fiercely beaked, with horrendous talons.

Most communal Indian dwellings are distantly spaced one from the other, and massed dwellings are unusual since each communal house must have fields about it for cultivation; as new forest is always being cut, burnt and brought into cultivation, centralization of house structures is not a usual tribal pattern. Yet here the conquistadors saw what they believed to be hundreds of houses laid out in formal street pattern; in the centre was a high building with an observation tower.

Philip von Hutten was the first white man to look upon the Omaguas, who through no choice of their own had been chosen to occupy the site of the myth of the Golden City. By 1611, it was an *idée fixe* in history: "South of the province of Venezuela", said one of the historians with a fine disregard for distance and geography, "are the Omaguas within the province of El Dorado".

The Omaguas, probably of Tup-Guarani stock, occupied the plains above the rivers between the Vaupés and the Japura and built their large communal houses of flattened bamboo with palm thatch. They were found using copper axes "such as they use in Peru", and they worshipped various gods, which were represented by painted figures on bark cloth and set up in a large communal house (the great house which Hutten saw). They were pottery-makers and, as well, water people skilful in passing the rapids. The dugouts, immense for the area, were as long as forty-five feet, hollowed out fron a single cedar log, often a yard wide. Since classicism now had its place by naming the fighting women "Amazons", the Omaguas were called "The Phoenicians of the Amazons".

They subsisted mainly on *cassava* – that is, manioc – prepared in huge inch-thick pancakes; dried and hardened, these *cassava* cakes last for weeks. They can be eaten as hard tack, put into stews or made into gruel by adding water and salt. It is on *cassava* that Philip von Hutten's men principally subsisted.

The Omaguas were warriors using spear and wooden

shields, and were also known for their skill in fishing, using the fish poison *barbasco.* The Portuguese, in 1631, found the first rubber being worked among the Omaguas.

All this naturally was unknown to Hutten when he and his forty mounted conquistadors looked down on the most populated village they had ever seen in all their years in the Americas. No more for it, this was "El Dorado". Being discovered, the priests blew their sacred bamboo trumpets; the war drum, made out of an artifically hollowed tree trunk, beat the staccato warning of attack. Then the Omaguas (Hutten thought that there were over a thousand) swarmed about them; hemmed in and unable to manoeuvre in the plaza, they retreated to the higher cleared area where they could use their horses and lances more effectively. The Omaguas followed, and in such mass that even their horses were ineffectual. All were wounded, Philip von Hutten seriously; they retreated and were set upon continuously until they reached the boundary of the Guayapés.

For weeks Hutten wavered between life and death. Although it was later seen that he would recover, still he would not be in a fit condition to command. Pedro Limpias now claimed the leadership, as the oldest, most experienced captain. But Bartholomäs Welser insisted that he was second in command, doubtless mentioning that after all they, the Welser, were the proprietors of the land. There are few details of the quarrel. Philip von Hutten allied with Welser, while the soldiers took sides between the two, and so in that atmosphere they began in 1545 the familiar long trek back to Coro. Even though he was badly wounded and wasted, and had to be carried in a hammock, Philip von Hutten's enthusiasm remained undiminished. So certain was he that the Omaguas had the city of El Dorado that he was planning to return armed with ducats and men to conquer them. Therefore possessed of fever from wounds and gold, he was carried to Coro. It was the dry season of 1545.

Neither the earth nor the events of living history stood

The Amazonian dugout, hollowed from a single tree and highly buoyant.

Kofanes chieftain wearing guacampo feathers in his ears and a jaguar-tooth necklace.

still while the five-year-long march of the Welser took place. Though they were swallowed up in the vast distances of time-space, the rest of the world was most obviously not.

In the Welser counting house of Augsburg, there had been at first no undue anxiety over the five years of silence. They had grown used to the vast hiatus that separated the Old World from the New. They trusted in the leadership of young Philip von Hutten. Still the Governorship of Coro had to be filled, and so the Welser sent out another of their kindred, Herr Heinrich Rembold, who was named factor and executive agent. Whatever his title, it mattered little, for he sickened and died within the year 1544 of his arrival. Whereupon the Council of the Indies, to fill the vacuum, named a bishop as an interim Governor. Yet even while he was going through the rituals of taking office, actual power fell to the scrivener-royal in residence, one Juan Carvajal.

215

Inga Indian, descended from the tribes Philip von Hutten encountered in the Amazon jungle.

Perhaps it will be recalled that Micer Ambrosius Dalfinger, of almost faded memory, had on his arrival in Coro in 1530 as the first Welser governor made out several official documents. These were always written out by Juan Carvajal. "Paso de mí" (Passed before me) it read and many papers had passed before Juan Carvajal in these fifteen years, so that he now was taking a proprietary interest in the Golden Man, not as such, but in the land which the expeditions had opened. He had himself long been disillusioned over the search for this will-o'-the-wisp; he felt that actual colonization, the raising of cattle and cotton, and such like, was the real worth of the land; ranching Indians and searching for gold was secondary. Consequently he opposed the Welser.

So, the wave of anti-Welser feeling throughout the small settlements in an around Coro was concentrated in the person of Juan Carvajal. This in turn reflected the Spanish reaction to the growth of the Reformation in Europe. The

216

intense religious feelings of the Spanish were evoked when Martin Luther broke his monkish vows and married a nun. Now, in their minds, Turk and Luther were equated with Judas. On the higher official plane, the Reformation was regarded, after the Peace of Crespy in 1544, as a cancer in the body politic, which must be removed by force. After several affronts by the Lutherans, real or presumed, Charles V set off with an army of 25,000 and defeated their army at Mühlberg on 13 April 1547. With that victory Charles V thought he had brought all Europe back into the fold of the Holy Roman Empire. Now since Spanish lives and Spanish taxes had to be exacted for this war, anyone who embraced Lutheranism was suspect. As many of the Welser group had sided with the Reformation, this made many suspect. So long as the Welser had the ear of Charles V, acquired through fresh loans and credits, they escaped the imperial wrath. The fact that Welser's daughter, Phillipina, was married to Duke Ferdinand of Tyrol somewhat eased their equivocal position. Still, the Welser were losing their power at Court, and Charles was listening more closely to his Council that he should abrogate the claims of the Welser to their leasehold on Venezuela. Thus since the least likely place for a secret is in the secret council chamber, this attitude became known to the Spanish officials. Slowly it percolated down to the lesser men, then overseas to the Americas, and finally into the implacable being of Juan Carvajal. He may well have had, as was said then and later, "a scrivener's soul" – that is, one who thinks and acts in small legalities – but, small as it was, it had to be considered.

The resentment of Pedro Limpias increased, as he later confessed, with the press of the empty days as they on the way back recrossed the flat anaemic *llanos*. He had been among the first to set off for the fief of the Golden Man. He had actually, when he travelled with Nicolaus Federmann, arrived at the "land rich with gold and emeralds" only to be balked of his share by having been anticipated by Gonzalo Jiménez de Quesada.

A capitán's share of the gold and emeralds given to him by Nicolaus Federmann had been, while justly shared, but small recompense for all his years of service. Now he had been deprived of the leadership of the last expedition. Jealousy set in with embittering hate, and it proceeded with overwhelming speed, producing an effect on Pedro Limpias as salt on ice; it accomplished with frightful rapidity the total dissolution of his being.

In the matter of emotions, there is a different reaction between German and Spaniard. When a German hates someone sufficiently and this someone is assailed by misfortune, a German becomes elated; he has *Schadenfreude,* malicious joy. In the Spaniard the reaction differed; he was not particularly overjoyed at his enemy's ruin, but he became rabidly uncontrollable in envy over his success.

Pedro Limpias was as ignorant of what had transpired in the colony while they were gone during the five years (1540–1545) as were the Welser's men, but he was soon made to know by Juan Carvajal, who was then attending to the formation of a colony a hundred miles from Coro. Limpias in his revenge revealed that Hutten had lost half of his men, almost all his horses, and furthermore was plotting against the King.

Philip von Hutten came on very slowly conducting all the wounded and sick. When he arrived at Acarigua, near the Tocuyo river (well-remembered since the time of Nicolaus Federmann), he found on the trunk of an immense ceiba tree near the road a carved sign under a cross:

Aquí estuvo Juan de Villegas . . .

Here waited Juan de Villegas for four days, waiting for Philip von Hutten. As he did not come he went on to Tocuyo where he can now be found.

218

When von Hutten found Villegas he was apprised of the new "situation". Although he himself was Captain-General and had been Governor-designate when he left, now there was a new "Governor". At first he refused to meet Carvajal, then he relented, and they met at vespers close upon Easter Day, 24 April 1545. After they had exchanged their various credentials and titles, good or bad, false or real, Juan Carvajal revealed that he was acting Governor of the colony, not Hutten. In that capacity Juan Carvajal wished to prevent him from continuing to Coro, whereas Philip von Hutten, Captain-General of Venezuela, insisted that he, unless there was a contrary order, would leave for the coast and there make his report to the King. He insisted that he and his soldiers who had searched for El Dorado for five years, during which time they had lost so many and so much, had the right to return to the coast. He wanted to rest his men and give an account to His Majesty and to the Herren Welser.

"Bélzares!", repeated in the Spanish pronunciation, "You hear that?" John Carvajal shouted to the soldiers. "You, all of you here are my witnesses that he said this governación was that of the Bélzares. Here there are no Bélzares, only His Majesty." To which von Hutten answered calmly enough: "By which they are here for His Majesty". Whereupon Carvajal ordered their arrest, but Philip von Hutten answered: "What you have ordered can only come from a judge, and I am the Captain-General of these realms." Moreover, he insisted he would proceed to Coro to make a report about his journey "for the king and the Bélzares".

The soldiers, now divided as much as were their leaders, stood, swords unsheathed, tense and expectant. At this Bartholomäs Welser went into action, lowering his lance and galloping toward Carvajal to run him through. As he got near, his horse, so weakened by the long ordeal, had not strength for knightly combat and stumbled. Then one of Carvajal's men fell on Welser. Above the din of falling swords came the voice of Padre Frutos de Tudela, who had accompanied the expedition: "Peace, for the love of God, peace. Do not kill each other."

Reason having triumphed over rashness, no matter how brief, the two parties drew up an agreement in which both sides resolved not to resort to arms. No action would be taken on either side against those such as Pedro Limpias who sided against the Welser, and the soldiers could make their own choice, either to proceed to Coro with the Welser or to remain with Carvajal, who would return all of their property including Hutten's important *Journal of the Expedition;* the march of the Welser would continue to the Coro under safe conduct.

The return to Coro had proceeded for eight days when they neared the Sierra de Jijira that separated the hinterland from Coro. Hutten had sent sixteen soldiers in advance with machetes to cut the undergrowth for the passage of the main group. Unknown to the Welser, so vast was the land and so unpopulated, that Carvajal under the urging of Pedro Limpias had sent his partisans to ambush the Welser. While one group of their men was cutting a path and another party was scrounging for food, Hutten and Welser had taken to their hammocks. They heard a shout of "Long live the King" and before they could arm themselves, they were in the power of Juan Carvajal. Hutten and Welser were put in chains with seven of their men. According to the testimony (for the proceedings about it, long, drawn out, detailed and lengthy in verbiage, are still preserved in the Spanish Archives), Carvajal was urged by his followers to delay no longer: bring them to justice, condemn and decapitate them.

It was Easter Sunday of 1545 when Juan Carvajal, to justify his actions, approached Hutten and Welser and shouted that they had done wrongs to His Majesty for which they would be castigated. At this, young Welser, still unaware of their perilous position, shouted back: "I have no fear of the King."

With that outburst of *lèse majesté* as his justification,

Carvajal ordered that justice be done. Two blacks sharpened their machetes and readied the first two Spaniards for decapitation. Again the padre attempted to intervene, demanding that they must confess before being beheaded.

"Dear little father", Carvajal replied, "let them confess in the other world." Accordingly, their heads were lopped off.

Now came the turn of Bartholomäs Welser, who interrupted the proceedings by saying that Carvajal was not the King, for only the King . . . Carvajal stopped him: "Here *I* am the King." Then turning to the negro executors he ordered: "Cut off the head of Bartolomé Bélzare." And it was done.

Philip von Hutten was readied. He asked to be allowed to confess, but Carvajal was adamant: "You can confess in heaven." At this Hutten raised his manacled hands towards the heavens and began to recite. The myth of the mirage of El Dorado had led him to lands never seen before by white men; he had traversed a good part of *tierra incognita;* he had wished to take part in great discoveries and conquests; and he sought for glory and only wished to return to his homeland after he had done what would honour their names and lineage. When he came to the end of his Latin invocation and pronounced the words "miserer mei", the headsman struck. Then he was drawn and quartered. Philip von Hutten had not quite reached the age of thirty-five when he had completed his "strange desire".

¹ *Indianische Historia.* Ein Schöne kurtz-weilige Historia Niclaus Federmann des Jungern von Vlm erster raise so er von Hispania vn Andolosia auss in Indias des Occeanischen Nors, gethan hat vnd was ihm allsa ist begegnet biss auff sein widerkunft inn Hispaniam auffs jurtzest beschriben gantz lustig zu lesen MDLVII (Colophon) Getruckt zu Hagenaw bei Sigmund Bund ic. [63 numbered leaves – 168×135 mm]. (The Charming and Agreeable

Account of the First Trip of Nicolaus Federmann, the Younger of Ulm, to the Indies in the Ocean Sea, and all that happened in that country until his return to Spain. Briefly Written and Diverting to Read.)

PART 3

'I HAVE A LONG JOURNEY TO GO...'

CHAPTER X

A Pilgrim Shadow

He met a pilgrim shadow
"Shadow", said he,
"Where can it be
This land of El Dorado?"
                        – Edgar Allen Poe, 1849

THE pursuit of El Dorado was now going to be revitalized by the very man who had profited most from it – none other than the redoubtable Gonzalo Jiménez de Quesada.

It was now 1548. It had been ten years since he, with Nicolaus Federmann and Sebastián de Belalcázar, had returned to put the matter of jurisdiction before the King. Federmann had died in prison, but Belalcázar, who was *persona grata* with Charles V of Spain, quickly had his audience and won his *gobernación* of Popayán and all else that he had founded and returned with dispatch to his new imperiums.

Quesada was far less fortunate. Early in the year 1540 he

225

had been in Seville and had deposited (so records the register of the Casa de Contratación) a large box containing 11,000 pesos-weight – that is, pounds of Chibcha gold – and five hundred and seventy-two emeralds which constituted the Royal Fifth and, having done so, he believed that he would, as had Hernán Cortés in Mexico and Francisco Pizarro in Peru, be made a Marquis with the governorship of the lands that he would call New Granada. Scarcely.

Alonso, the son of Fernández de Lugo, who had been governor and financed Quesada's gold-gathering iconoclastic anabasis into the realm of the Chibchas, stood firmly in his path. He was well-connected. His wife was rich. Her sister was married to the secretary of the King. So, fearing all this, Quesada never went personally to Court, but presented his petition "by means of other hands" for he had been made aware of the *influencia de faldas* – that is, the "petticoats" of those two sisters.

Charles V, on a State visit to Ghent (arriving with so great a company of troops, grandees and bishops that, according to a witness, it was as if God was arriving out of Paradise), there conducted the State's business and there adjudged the case of Lugo versus Quesada. "I have studied the various petitions", he directed, "and have so ruled that Alonso de Lugo shall have the governorship of New Granada."

"But also", as the chronicler wrote, while the conqueror of the Chibchas was "dividing his time between pleasure and petitions, documents of other indictments were building up against him." Quesada was accused of torturing and then murdering the grand Zipa, for which the *residencia,* a form of impeachment, demanded that he answer the charge within three days.

"On behalf of the King", the official crier gave out in his sonorous voice to a roll of drums, "on behalf of the King, do you, Gonzalo Jiménez de Quesada, answer before the Royal Justices."

With that Quesada evanesced to France, where he began

226

to actively write his histories. Then later it was Italy. He found Genoa filled with Spaniards, for it was controlled by Spain, as well as Porto Ercole, an entrepôt to Tuscany; then, he went on to Rome and Naples. Always there were Spaniards and always some news of New Granada. In Rome, he had read a Fugger News Letter which told of the death of Philip von Hutten and Bart Welser, so by the time he returned to Madrid in 1547, since he had learned that the charges against him were beginning to fade away, he then heard more of the intense legal activity on the part of the Welser.

Moritz von Hutten, Bishop of Eichstätt, was demanding justice. He wrote to one, whose name has been effaced, yet must have held high office, for it read: "You will be travelling to Spain by order of the Emperor with the Archduke Maximilian of Austria, so this would be a good opportunity to inquire further into the death of my brother Philip . . . You have learned of the awful death of my brother during Easter week, 1546. This terrible deed against God and the Law was committed by a Spaniard called Juan Carvajal."

There also remained a fervent belief in great treasures. "In addition, it was reported to me that my brother, Philip, possessed gold and emeralds ... These valuables now belong to me and my brother, Wilhelm von Hutten, his legal heirs. I would like you to inquire, secretly, how much gold and emeralds were in his possession."

The Huttens, who were well-connected – Philip had been educated at the Spanish Court – wrote and demanded of Charles a redress "so the Emperor, on our demand, has sent an order to the Council of the Indies". When Charles V was travelling with his peregrinating Court to an imperial city near Ansbach in March 1547, Moritz wrote to the Bishop of Wurzburg inquiring "whether it would be a good idea if the two of them, both Bishops, with other Noblemen, should not go to Nürnberg to see the Emperor personally about the matter".

In 1548, Bishop von Hutten was again writing to an

unnamed German Prince repeating the events, and begging him to remind the Emperor that he give an order to the Council of the Indies to find and hand over to the Casa de Contratación in Seville the gold and emeralds as well as the journal, manuscripts and maps of the "newly discovered lands" and to "return these things to the legal heirs".

Many reams of legal paper were consumed in this involved battle. These still lie in large piles in their neat boxes in the *Archivo General de Indias* in Seville. The language is exacting and legal, yet passions burn through and across the pages of all this dry-as-dust legal verbiage stalks the spectre of the Golden Man.

The pursuit of El Dorado should have expired with the deaths of Hutten and Welser. But there were others to keep it alive, Quesada's brother Hernán, who had assumed the overlordship of the land of the Chibchas that Quesada had conquered, found new enterprises while Quesada betook himself to Spain to have, as he believed, his rights of conquest confirmed. Quesada's hoard of 185,962 pesos of gold, and his handsome gathering of one thousand eight hundred and fifteen emeralds, had exhausted all of Chibcha wealth on the surface and the Spaniards could not understand that the gold and emeralds had been an accumulation of centuries.

Hernán was the first to put the two facts together: the Golden Man and the lake. He conceived the idea of lowering the level of the lake, which would then expose the sediment around the shore. If the Indians spoke truly, there would be much treasure. Since the only water-conductor was a sort of natural bucket made from the hollow gourd of the calabash vine, Hernán arranged a human machine; the Indians were stationed one yard apart from the top of the lip of the lake to the bottom; a gourd was filled with water, passed from hand to hand until it reached the top, then the empty calabashes were returned. Within months this operation, done in the dry season, had lowered the surface sufficiently to expose the darkened heavy shore-sediment of Lake Guatavita. There Hernán did find a small amount of golden offerings, mostly those called *tunjos,* which were of base copper, with only a slight golden skin. But pure gold, having three times the specific gravity of iron, would with the passage of time have slipped down the mud banks into the deeper part of the funnel-shaped lake. After much herculean labour, Hernán did not find any fortune, but he definitely established the certainty that golden ornaments were thrown into the lake of Guatavita. Here then, if the process of logic had been advancing orderly, inexorably from cause to effect, this was the repository of the gold of the Chibchas; it made understandable the phrase, "there was no more gold on the surface".

It had been extremely laborious. Then, too, it was not the sort of endeavour that would appeal to one who dreamed of conquest. It was, one must see, also a matter of pride. A gentleman might lead an army for conquest, but the *hidalgo* class disapproved of a menial occupation which would cause a gentleman to lose caste. Thus Hernán de Quesada, who spent months merely superintending a water-lifting process, was certainly in this category; it was definitely menial.

Although he now had the key, still, like all the others, he believed that the Golden City lay down there somewhere in the vast *llanos.* There being nothing else for it, he assembled an expedition in Tunja, which had been the capital, so to speak, of the Zaque of the Chibchas, and on the morning of the 13 September 1545, with two hundred and fifty men and two hundred horses, and the usual Indian retainers, he set off to find the Kingdom of Gold.

They crossed the heights, descended to the plains and were amazed there to find, from the Indians who acted as guides and carriers, that Georg Hohermuth of the Welser Company had been there in 1536, so they followed their spoor. With the high misty *cordillera* on their right and the broad grassy *llanos* on the left, they advanced southward. Neither the incessant rains, nor the attacks of Indians, nor the deaths already taking place, changed either his determination or his dream. The one memorable moment in the expedition, when hunger was upon them, was the ritual sacrifice of the conquering ass Marcobaré. He had been part of the conquest ever since he swam ashore in Santa Marta from some shipwreck and had been taken, like a Pegasus upward, by the Indians and recovered by the Spaniards, who called him Marcobaré after the chieftain who had him. He went through the whole conquest as *El Asino Conquistador,* his braying always carrying a note of safe conduct. When he was first discovered and his discoverers were hungry, they wished to eat the author of the bray and this was not allowed. Now, five years later, he was to go into the soldiers' stomachs at least with what can be called the benefit of the clergy. On his last expedition, he had faithfully carried a worthy friar, named Vicente Requesada, through mountain, swamp and grassland. Pushed to the extremes of hunger, the soldiers turned hungrily to Marcobaré. The friar pleaded for the conquering ass. He reminded them how he had carried Sergeant-Major Salinas, how he had borne men and goods for Quesada up to conquest, and how his braying was the soldiers' guide post. The friar even offered himself in its stead but he begged in vain.

With the conquering ass in their stomachs, Hernán's army went on to the Caquetá river.

The lower Caquetá river, before it enters the Amazon, runs parallel with the Vaupés, where Philip von Hutten had passed in 1543. Between these two rivers was an upland grassy plain. Along the rivers and the immediate land behind the jungle was an unyielding phalanx of trees, broken only here and there by the foliage of an acacia, with finely divided tremulous leaves, or the large, star-shaped leaves of the *cecropia;* trees were festooned with brilliant begonias and red-flowered vines, exhaling a subtle perfume, climbing above the lower trees to reach for the sunlight. The area was heavily wooded, except for occasional stretches of high plateau-savannahs. All rivers and streams were fast-flowing, rock-bedded, difficult to either ascend or descend.

Hernán's group sought for the City of Gold in Mano on the upper reaches of that river, then, still on the scent, he crossed the Andes and traced his way to the small settlement of Popayán in the upper Cauca river, and so made his way back to his starting point. He had been gone sixteen months, travelling fifteen hundred miles, and all his horses lost, which was in itself a small fortune; of the two hundred and fifty men, only eighty survived. Preternaturally aged from his misadventures, financially in want after the last débâcle, he was on his way by boat down the Río Magdalena to see the newly-arrived Governor, when (while playing cards under an awning on the ship's deck during a rainstorm) a bolt of lightning struck the mainmast; he was killed instantly.

"The bolt", someone remembered, "burned his hair and beard and all the hair on his body (for he was very shaggy), and it burned all his clothing, and he was left naked; and those parts of his clothing that were left were in bits no longer than grains of sand, all burned and likewise his entire body, apparently with a blow; Hernán Pérez de Quesada left life with skin jet black."

The Welser themselves also kept the pursuit of El Dorado alive. Martin Luther was a poor physicist when he envied the dead for being at rest. He was wrong. The dead for being at rest. He was wrong. The dead have much to do, for they prepare life for the eternal recurrence.

The Welser pressed their claim over the jurisdiction of New Granada, insisting that their patents included the land discovered by their vassal, Nicolaus Federmann. Obviously nez de Quesada. It is known that during the years 1547–8, the historiographer of all these discoveries, Oviedo, met Quesada in Spain and refers to him as an "honourable man of good understanding and very able".

Many details of the discovery and "pacification" of the

231

Vegetation and huts on the banks of the Caquetá, a tributary of the Amazon, where Georg Hohermuth, Philip von Hutten and later Jiménez de Quesada were led by their strange desires.

Chibchas came from Quesada's manuscripts and large note-book, which Oviedo borrowed for many days, from which, as historians do, he freely copied.

Quesada still carried the scent of American forests in his beard and person, and all this talk of the past with Oviedo opened up the gates of memory. Amid the ruins of his career his pride was reborn and the dream of El Dorado again filled his mind. Once more he addressed himself to the King and asked for beneficial employment in New Granada in the lands that he had discovered for the Crown. This time the King and Council answered promptly: he was to have the title of Marshal – an empty one – and with it a coat of arms. The escutcheon was to have a snow-covered mountain rising out of the sea (that is, the snow-covered Sierra Nevada of Santa Marta) and many emeralds scattered on the waters, "in memory of the emerald mines you found". A golden lion rampant on a red field, with a sword between its paws "and all else with accessories with ornaments of gold and silver". He was to have an annual stipend of two thousand ducats, and Indians from the town of Moniquita to be held in *encomienda* – that is, the usuf-ruct of their labours. With that the lawyer of Granada returned to America. The year was 1549 and he was fifty years old. The Villa de Santa Fé, the village that he had founded, after ten years had long since taken on the aspect of a city: streets, a church, a fountain, a much-used gibbet. How different now than when he first planted cross and banner!

The citizens of Spain had followed its policy to conquer then populate: cities grew, stone buildings took the place of wooden ones, domesticated animals of the Old World fructi-fied and were to be seen all over the fields and *páramo*. Old World cereals – wheat and rye – grew beside the native maize, and fruit trees were trans-shipped and planted. Bananas brought from Africa as early as 1535 grew in tropical abundance. Spain was giving its New World – civilization.

Into this new Bogotá the Marshal Quesada settled, if not in full contentment, for his resources were limited, yet with a sense of satisfaction. He had nothing for luxuries. The coat of arms, given to him by the King, were never carved in stone over the door of his modest dwelling, and though young in feeling, he made no effort to marry or to procreate.

It must not be thought that the search for the Golden Man had ended with the deaths of the men of the Welser. Far from it.

There were still many old companions of arms about, most of them with estates, kept up by the work of their Indians held in fief, and from them, he found inspiration to begin to write his personal history of the conquest.

While Quesada was occupying himself writing his *Historical Compendium,* and a personal account, called *The Rastos of Sueca* – both unfortunately lost – the nephew of the newly arrived Governor of New Granada now entered the lists.

Pedro de Ursua, an *hidalgo* from the city of Pamplona in the kingdon of Navarra, was still young – he had yet to reach twenty-three – impressionable, and of rapt imagination. Of a certainty, he felt that he, where all else had failed, would find the Golden Man and his Golden City. El Dorado, now implying a land of inexhaustible riches, allowed no restraint to be placed on the imagination. There was a sort of organized frenzy about young Ursua, who made a final end of the scattered bands of resistance among the Chibchas. That done, he descended into the Muzo, emerald country, there to do battle with the anthropophagous Panches.

Muzo lay in a lush, humid jungle area between the mountains and the great river and was another of the areas whence come the finest emeralds. One of Ursua's captains found an emerald embedded in the horseshoe of his mount, whereupon Ursua, because of information wrung out of captives, began to loot graves as soon as their locality was revealed to him.

235

By this time, Pedro de Ursua's reputation as a disemboweller of Indians had grown to such proportions that the Panama administration invited him to try his well-seasoned extermination techniques on that Isthmus that was the land passage to Peru. No matter who one was, a Vice-King of Spain, or Vice-God, you disembarked at the small fortress-seaport near Porto Bello on the Caribbean side, and were poled up the Charges river in the rainy season; or in the dry you took the Charges trail to cross the narrow seventy-eight miles between the Caribbean and the Pacific. From the very first moment of the introduction of negro slaves in Panama, many had escaped and by 1552 they were sufficiently organized to attack convoys going from one ocean to the other. As gold and silver was now pouring out of Peru in immense tonnage, the King's Council took notice of the actions of the *cimarones.* So this became the first item of business on arrival of Don Andreas Hurtado de Mendoza, appointed as Viceroy of Peru.

There was Pedro de Ursua awaiting his arrival. The Viceroy was impressed by his past merits and gave him command to extirpate the *cimarones.* And this is precisely what he did. In two years, as a reward, he was invited by the Viceroy to come to Peru. So, in the waning days of 1558, he carried the saga of the Golden Man once more to Peru.

In Lima, the Viceroy succinctly explained his problem. The various upheavals in Peru since the time of the civil wars between Pizarro and Almargo and those that followed had left him an immense number of "disorderly rabble", of which, please God, he should like to be rid.

The fever of El Dorado being re-awakened, it should be searched for, and as this was an enterprise that demanded a strong leader, Pedro de Ursua was to be such a one. The Viceroy would allow him to draw from the royal revenues such that he thought he would need. As for volunteers, there was, as the Viceroy had hoped, no end. The fever, which had almost destroyed Venezuela, would now, contrarily, save Peru. Pedro de Ursua was allowed to style himself Governor of Omaguas and El Dorado.

It had a denouement like almost all else in our story: an epic of mismanagement. They set out with hundreds of horses, cattle, pigs and women, with a retinue of men, the dregs of Peru, officered by "doughty champions with elastic consciences". The ships built of green wood on a river of the Upper Amazon proved to be unriverworthy, so that only forty of the three hundred horses could be put aboard, cattle on which they planned to live were left behind, violence broke out over the enforced delays, and an officer was murdered. Whereupon, Pedro de Ursua hanged all the suspects, innocent and guilty alike, festooning the trees with their bodies.

Then they floated downward to where the Napo and Marañon rivers are confluent, and the stream, now swollen into immensity, becomes the Amazon river.

Christmas of 1560 was spent at Machiparo, the first River Amazon settlement (San Fernando de Machiparo) which had been previously set up by Francisco Orellana in 1540. By this time the Machiparo Indians had seen so many searching for the elusive Golden Man through their lands that starvation, theft, and murder were routine. But until now they had never seen so dangerous a human fauna as was left to wander in their villages.

It was an unusual fact that one of them, Lope de Aguirre, did not believe in El Dorado. Life had left him without belief in anything. He had been involved, in his twenty years in Peru, in every kind of violence, and three times had faced the hangman.

Lope de Aguirre had been born at Oñate, in Guipúzcoa, which is Basque country, and having a way with horses, he had come out rather early in the conquest to Peru, and when he was not involved in this or that, was trainer of war horses. A man remembered him as being "small and spare in body, ugly with a black beard and fierce, eagle's eyes".

Fifty years of constant conflict had given him a physical

237

constitution which seemed to inure him from assaults of hunger or cold, thirst or death. He was just the sort of man, since wrong-doers always enjoy luck up to the end, that could make exploratory history, for he was to discover the link between the Negro and Orinoco rivers for which others would search for two hundred years.

Aguirre's plan, which he unfolded to those who would listen, was simple – and violent. Kill all the officers, cause an uprising of all who hated the governing class, seize power, and proclaim a new American kingdom.

When they reached the Omagua territory, now in time's alchemy, El Dorado, Aguirre's mutineers surprised Pedro de Ursua in January 1561, and sliced him up. Other officers were treated in like manner.

Then they floated down to the place where the black waters of the Río Negro joined the whiter waters of the Amazon, and reached Manoa. There, having learned from some Indians, who had come down from the upper Río Negro to trade, that there was a secret way to pass from the Negro to the Orinoco by boat, Aguirre determined that as their goal. He was now to prove for the first time the riverine connection between the Orinocan and Amazonian water systems.

The tributaries of the Río Negro drain the high massif between the Sierra Parima and the mountainous part of Guiana. It is also fed from the *llanos* principally by the Vaupés, which has so often appeared in the search for the Golden Man. The Río Negro is a dark body of water framed between wide expanses of jungle which come down to the river's edge. Annual floods can raise the river up to thirty-five feet above normal, deluging everything with black water. At places the river is so wide that jungles appear only as indistinct walls of gloom. Four hundred miles upward, more or less on the equator, the Río Negro turns in a northerly direction, and where now stands San Carlos de Río Negro, one of the slender arms of the Río Negro makes an abrupt westerly turn. This the ships of

Lope de Aguirre followed for thirty-five miles. It was the secret channel, used by the Indians, going from one river system to the other, for that river then flowed into the Casiquiare. The Casiquiare is a stream without a counterpart in the world. It joins two rivers, the Orinoco and the Amazon, both of which flow in opposite directions. It has not a reversible current; it is simply an arm of the upper Río Negro which connects with another stream by only a short portage to the upper arm of the Negro.

It may well be that Lope de Aguirre was mad, yet the journey opened up a huge section of South America. Moreover, it was done under circumstances which demanded madness, since the mere problem of physical motion, not to think of it even in human terms, brought them to the edge of insanity. As planned, Aguirre eventually arrived at the island of Margarita close to the delta of the Orinoco, but the grandiose conspiracy collapsed. Therefore, arming more of the like that he had with him, he moved to the mainland and found lodgement at Barquisimeto, the well-remembered settlement beyond Coro which, since the times of Federmann, had been the disembarking point for expeditions outward bound to discover the Golden Man. This Aguirre now seized and declared his independence from Spain. That was his last escapade. He was killed, and his head was cut off and exhibited in a cage hung at the *cabildo* at Tocuyo. His memory as an evil spirit survives even now in Venezuela, for when at night the jack-o'-lantern lightning bugs dance over the marshy plains, the solitary wanderer crosses himself and whispers: "The soul of the tyrant Aguirre."

All these events welled up to Santa Fé de Bogotá and to the attention of the old conquistador Quesada. His principal enemy now was time, attended by poverty. His means were slender and no matter how often he pleaded with the Spanish Court, his emoluments were not increased. He had looked with envy on Sebastián de Belalcázar, who had returned from Spain in 1546 in full panoply of power. By letters patent he was *Adelantado,* that is, Governor, for life of all the territory from Quito north to the territory of Cartagena. Along with his titles, he had brought livestock, seeds, artisans, a legion of priests, along with whole families. Then to his surprise, he found that another, during his absence, had moved into his territory. Although the usurper had been his companion for years, and was gently born, Belalcázar, on the night of 4 October 1546, surprised Jorge Robeldo, and marked him for death.

"He was so much liked for his goodness to us that we looked upon him as a father," wrote Pedro de Cieza de León. But Belalcázar summarily beheaded Robeldo and his followers, and "to prevent the body of Robeldo and others from being eaten", went on Don Pedro, "they burned the house over their bodies". Robeldo's widow, Doña María, was a delicately-nurtured young lady but when she learned this, she became implacable. Belalcázar thought that he had conquered everything, as indeed he had, but what would bring him down was Doña María, Robeldo's wife. She pursued Belalcázar relentlessly through every court, through every council, until at last he was summoned to trial. In 1551, having been condemned, he started under bond for Spain down to the fortress city of Cartagena. There he sickened and died – broken, penniless, friendless. Only two followers cared enough to buy four yards of coarse muslin and paid a nameless woman two pesos to make him a shroud.

One by one, the old conquistadors were going, in the manner of the ancient Spanish nursery rhyme:

> O mother, my mother,
> my hair, my hair,
> one by one hairs fly away,
> in the air.
> O mother, o mother,
> my poor hair.

But it was the presumption of Pedro de Silva that

awakened the old conquistador, Quesada, from his slumbers. The very territory that he had won was about to be taken over by an upstart lately come on the scene. Pedro de Silva, a native of Jercz (where wine was made into heady sherry), had gone out to Peru, appearing as one of those which the poet-novelist Miguel de Cervantes complained: "The Indies shelter and refuge Spain's despairing, shrine of the mutineer, asylum for the murderer, chips and a green cloth for the gambler." Silva had taken part in a scheme approved by the Viceroy of Peru, by which wealthy gentlemen of Lima were given letters patent "in order to possess themselves of part of the great riches of the Amazonian Empire". As all such, these had failed. However, Pedro de Silva, who had made his fortune on the frontier city of Chachapoyas in Peru, who had taken part in the first disastrous enterprise, now himself believed in the reality of Golden Cities and Golden Men. Nothing else for it, he must to Spain to obtain permits, letters patent and the royal seal. The land grants of Spain in the Americas still, because of the misconceptions of the geography, overlapped. Pedro de Silva intruded into New Grenada.

He prepared for the expedition. There was no difficulty in financing it! People sold their homes, chattels, and debentures to invest in the enterprise; so much so that at the time of embarkation, Pedro de Silva was saddled with six hundred people; more than a hundred were coming with their wives and families.

Then the usual thing happened. By the time they had gone through a chain of Dantesque horrors, and had reached the island of Margarita, off the coast of Venezuela, which only a few years previously had witnessed the sanguinary descent of Lope de Aguirre and his "men of Marañon", they were torn by disagreements. On a day in May 1569, one hundred and fifty would go no farther. As the expedition moved toward Coro, death finally depleted his company. The only survivor, and one who will again reappear and find a certain literary immortality because of

241

his wonderful weaving of the fantastic tale of Manoa and the kingdom of gold, was Juan Martín de Albujar.

Juan Martín de Albujar will add singular idiocy as spice to Sir Walter Raleigh's quest for the "large and beautiful Empire of Guiana".

And this act awakened the old conquistador. Instead of recalling the horrifying experiences which he went through, contrariwise Quesada was all credulity and himself convinced that El Dorado was located "out there".

It was at this point in 1569 that the citizens of Bogotá, in the belief that the discovery of El Dorado was part of their inheritance, prevailed upon Gonzalo Jiménez de Quesada to lead them in pursuit of it. He was now seventy years of age. Well preserved, "erect and gracious", and of a certainty still a good horseman, it happened that he himself had been deluging the Court with petitions to raise his pension: "On a certain occasion at Court", he wrote, "there was talk of giving me a reward for my services, and after some discussions, it was agreed that I and my heirs should be given subsistence in perpetuity so that memory of my services might endure, as did the similar services of the Marqués del Valle (Cortés) and Pizarro, to each of whom were given twenty-one thousand vassals and fifty or sixty thousand ducats of pension, and very important titles, though they had discovered and settled provinces no better and no richer than those I have brought."

Much had changed in the years since he had left Spain. Philip, the heir apparent, had married Mary Tudor, one of the daughters of Henry VIII, on one of the rare sunbright days of 1554 at Winchester Cathedral, and so was, albeit briefly, able to sign himself, "I, King of England".

In the same year, 1554, the courts released some of Quesada's rights. It seemed that the mad Queen Juana had been dead for so long a time that, when her death was announced, it caused all those who could to remember that she had been that gently mad Queen, even when Quesada was a law student at Salamanca University.

242

The next year (1555) Charles began his long series of abdications, first as Holy Roman Emperor, then as King of the Two Sicilies, as Count of Flanders and so on, in preparation for his retirement from public life into the Hieronymite Convent of Yuste. At least with that King, Quesada could sometimes ask and be granted an audience, but from the new King, Philip II, he was much distanced.

Philip II was well trained for the office by his father (who left him a series of maxims and guides to policy). Fair-haired and blue-eyed, although of passive countenance, he had the protruding Hapsburg jaw and lip. Still, he was far different from the gloomy tyrant of the Escorial invented by the English to justify their piracy and senseless destruction of Spanish cities throughout the Americas. The Venetian Ambassador, Michele Soriano, thought him "always of such gentleness and humanity as no prince could surpass; and although he preserves his royal dignity and gravity in all his doings, as nature and habit incline him, he is none the less gracious for this; on the contrary, his dignity and gravity only serve to enhance the courtesy with which he treats everyone".

Philip spoke several languages, was a book collector, played the guitar (for which instrument he composed), and was so excellent a chess player that he gave his chess master, Ruy López (the perfector of the famous Ruy López gambit), spirited opposition. He rose early, retired late, and was constantly at work, trying to hold all threads of government which now, as it was so greatly over-extended, were often inextricably entangled.

The King was guided by a series of councils, each departmentalized under justice, finance, military orders, the Indies and the like. These councils were advisory and consultative, not policy-making committees. Final decision lay with the King alone. Every detail, no matter how unimportant, passed through his hands; for instance, the cost of canoes for a small fortress at Puerto Bello in Panama; the building of a bridge across the Rimac River in Peru; the disputed costs of some remote expeditions or pleas. All this while he had to make decisions of incalculable importance on the wars against the Turks, the Netherland revolts, the second Battle of Tunis, and the great Armada. Now he was forced to listen to Quesada.

The phantom of El Dorado again took fever to Quesada's blood and brain. It remained like malarial germs which take refuge in the spleen, issuing from time to time into the bloodstream and bringing on the tertiary ague. Who should have known about the nature of the Golden Man better than he? Everything that the Indians had told freely or under torture had been proved. There were no gold mines in the Chibchan territory; it was obtained by barter. There had once been a Golden Man, purely ceremonial, and the golden ornaments which Quesada himself had harvested had been the accumulation of a century. Residual gold lay in the bottom of the sacred lakes, principally at Guatavita, which his own brother, Hernán Pérez, had proved.

He was close to seventy when the royal decree arrived in one of the post boxes called the *cajón de España,* the mail boxes of Spain. It was dated, from El Escorial, 15 November 1568. He was to be made Governor of the Province of El Dorado, his stipend was to be raised to four thousand ducats annually, he was to have more Indians, under *encomienda* – that is, large areas of allotted Indians to his "care", and, as well, the towns of Mariquita, one of the first settled by him, and Tunja, where he had found so large a fortune of gold and emeralds. His new territory was to be extended four hundred leagues – that is, one thousand two hundred miles eastward – and be called the Province of El Dorado. His fief was to be extended from the Andes to the waters that surrounded the Isle of Trinidad. More, if he found it, he was to have the title of Marqués. At the age of seventy he was septuagesimally fuddled like Don Quixote de la Mancha of celebrated memory. "His brain was addled from dreaming too long" over the whereabouts of this land of El Dorado, so that his wit, like that of Don Quixote, "was almost wholly extinguished so that caused him to fall into one of the strangest conceits that ever a madman stumbled on in this world". Quesada guaranteed that he would raise four to five hundred men, at his own expense, completely equipped and all fully supplied, bring along eight priests and – "I will also take five hundred married men, wives and workers and I will take no less than five hundred cows, four hundred horses, a thousand pigs, three thousand sheep and goats, five hundred negro slaves, both male and female. . . ."

Said Erasmus, writing *In Praise of Folly:* "Folly is the only thing that keeps youth as a stay and old age far off." Old capitáns flocked back for service under Jiménez de Quesada; the people of Bogotá pressed money into his hands, even though against all the indications of reason; they were convinced that out there – somewhere – was the mysterious Golden City.

The very quality of this human service, as well as the quantity of the bipeds and quadrupeds, formed it into the fairest company ever assembled in the conquests. Of the eight priests, two were to be the historian-scriveners, and it is only through them that posterity, that repository of man's foibles, knows what occurred on the fantastic voyage of Don Quixote-Quesada.

Of the first, Fray Antonio de Medrano, who would die on the march, little is known except "that he lived fifteen years in the Indies". Pedro de Aguado, who then took up the record, is better known. Having, in 1573, been elected Provincial of the Seraphic Order of Franciscans in Bogotá, Aguado had the good sense to turn back from the terrible march before it was too late, undoubtedly judging that martyrdom – in cases like this – must be left to those who, knowing not how to doubt, so use their simplicity as an excuse for their pigheadedness. He turned back and later wrote, so that it is thanks to these two – Medrano and Aguado, – that we know the reasons why.[1]

In April 1569, after the usual solemn ceremonies, the

army of men and women, black slaves, a retinue of carpenters and masons (for Quesada was ordered to build sugar mills on the rivers and plant sugar cane), Indios, pigherders, cowmen, pigs, cows, sheep, goats and eight friars – all riding amid the odour of sanctity – left Bogotá, forward, and downward. It was a joyous beginning. Many inhabitants of the city followed them for a while out of the city, until they came to Pasca, a Chibcha village, well remembered as the place of exile of Capitán Lázaro Fonte. After Casa Suma Paz, the high-placed, had been passed (which it may be recalled was where Nicolaus Federmann of Ulm had, like an apparition, appeared before Quesada's Captain Lázaro Fonte in 1539 with his skin-clad seekers for the Golden Man), there followed a descent from about 12,000 feet, down through the varying landscapes of forest and grassland, until they reached the valley, where the Güejar river began to form and to flow down into the flatland of the *llanos*. It had taken them twenty days to come ninety miles. There they encamped at a place called Mesetas, waiting for the slow-moving herds of pigs, sheep, goats, cattle, to catch up.

The rains had not yet fallen. The grass was high, brittle and volatile. A spark set off the grass, a steady wind enlivened the fire, which travelled in the underbrush and the trees along the rills. Within moments, the expedition was engulfed. Much of the livestock was consumed, and a barrel of powder exploded and sent unequal parts of people and expedition stores into the air.

When he had reorganized his company – which diminished with each mile covered – they moved into the settlement of San Juan de Llanos. It had first been called "Nuestra Señora" (Our Lady) by Micer Georg Hohermuth, who had travelled there in 1535. It was re-occupied by Nicolaus Federmann, who renamed it "Die Schmiede" (The Forge), for there he had his ironmongers set up a forge to shoe his horses before the ascent of the Andes, in 1539, to search for El Dorado. It had again been occupied by Philip von Hutten, in 1544, and renamed San Juan de Llanos; so it remained, and thus it is today. There the expedition rested. Nerves were fretted, a duel was fought between two soldiers, desertions began, those leaving making off with horses and cattle.

Now there stretched out before them an endless sea of grass, higher than a man's head, so that Indios were sent ahead to trample it for passage. The direction was east-south-east, and they moved by blind reckoning. Yet what possessed the principal guide, Capitán Pedro Soleto? He had been on such an expedition before, he knew, and yet perhaps he did not know. At least he led them without plaint.

The insects were as thick as peas in a pod. In the daytime, they were plagued by the pium and marium, two very minute flies, which were annoyingly irritating; hands, neck and feet were painted with bites. The bite leaves a small pustule filled with blood, causing inflammation and scratching and a secondary ulceration and infection.

When the flies left off at nightfall, then came the mosquitos, transmitters of malaria and yellow fever. Vampire bats followed the host of animals – small, leaf-nosed, night-dwelling mammals. They preferred to pierce human toes, ends of noses, and lap up the blood as it came out. Horses and pigs were especially vulnerable. If not vampires, then jaguars, which devoured new-born calves, horses, pigs, lambs. Perhaps never in the biological history of the *llanos* were the carnivores offered so continuous a treat. Crocodiles waited, floating with only their eyes awash, to pull down anything within their range.

So weeks became months, months turned into a year. Long before they had reached the point of no return, desertions began. The guilty were hanged. The desertions continued. Quesada then decided on a new policy – let the discontented return.

"There is no one to stop you, Capitán Juan Maldonado," Quesada said. So surrounded by a corps of the moribund

and the despondent, Maldonado began the long journey
back. Six months later he reached San Juan de Llanos.
There were only a few survivors.

Then Fray Medrano made his last entry in his *Book of
Voyages,* turned them over to his colleague in God and
died.

While travelling beside the white waters of the River
Guaviare (Huaybero), rushing down over rocks in foaming
cascades, Quesada and his remaining men met and defeated
an onrush of Puinabi Indians: a well-aimed bolt from
someone's crossbow caught the chieftain in the chest and,
as was their custom on the death of their leader, they fled
the field of battle; so outrageous fortune even deprived Don
Quixote-Quesada from dying in harness. Further on, the
white waters of the Guaviare met the black waters of the
Río Negro at Atabapo, as it was called, from a river which
poured in above it and is now named San Fernando de
Atabapo. A convent would be built there in time, and it
would acquire some local fame. Then, it was a collection of

The jungle night is full of bats. Few are blood-sucking. This one is the real
vampire, seen here lapping up blood freshly drawn from a steer.

Indian dwellings. All about the rivers were very low hills and taller mountains; therefore in December 1571, when Quesada had arrived, the lands were inaccessible in any direction except by water. The chimera of the Golden Man evanesced in the white and black waters.

Here Quesada agreed to turn back. Can one recall how, three years before, they had set out as so gay a company? Of four hundred Spaniards, only sixty-four survived; of the priests, two; of the fifteen hundred or more Indians, only four lived. Of eleven hundred horses only eighteen were alive, and these formed the small squadron of twenty five, who, with Gonzalo Jiménez de Quesada, limped into Bogotá in the last days of 1572.

The winter years were on him now. His lands, estates and *encomiendas* were encumbered with debt. The title of *Marqués* had escaped him. He was ill with rheums and phlegms so that even the low-placed tropical warmth of Mariquita (on a direct line with Honda, the highest port of navigation on the Magdalena river) did not fully dissipate the cold within his bones. Yet he kept his pride and spirit even though abject poverty brought him slowly downward, like a wintry tree deprived of its foliage. "He is poor and needy," wrote Hernán Vanegas, one of the conquistadors who lived in Bogotá, where he has the usufruct of "two thousand Indians, *más o menos*" – that is, more or less. "He has no possessions nor house of his own in which to live in this city of Santa Fé de Bogotá. Capitán Juan Tafur, a horseman and a person of capacity, who was himself not too well off, because he was deprived of his property in Pasca, said, 'Quesada is poor and much encumbered with debts.' "

And another who knew him then declared: "I do not know of any goods or chattels which belong to the Governor, nor even a house to live in, save for the tribute which he has from his Indians, and even this is pledged on account of the heavy expenses of his recent expedition."

Yet he was called out time after time to dispel this

249

uprising or that, "turning me aside from my work", Quesada wrote in one of his last petitions to the Crown, "I had in hand".

The work that Quesada "had in hand" was his *Historical Compendium,* his autobiography and the period of his discoveries; recording his entry into the realm of the Chibchas, his time in Spain, his triumphal return, the last expedition, and the disastrous search for El Dorado. The book was long in the writing. Oviedo, the historian, had seen part of the manuscript in Madrid between the years 1547–8 and, as we saw, had borrowed and presumably copied much from the "large, unbound memorandum book". It is lost. He also composed another, the title of which is *Los Rastos de Suesca,* which could be said to be periods at Suesca, for it was a large village just outside of Bogotá, where Quesada had his *quinta* or country house. It too was seen, used and quoted by historians. It was even given a licence to be published. "We have been informed," said the king, "that you" . . . using the imperial tense, *vos habeis,* "have composed a book entitled *Los Rastos de Suesca* about affairs touching the Indies. It appears to us that it will be useful and serviceable . . ."

Quesada was mortally ill with asthma, "of which I have been affected for twenty years", slowly turning into bronchial embolism, which made him unaware of time and death. He never knew – how could he have then? – that Miguel de Cervantes, who had immortalized knights such as Quesada in Don Quixote de la Mancha, knights who fell "into one of the strangest conceits ever stumbled on in this world", was now himself possessed of the dream of El Dorado.

Andreas Sánchez, the public notary, was summoned to take down Quesada's will and last testament, for, like a true lawyer, he had always put off making his will. It was drawn up the day before he died. Don Andreas arrived with quills, ink, paper and witnesses to take down the will and last testament of the Knight of El Dorado. It was simple.

250

"I, Don Gonzalo Jiménez de Quesada, *adelantado* of this New Kingdom of Granada, which I, as Captain, discovered, conquered, and settled in these Western Indies, along with many soldiers and gentlemen of the said armada who came with me . . . believe in the Most Holy Trinity, the Father, Son and Holy Ghost. . . .

"At present, I find myself very ill of body, albeit sane in mind, to dispose of whatever was fitting." His estate was small. He was in debt to the sum of 60,000 ducats for his final expedition. It was to be paid. He asked there be put aside a sum of money to maintain a jar of water near the knoll of Limba, where he once thirsted mightily. Having never married and his heir and nephew, Gerónimo, on "whom my hopes in this kingdom were centred", having been killed while "pacifying" the *Panches,* there was no one close to him but his niece Doña María, married to Colonel Antonio de Berrio, who was in Spain. "As your Majesty has done me the kindness of allowing me to name a successor to the grants of land . . . I hereby name as my successor, Doña María, daughter of my wife's sister."

There was a specific charge that his successors, having come by his death into the province of El Dorado, which stretched from the Andes to the Guianas, must continue the search for it. Even as he was laboriously writing out signature and expiring, at the age of eighty years, on 15 February 1579, his last thoughts were on "that great and magnificent city called 'El Dorado' ".

Should not the phantom, which he pursued through most of his life, have now expired with him at his death? In all unreason, is this not the way myths should expire, going out with the ones who had given them life? It was to be very different.

The lunacy of El Dorado he left to his heir, Antonio de Berrio y Oruña, who, by a strange concatenation of cause and effect, would surrender the same passion to . . . Sir Walter Raleigh, Gen'.

251

[1] Medrano, who died on the trek, wrote *La historia de Santa Marta, Nuevo Reino de Granada* and Aguado, *Historia de Venezuela.* The books were not published until 1906, but they seem to have been known in manuscript, and most of the contemporary historians made full use of them.

CHAPTER XI

'The Discoverie of the Large, Rich and Beavvtiful Empyre of Guiana...'

Men shall find in El Dorado-Guiana more rich and beautiful cities, more temples adorned with gold than either Cortés found in Mexico; or Pizarro in Peru. – Sir Walter Raleigh (writing in 1595)

Antonio de Berrio, Governor of the province of El Dorado, had that very morning of 4 April 1595 reported to his King, Philip II; the new settlement of St. José de Oruña – named after his wife to whom he owed his titles and lively prospects – near the Port of Spain, Trinidad, was now settled. It was on that very day that an Indian runner reported that four English ships had sailed up to and anchored in the bay.

Colonel de Berrio, having served for forty years in the King's army, reacted martially: he dispatched an officer – his nephew – with eight soldiers and twenty-five Indians to make proper reconnaissance. On arrival, they saw four ships, each about three hundred burden, flying the ensign of Queen Elizabeth of England. Accompanied by two Indians as interpreters, who spoke – no matter how badly – Elizabethan English, the Spanish officer questioned a group of Englishmen from the first ship who came ashore bearing a white flag of truce. "They had not come with the intention of doing harm," they said, "but only in search of refreshment."

Capitán Rodrigo de la Hoz was courteously invited aboard with his men and he was rowed out to the flagship. Hanging from the mizzen was the personal flag of the Admiral: five silver lozenges on a field of blue, the standard of Sir Walter Raleigh (Knight, Captain of Her Majesty's Guard, Warden of the Stannaries, Lieutenant-General of the County of Cornwall). There the astounded Spanish officer came face to face with the formidable "Milor Guaterral", as they called him. His name was high on the wanted list of Spain, for he was well known for his piracies and raids and burning of fleets and cities.

Age had now touched him, for the weeks in the Tower during the year 1592 had tumbled his pride. He was no longer that Raleigh, the courtier, when at thirty-five he was considered a "dangerous and magnificent man" – that Raleigh that stares out from his portrait painted at this time. dark eyes, bold and alive, a well-trimmed moustache and beard, a jewelled earring dangling from his left earlobe, a costly raiment of heavy brocade, a black velvet cape set with strips of small selected pearls, and his prominent virility nested in an elaborately jewelled codpiece.

Raleigh reflected his age as the age reflected him. It was the moment of Bacon and Shakespeare, the time of Marlowe and Spenser, and Raleigh in his personality contained all of that age's contradictions. He could display his literary subtlety and versify as well as most, as shown in *The Ocean's Love to Cynthia.* He was at home in the savagery of the city, where he witnessed contests of dogs and mauling bears; his flowing black hair and one bejewelled ear, if such could then be considered effeminate, mattered little in bat-

254

Portrait of the greying Sir Walter Raleigh about the time he set out on his voyage of discovery to Guiana. A variation of the portrait described in the text, from the Original by Guido Zucchero, in the collection of the Most Noble the Marquis of Bath. (Mary Evans Picture Library)

tle, for he entered war with consummate energy and consummate capacity. Delicacy, brutality, piety and lust were all synthesized into the person of Sir Walter Raleigh, as well as the age's naïveté – the lunacy of the Golden Man.

Now – that is, in the years 1592–5 – he had fallen into temporary eclipse at Court because of his affair with, and then marriage to, Lady Throgmorton, one of the principal ladies-in-waiting to the Queen ("one of her tiring women", as Elizabeth R. called her). He had spent a few weeks in the Tower followed by royal dismissal and – "It seemeth," wrote Anthony Bacon, "he lost his place and preferments at Court, with the Queen's favour, *such was the end of his speedy rising . . . at which many will rejoice.*"

The three years 1592–5 were of uncertainty, chiefly over the possible incubus of debt, since his solvency depended on royal perquisites. Such gains rested on his ability to retain that which the Queen, with such largesse, had given him. This uncertainty had wrought the change in his face. At forty-three, in 1595, his fine beard and upturned moustaches were greying, as was his lustrous black hair; his dress was less luxurious, only the starched linen lace neck ruff and sleevelets reminding one of his former elegance. And so he was portrayed on the eve of his "discoveries of the large, rich, beautiful, Empyre of Guiana" by Guido Zucchero, an Italian portrait painter then in England. There Sir Walter Raleigh stands, his right arm akimbo, the other arm leaning on a globe of the world with his index finger pointing almost carelessly to the Island of Trinidad where his ships on 4 April 1595 actually lay at anchor. What he had not lost "in the winter of his life" was a knowing quizzical look, almost contemptuous, which the painter caught in his portrait.

Antonio de Berrio waited impatiently for the return of his men, and when he had no "tidings of any kind from his nephew", another group was sent. These as well were invited on board the ships. "All of whom," Walter Raleigh wrote, "I entertained kindly and feasted after our manner:

256

by means whereof, I learned from one and another as much of the Estate of Guiana (El Dorado) as I could, or as they knew, for those poor soldiers, having been many years without wine, a few draughts made them merry, in which mood they vaunted of Guiana and of the riches thereof and all, what they knew of the ways and passages thereto."

At dawn the next day, after dispatching at Poinard Point the drunken Spaniards, the English "fell upon the place", as the official Spanish report reads, "at daybreak, slaughtering all on whom they could lay hands". Then they destroyed the city. As Raleigh admits: "I sct their new city, St. Josephs, on fire." This was, it was stated, a reprisal for eight of his own men having been killed the year previously.

The real prize was the capture of Don Antonio de Berrio and his principal aide, Alvaro Jorge, aged sixty, and just returned from a long trek from Bogotá. After calling all the Indian chieftains of Trinidad together, Raleigh, through his interpreter, told him that he was the servant "of a Queen, the great Cacique of the north and a Virgin." Thereupon, he had taken an engraving of the Queen "and fixed it", read the Spanish report, "on a very high pole bearing the Arms of the said Queen". An act of possession under which excuse the British possessed themselves of the Isle of Trinidad two hundred years later.

As to his prisoner, Raleigh acknowledged Antonio de Berrio as a "Genᵗ. [meaning, of course, like himself, a gentleman], well descended and having long served the Spanish king in Milan, Naples, the Low Countries and elsewhere, very valiant, and liberal, and a Genᵗ. of great assuredness, and of a great heart; I used him according to the small means that I had".

Raleigh secured information. Just how it was extracted is not mentioned. The official Spanish report confirms that the General (that is, Raleigh) treated Berrio well, entertaining him with banquets whilst persuading him to divulge the contents of the letters he had written . . . describing the riches of the country of "Guiana-El Dorado".

Raleigh being ceremoniously welcomed by the Cacique of the Arromaia region, who orders presents to be brought. "I made them understand that I was servant of a Queen [Elizabeth] who was the great Cacique of the north, and a Virgin". (From Theodor de Bry, *Americae Pars VIII*, 1599)

It is not difficult to place oneself in Antonio de Berrio's position, nor the state of his mind. He himself has told much of it in his own *probanzas de servicios* – that is, his proof of services to the King. He explains that, having been born in Segovia (that Roman-founded city which still uses its famous aqueduct built by Agrippa in the time of Augustus), he began to serve in the army first in Italy, at the siege of Sienna, which had rebelled gainst Charles V in 1552, then in Germany and Flanders. He helped put down the rebellion of the Moors in Granada where he was Capitán and Governor of Alpujarra. He served in Africa at the taking of Tunis and he judged himself then – he was writing in 1594 – "either the oldest or one of the oldest soldiers of Your Majesty". Berrio married late in life to María de Oruña, the niece of the old conquistador of the Chibchas, Gonzalo Jiménez de Quesada, but not so late it seems, for he was able to sire eight children. One can imagine the surprise of this old soldier who looked forward to a meagre pension, tied down with a large family, to suddenly have drop, virtually out of the skies, the Golden Man himself. In the notice of the death of Quesada, he found that the will and testament left the whole province of El Dorado to his niece, and therefore himself. "So when advancing age demanded rest," he wrote, "I went instead to the Indies to inherit the estates of the Kingdom of New Granada . . . which by warrant of Your Majesty were bequeathed to my wife . . ."

Still the search, meanwhile, for the Golden Man did not disappear. A century of repeated disasters made no impression, for nothing seems so eradicable in the human mind except what is *false* or fabulous.

"On arrival in this Kingdom (of New Granada) in 1580," wrote Berrio, "I began to gather munitions, stores, men, for the enterprise." And where would Antonio de Berrio search for El Dorado? In the *llanos,* the kingdom of the Omaguas which Philip von Hutten had seen attacked in 1544. It is interesting to speculate why he chose this direc-

Raleigh presents the wife of the Cacique who had pledged his support to his
Queen and country and aid in the search for the Golden City of Manoa.
(Theodor de Bry, *Americae Pars VIII*, 1599)

tion, while others continued to be obsessed with the Lake of Guatavita. At this date Don Antonio de Sepúlveda was engaged in an assault on the lake.

Don Antonio Sepúlveda, like Hernán de Quesada before him, appeared at the edge of Lake Guatavita in 1578. He had made a modest fortune as a wine exporter, bringing over the wines of Spain in wooden casks to Santa Fé, where, of course, they fetched astronomical prices. The idea of exploiting the lake was suggested by Capitán Lázaro Fonte, that old conquistador whom Quesada had banished to Suma Paz after Fonte's rebellious insolence, and with whom he had been reconciled when Fonte warned him of Federmann's approach so many years before. Fonte had, in secret, searched the narrow shore of Lake Guatavita and by digging about had found some gold and emerald-studded jewels under the lacustrine mud. He had confided this to Antonio Sepúlveda and proposed a working partnership, but before its fruition Fonte had yielded up soul and body. Nothing for it, Sepúlveda betook himself to Spain, secured permission from the Council and, in exchange for giving the Crown one-fifth of all found, was given the exclusive concession to search the Lake of Guatavita for its treasure.

With that Royal Cédula in hand, it was not difficult to raise additional capital; which he did, giving his vast chattels as security. Indians were assembled, houses built to house them, and they were set to work with mattock and pickaxe, to cut the fifty-foot rim of the lake crater. They worked like harvester ants. The earth prised out was put in their poncho-like *ruanas* and carried away. In time, months at least, a large V-shaped slice was cut down into the lake crater.

As projected, when they had made a deep cut, the water poured out, taking with it a fair number of Indians. On the edge, buried in the mud, were golden images and an emerald as "large as an egg" and gold, and more gold. Whereupon, Antonio Sepúlveda, who had at last, by an application of pure reason and empiricism, proved that this *was*

Sir Walter Raleigh (spear in right hand) at the burning and sacking of San José de Oruña, founded by the Spanish explorer-captain Antonio de Berrio in 1592. "I brought Berreo and his companions with me aboard [they are seen walking with manacles] and . . . set their new city S. Josephus [José] on fire." Drawn by Theodor de Bry, *Primo Descriptionem . . . Americae Pars VIII*, 1599 (British Museum)

the Lake of El Dorado, ordered the cut to be lowered further. Thereupon, the sides, improperly banked, caved in, burying the Indian workers. Funds gave out, the Royal Treasurer claimed all that had been recovered, the lake filled up again, and Don Antonio Sepúlveda – with all his chattels mortgaged – got himself to a hospital to die, there being no means left to him, nor anything else, nor would anyone afterwards run the risk then of taking the job of searching for the gold that actually lay at the bottom of the lake of the Golden Man.[1]

But Antonio de Berrio wanted to search an area to the east of Guatavita. Why had the illusion of the Golden Man and the Golden City been transferred from a place high in the barren Andes, where at least the Golden Man was known to have made his ablutionary rite, into a vast unknown area fifteen hundred miles eastward?

The reason why came from Peru. After the Lord-Inca Atahualpa had been ransomed, then garrotted after the gold had been distributed among the conquistadors, all immediate effective opposition to the Spanish conquest ended. Cuzco was occupied in 1534. Manco Capac was made, they assumed, a puppet Inca, then he, Capac, escaped and began the long siege of Cuzco. When it was broken, he disappeared with his principal men to a prearranged stronghold in the inaccessible montaña of Vilcabamba. The neo-Inca State existed until 1571, during which time they kept up trading relations with the "savage" Indians of the Upper Amazon, so that bronze tools, axes, copper and gold were continually exchanged up and down the trade routes, both on river and on land. Inca-produced silver was found by Sebastian Cabot on the great river that flowed down past Argentina, and so the river was named La Plata out of the belief that silver came from there. Doubtlessly, the techniques of working silver, gold and copper were learned by the more talented forest-dwelling tribes so that golden objects continued to pass along. Diego de Ordaz, the famous companion of Cortés in the conquest

The first illustration of the Lake of Guatavita as drawn by Alexander von Humboldt in 1801, *Vue de lac de Guatavita*. The sides are more precipitous than they appear from Humboldt's drawing. At present there is no evidence of "les restes d'un escalier servant à la cérémonie des ablutions".

of Mexico, who sought out a Golden Empire in the Amazon as early as 1535, found an emerald "as large as his fist" in an Indian canoe on one of the Amazonic rivers. This could only have come from Colombia. Then (which may well have been true), the Spaniards believed that the Incas had buried gold which was to have been brought to Cajamarca to ransom their Inca, and for years expeditions eastward out of Peru went up and down the jungle ways looking for a kingdom they had already conquered.

The kingdom of women, the Amazons, was another illusion which came out of Peru. In the Inca religion, the Sun Maidens, called Nustas (chosen women), chosen for talents and comeliness, were, at an early age, confined to houses, close to the Sun Temples, which they served. At each Sun Temple, the Chosen Women were in attendance, ruled by a *Mamacuna.*

Incas and their chieftains would often take their secondary wives, the Ñustas, from the Sun Temples, but to the common man they were sexually inviolate. At the height of their expansion, the Incas maintained fortress-cities as far east into the jungle as Paraguay; there were frontier guards on the Upper Amazon, and wherever the Incas were, there were Sun Temples and where there were Sun Temples, there were Chosen Women. This religio-social fact was the basis for the Amazon legends; from the very beginning of exploration, as they entered the forested areas of the Upper Amazon, the Spaniards heard of "cities, built of stone, with large gates . . . peopled only by women . . . among them there was one who reigned over all the rest . . . they were rich in gold and silver, there were very big buildings consecrated to the Sun".

The myth of the Amazons came out of a confused knowledge of the Inca "Chosen Women", who were enclosed in a kind of convent from which men were excluded. Forest-dwelling Indians who had trade relations with the Incas, exchanging jungle-products for worked metal, had first-hand knowledge of such institutions, and the legendary theme of women-without-men entered most primitive social histories and remained there to be given to the myth-hungry seekers of El Dorado.

Antonio de Berrio set off on his search for the will-o'-the-wisp in a military fashion; there would be no Indians, women or sows, but one hundred mounted men, well provisioned. He set off in January 1584 from Tunja, which still retained its fame from the famous rape of its tinkling golden plate and thousand emeralds. He made his way to 6° N. latitude, and reached the upper reaches of the Casanare river. There twenty men turned back; yet undaunted, down he went two hundred leagues, until the river had its confluence with the larger Meta, one of the principal tributaries of the Orinoco river system.

Below, where the Meta joins the Orinoco, Berrio saw before him forested mountains as high as 4,800 feet rising out of the plains. Attacked there by the Yaruro Indians, he repulsed them with a loss of three soldiers, captured several and, through his interpreter, learned that "in the mountains, to the east, there is a very large laguna (the transposed lake of Guatavita).

"So, on Palm Sunday, 1584, I discovered the cordillera . . . so ardently desired and sought for seventy years past." Then he was told that on the other side "were great towns and a vast population". So, in Berrio's imagination, he had found the Golden Man and the Golden City. For El Dorado, now a great city, had now and long since been superimposed on the Golden Man, the legend moving from the west, where it was close to Bogotá, to a thousand miles east, where it was not. It was the essential concomitant of El Dorado and its lake to be surrounded by mountains.

"All searched", wrote the sceptical historian Oviedo, "for the great Prince, noised about in those countries, who was always covered with powdered gold . . . fixed on the body by means of an odoriferous resin . . . the Prince washes himself every evening and is gilded anew in the morning, which proves that the Empire of El Dorado is infinitely rich in gold mines."

And so, lake, city and gold mines became inextricably linked in the search. Berrio went down to Baraguan (Orinoco) – "the greatest river I have ever seen" (quite correctly, for here the Orinoco is more than three miles in width) – waited there on the banks for four months until the flood waters subsided, then set off with fourteen men to find and climb the mountain with the great laguna. He failed, yet he picked up some rocks which he believed contained golden flecks. Therefore Antonio de Berrio, not wishing, as a good commander, to "venture further to sacrifice my people and myself", returned to Bogotá. He had been away seventeen months and lost only "eight Spaniards, three to five Indians to sickness".

The second expedition occupied Berrio for twenty-eight months – that is, from the summer of 1585 to the spring of 1588. In Bogotá, he re-equipped himself and found new recruits, for with the new discoveries of the whereabouts of the lake sought by Quesada this did not present difficulties. Again, having crossed the wide *llanos* and reached the Orinoco, he tried to reach the Sierra de Machpichi, whereat the golden laguna lay (5° N. latitude) and failed, but he found where the mountain chain ended. The expedition came abruptly to a close and one of his captains mutinied and fled with the majority of the men.

Once more, after travelling 1,200 miles over land, Antonio de Berrio was in Bogotá where he received "fresh orders from Your Majesty, which he encouraged me to start on a third journey". In 1591, he embarked with more men and more equipment and by now had acquired the skill of going from Bogotá to the banks of the Orinoco in record time.

Again, he tried to cross the wide Baraguan-Orinoco, but was thwarted. Most of his twenty canoes were lost, and thirty-four men deserted him, with horses. When a disease killed almost all of his Indian carriers, he ordered the rest of the horses to be destroyed, the meat to be smoked over the fire for food, and commandeered canoes from the Caribs with which to go down the Orinoco river until he reached a tributary called the "Caroni" (which will figure large in the beautiful, rich and wonderful city of Guiana of Sir Walter Raleigh). There he came into contact with the feared and dreaded Carib Indians.

The Caribs "confirmed all the information which I had received higher up" about the lake, the large population and for the first time, the word "Guiana". The Guianas were so numerous, said the Caribs, that they feared to ascend further. Antonio de Berrio then descended the Orinoco and "came out at the arm" – that is, one of its myriad channels – and "I came out of the one that faces the island of Trinidad".

Trinidad, which was first seen in 1497 by Columbus (who skirted its coast and named it) lies just north of the mouth of the Orinoco and is largely flat or undulating except for a range of small, hinterland mountains. Raleigh though that it "hath the forme of a sheep hook". The Gulf of Paria, which points like an extended index finger, causes a rough and uncertain sea for navigation; "the Dragon's mouth", it was called, and makes the route to Margarita Island – once famed for its pearls, and then an administration centre – a difficult one. Much of the shore and rivers of Trinidad are dominated by mangrove swamps, slender reddish roots awash in the low tide to which oysters cling, so that when Raleigh wrote "their oysters grow upon these roots", he became the butt of great jests over "tree-growing oysters". The island was noted for its pitch lake, a seepage of black viscous asphalt, much in demand for caulking canoes – and, naturally, an important native trade item. Raleigh became aware of it and found it "most excellent, good and melteth not with the sun".

Berrio in his inventory told that there were 35,000 original inhabitants – "the land is very abundant in sulphur, maize, quantity of cotton . . . but the best features are its nearness to the mainland, its numerous population, and its large supply of canoes, so that as many people can be taken for a single journey, as we should desire" (to seek out El Dorado).

When Antonio de Berrio arrived at Trinidad, in 1592 ("with twenty men and all of them ill"), he found that it was uninhabited by Spaniards and the Indians friendly. He asked the Council of the Indies that he be allowed to settle it immediately to use it as a base for an assault "of the great cities and riches of El Dorado".

It was not so easy to say "let there be a settlement" and thus possess one. Berrio was in another's territory, which was administered from the island of Margarita (one hundred miles north-eastwards); so there went Berrio in October 1591 to obtain permission; and there, too, he learned of the death of his wife in Spain.

While this was being resolved, Antonio de Berrio, accompanied by seventy men, travelled up the Orinoco, then into the Caroni, in search of El Dorado. He made peace with

Indians of the Orinoco with wild pig and other spoils. Drawn by Rugendas.

the Arowak Indians, whereupon he stated "that I shall try to penetrate into the interior of Guiana, by means of their chief, Moriquita, whom I have in my power".

Berrio declared that this Guiana "held the greatest wealth and grandeur that the world holds. . . . If the place was as large as Seville, why had it not been entered"? It was a rhetorical question which Berrio answered by describing the number of rivers, cascades, waterfalls and inundations, "but the Indians tell the truth . . . and as I have travelled . . . more than seven hundred leagues (2,200 miles) by land and water . . . and have spent ten years in continuous labours, I am well informed and know the facts".

In his letter to Philip II dated the first of January 1593, he told him that he must have ships of a certain draught, contact with a merchant "who is not a buccaneer, but a man of courage; to send him trade goods, axes, cut-glasses, gilded knives, trumpets, hawk bells, mirrors." Then he suggested that "I desire Your Gracious Majesty to become an investor yourself, before I discover the gold". It seemed incredible that all this would be read by the King himself.

What now possessed this conservative, aged – Berrio was now seventy – army colonel, whose whole career was based on realistic military terms, to petition a royal investment in an El Dorado not yet found? The explanation was his discovery of Juan Martín de Albujar.

Now it was not unusual to see Indians in feathers and painted, with their ears pierced, coming and going to the Isle of Margarita, for it was the source of pearls and many came to bring pearls to trade or sell. But one Indian chief was heard saying his orisons during Mass in perfect Spanish. When brought to the officials he had a marvellous tale to tell. He was the only survivor of the ill-fated expedition of Pedro de Silva, that expedition which had roused Quesada from his reveries to begin again the search for the Golden Man.

Juan Martín came from the Moorish-Spanish town of Albujar, and since Juan Martín is as common as the name

"John Smith", he added that nobiliary particle, "de" – not to suggest genteel birth, but merely to distinguish himself from the myriad other "Juan Martíns". He was captured by the Caribs, and turned native; pierced his ears and his nose septum, passing through it good gold ornaments; married, had children, and became a local chieftain. After living on the Upper Caroni for ten years he yearned to see again his own people. He therefore moved from tribe to tribe and finally he went in a canoe bound for Trinidad, then by the same conveyance to Margarita. By the time he repeated his story to Antonio de Berrio it had grown wondrous. He knew about the El Dorado legends, and had often been at the great lagoons where, during the river's periodic inundations, he had seen great expanses of water. He had, he said, been led blindfolded into the presence of the Inga, or emperor, who, treating him with kindness, had sent him back laden with gold after seven months' residence in El Dorado. There were untold riches. The Inga was covered with gold-dust. Unfortunately, Juan Martín was so overjoyed to be among his own again that, during the time he was drunk, someone had stolen all the gold from El Dorado. Antonio de Berrio never referred to Juan Martín de Albujar in his letters to the King, but Walter Raleigh alleged that a sworn copy of Juan Martín's story was in Berrio's possession.

The settlement of San José de Oruña on Trinidad was being built by Berrio in 1593, when he realised that he must, before he was forestalled, send an expedition up to the El Dorado to make a formal claim. The one selected to lead it was Domingo de Vera.

Vera was young, impressionable, doubtlessly energetic with a soaring imagination that never would permit an ugly fact to spoil a beautiful theory. This was to bring death to thousands. In April, Vera set off with thirty-five men from Trinidad, up the Orinoco, turning into the River Caroni and taking "formal possession of the land in the name of Antonio de Berrio and the Crown". He moved near to

272

Sierra Piacoa, made inquiries about the great lake and there heard of Gran Manoa. There, so read his report, was a great salt lake known to all as "the sea", whereat, a generation or so ago, people arrived who went fully clothed; also that among the Guianas was a tribe "whose shoulders were so high that they were almost at level with their heads". This was, in point of anthropological fact, a Cubeo ceremonial mourning bodypiece in which body costumes made of bark cloth cover head and shoulders and give the appearance of a headless body.

There was as always some gold, so that when Vera reappeared in Trinidad in May 1593, with golden ornaments and a confirmation of Juan Martín de Albujar's tall tale, the septuagenarian heart of Antonio de Berrio overflowed: "I know not whether the silver-smiths of Spain could fashion conceits so life-like and of such perfection as the Indians make." Therefore, Domingo de Vera was sent to Spain to seek an audience with the King and secure all the necessary assistance for the final assault on the Kingdom of El Dorado and the lake of Gran Manoa. Meanwhile Antonio de Berrio waited impatiently at his new settlement of San José de Oruña during the years 1594–5 for his return. Then, as if to fulfil his remark that "the devil himself is the patron of this enterprise", Sir Walter Raleigh arrived.

"Many years since," Raleigh wrote, "I had knowledge by relation of that mighty, rich and beautiful Empire of Guiana and of that great and Golden Citie which the Spaniards called El Dorado."

"Many years since" had been literally only one year when, in 1594, Captain George Popham, privateering as usual, had captured a Spanish vessel and discovered documents: "There have been certain letters received here of late of a land newly discovered called Nuevo Dorado . . . they write of wonderful riches to be found in this Dorado and that golde there is in great abundance."

Sir Walter Raleigh's captain had found the reports of Domingo de Vera, the wonderful thousand-and-one-night

273

tales of Juan Martín de Albujar and other reports that gave a form of official substance to El Dorado.

This was Raleigh's key, and with it he opened the door. He had a superb library. He read in Latin, French, Spanish, and all that was new in the realms of thought gravitated toward him. Moreover, he "could toil terribly", and he had on hand books published about the Incas (Pedro de Cieza and López de Gomrara, *A fruitful and pleasant history of the conquests of Mexico*). Peter Martyr's *Letters* (appearing in English as early as 1555), André Thevet's book on Brazil (geographically near the "wonderful riches"), which was titled *The new founde worlde or . . . wonderful and strange things,* were read avidly by Raleigh who combed the available maps and formulated his El Dorado "enterprise". He had full need of it, for during the years of 1592–4 he was in disgrace with Elizabeth Regina. The days in the Tower following his secret marriage revealed a side of his character not often seen in his proud, haughty man. His mental state bordered on hysteria and he often wrote letters to Robert Cecil, the Secretary of State, pouring out his misery. He wrote letters to the Queen of exaggerated flattery, likening her to a Venus ["the gentle wind blowing her fair hair, her pure cheeks like a nymph"]. All this about a woman nearing sixty with close-cropped hair, pock-marked face, horribly made-up, a formidable woman rather than feminine, and one who – like many women in their wintry years – hated in direct proportion as she ceased to be able to have herself loved. "The gentle wind blowing her fair hair" – even this touched Elizabeth not. So low did he feel his estate, he vowed that if let out of the Tower to gain royal favour again and to serve his gracious sovereign, he was even willing to ship out as a "poore mariner". This more than all revealed his mental state, for Raleigh loathed the sea – that "pasture for fools". He was easily seasick, and he hated the stench of the forecastle. His description of one of his journeys in an open boat said: "There was never any prison in England that could be found more unsavoury and

Emeralds as diadems. Two emeralds and a quartz gem set in cast gold, found in Coclé, Panama. (Peabody Museum, Harvard University)

An emerald lying in the white quartz of its birth. Found in bituminous shale, it is the most costly gem-stone and is found only in Colombia.

Two scenes from the magnificently illustrated Köler Codex composed by Hieronymous Köler of Nuremberg. He accompanied Hohermuth on his expedition to Coro, and recorded details of the journey in words and pictures.

(top) The three members of the Welser expedition riding towards Seville for embarkation.

(bottom) The *Victoria*, flag-ship of the Welser expedition, arriving in Coro, Venezuela.

Queen Elizabeth I, by M. Gheeraerts the younger. The handsome Raleigh was favoured with titles and a knighthood, but the Queen's displeasure on occasion was made equally clear. (National Portrait Gallery)

loathsome, especially to myself . . . and cared for in a sort of differing." He had no sea command during the invasion of the Great Armada, and when he was one of those who was to hang on the tail of the retreating ships he was the first of the sea captains to complain and give up. Not without civil sneering was he dubbed "Jonah" by Robert Cecil. Queen Elizabeth gave him her private anodyne as "water", the thing he most detested. Take away, said one of his biographers, the purple prose that coloured all of his exploits at sea, and his actions are "exceedingly bare".

But the El Dorado enterprise was to be different.

Raleigh had need of something startling, brilliant, such as the discovery of gold-rich country and the opening of an empire to the Virgin Queen. Its coming could not have been more timely, for Raleigh was unused to his present contretemps, having "travelled many roads with ease".

He was born in 1552 (although the exact date is not certain) in Devon, at Hayes near upon Budleigh Salterton, in a house which is still existent and habitable. His father, also a Walter, was a Devonian squire of a blood not as blue as Sir Walter's latter-day fame would have his contemporaries believe, yet he was affluent enough to send his son to Oxford and otherwise finance his first years. In Devonshire, that incunabula of British sea captains and supremacy of the ocean-seas, the elder Raleigh married three times, and so Walter Raleigh, the second, became related to Gilberts, Grenvilles, Courtenays, St. Legers, Russells, all of which connections became his social ladder to aid his rapid rise.

All men dream, but not all men dream alike, least of all Walter Raleigh. He was, as many in that lively creative period, fully literary. He had matured early, as boys then did, coming down from Oriel College, Oxford, at the age of fourteen, equipped with what would now be judged uncommon learning for one so young, but which in that time, for one of his social position, was not at all so extraordinary.

Yet wherefrom the inheritance of mind, his sense of

poetry, his subtleties, the incredible range of his curiosity? They were not from his father – a reduced Devonian country gentleman – and not from his mother. Then whence? It was not among military commanders nor admirals nor even pirates where he lived; "the country of his mind" was with Marlowe, Spenser, Ben Jonson, Shakespeare. When he was for the last time in the Tower and writing his gargantuan *History of the World,* Thomas Hood wrote to him:

> In greatness thou art lost
> As in a wood
> Treading the oaths of flattery and blood.

At fifteen, Raleigh was a soldier – certainly no common foot-slogger, but a subaltern in a volunteer English army to aid the Huguenots in the Netherlands.

This demi-war, an attempt to detach the Netherlands from Spain's influence, became one of the irritants that led to the Spanish Armada. Philip II had inherited from his father an implacable distaste for heterodoxy in any of its forms. He then had his hands full fighting Moors in Spain and abroad, so that when England intervened in the Netherlands and France, he was unable to give the newest involvement the full Spanish treatment. So it was here that young Raleigh had his first high moments in doing service to his Queen by offending the King of Spain.

After he had spent some years in France and had reached his majority, Raleigh went to sea on a rather profitless expedition led by Sir Humphrey Gilbert, his half-brother. Two years later he had his first taste of Ireland and attracted by his *brio* the notice of his officers (and the Queen) over his dash and daring.

The Earl of Leicester, a Privy Councillor to the Queen, sensing that he found in Raleigh a man to reinforce his hold upon the Court, placed him there as his protégé. While Drake and Hawkins made their fame and fortune by raiding the Spanish Main and putting to torch and rapine the

American cities which Spain had so painfully built, Walter resided at Court close to the Queen. She had a nice eye for handsome men, and she kept Raleigh in assiduous attendance, for all agreed on his good looks and the strength of his personality. Raleigh remained a courtier. His real talents lay unutilized.

Now it is true that despite the pirates, most of the Spanish fleet got to safety. In one of the Fugger News Letters, dated from Madrid, 26 September 1583, it was reported: "The Spanish fleet, praise to God, arrived without misfortune . . . carrying fifteen million ducats of gold." In 1587, a Fugger News Letter dated from Antwerp, which the Queen could clearly read, stated that the whole Peruvian fleet of one hundred and seventeen ships "have arrived with fourteen millions in gold and silver".

These reports aroused Walter Raleigh's gold lust as it did many involved in piracy, for one of his chief sources of income was obtained from privateering. Robbery at sea was a profession, organized by courtiers and businessmen, for who could forget the profit on one of Drake's voyages, a neat 4,700 per cent for an investment? Raleigh always had ships at sea bent on freebooting.

Walter Raleigh quickly insinuated himself into the goodwill of the Queen. She heaped her royal favours on him; he was knighted; he won the coveted right to "farm the wines" – that is, a monopoly of all wine imports into the isle. He was given the exclusive licence to export "all woollen broadcloths", by which he waxed rich. He became Vice-Admiral of Devon and Cornwall, Lord Warden of the Stannaries (the tin mines in Cornwall), and for his early prowess against the Irish rebels, an estate there of 12,000 acres, the forfeited estates of the Earls of Desmond, at Kilcolman in County Munster.

Even in that age when rapaciousness was part of Elizabethan social life, Raleigh gained an early and ugly reputation for rapacity. "I would rather trust the Devil with my soul", said one who had had his fill of Raleigh, "than you with my goods."

278

His enemies seemed to be legion, but this might have been only proof of this highly strung man's unquenchable energy; "he can toil terribly", was Cecil's view of him.

There was also a ruthless logic in Raleigh's thoughts and actions, and, as he was fearless, he disliked being crossed. He had a gift of repartee – a "scathing tongue" – which was like the riposte of a rapier. Consequently, many who would have liked to esteem him for his quickness of mind and overwhelming generosities were put off by his singular disregard for others' feelings. Seldom did any man ask more from life than he, and seldom had life a greater spite in denying it. He had a form of genius. He could write soaring prose and his verse even in those times was of the best. His thoughts were daring; he could give out the most abstruse metaphysical arguments and then, in turn, be a man of action. He used high-handed bribery, could lie unblushingly, grovel, whine and then raise himself high in quixotic knight-errantry. There was in this Raleigh several men who might have grown great and done fine things had his dual natures not been forced to prey one upon the other in so intolerable and indissoluble a union.

The fabled riches of the Americas fascinated him. His first folly cost him £40,000 when he sent out a fleet at his own expense to seize land north of Spanish Florida. In 1585–7 he fitted out two other expeditions in an attempt to colonize this "Virginia"; it ended in the death or dispersion of the first colonists. Sir Francis Drake did the knightly thing by collecting the last of the disillusioned and bringing them back to England. Tobacco and potatoes, although he had nothing to do with their discovery, were Raleigh's sole reward for the time and the £40,000 spent, which was somewhat retrieved by his exploitation of these two crops which he drew on his huge latifundia in Ireland.

In the summer of 1592, while Raleigh had his privateers out on one of his largest acts of piracy, he got Lady Elizabeth Throgmorton with child. Now Raleigh was not a sensual man. He certainly was not known as a womanizer, but that Sir Walter should debauch one of her ladies-in-waiting infuriated the Queen. This frail, blue-eyed, honey-haired, only daughter of Sir Nicholas Throgmorton had ornamented her Court for years. She was regarded by Elizabeth as a sort of vestal virgin. It was not alone the result of jealousy – even though Time's unpleasant hand was on her face – she regarded manners and morals as a royal responsibility. As aforesaid, Anthony Bacon gave away the scandal in a letter dated 30 July 1592: ". . . Sir Walter Raleigh, as it seemeth hath been too inward with one of her Matie's maides . . . he will be speedily sent for . . . he escaped from London for a time . . . All think the Tower will be his dwelling." And in that Tower Raleigh remained in utter anguish. First his captains had missed the Spanish treasure fleet, which was announced by a Fugger News Letter (dated 1590) from Venice saying "that a fleet had arrived in Lisbon with eight millions in gold . . . they had sailed north farther than usual to avoid the English ships waiting for them".

But later, the dispositions of his pirate ships resulted in the richest single capture ever made at sea. The *Madre de Diós,* one of Spain's largest carracks, had a cargo of spices, bullion and other material that staggered London's imagination.

When it was brought into Plymouth harbour, the people fell on it and before the investors or brokers or traders could get there, the sack was general. The Queen was furious, since she was a prominent stockholder, and eventually it was seen that one man alone could unravel it – Sir Walter Raleigh. And he under charge of a keeper of the Tower was released to go to Plymouth. Sir Robert Cecil, who liked him not, nonetheless observed the effect of his presence on the common man: ". . . the number of hundred and forty goodly men all the mariners came to him with such shouts of joy".

In the end the Queen got her enormous profit, but Raleigh sustained a great loss. This was even more grievous since he took the greatest risk. But then, at least he was out of the Tower.

In 1594, as written, one of the captains in his employ, George Popham, captured a royal Spanish ship off the coast of Venezuela. There among the captured ship's papers were reports of Spanish expeditions to search out El Dorado, and the King of Spain's enthusiastic response to these plans. So certain was the lost Golden City that Quesada's heir, Antonio de Berrio, as Sir Walter Raleigh read, had been promoted to be "Governor of Guiana and El Dorado".

All this, as he read it, was calculated to set Raleigh's imagination afire; his noble heart pounded the more as he read all that could be obtained, and along his veins the sounds beat out El Dorado, El Dorado. There would, he said, be undying fame for "the one who will endow his country with the knighthood of El Dorado". Although he had vaguely read what happened to the men of the German Welser and fully knew what happened to many of the Spaniards who had sought out all this, still his own plan seemed "Feasible and Certain" – as so it did to the bankers. For the prospect of gold, bankers have always been venturous. Among those who gave liberal furtherance to Raleigh's enterprise were some of the most prominent men of the realm and some of the most influential members of the Court. The glamour of the marvellous, coupled with the glowing descriptions of the great empire of Guiana with its inexhaustible riches, sufficed to secure all the money and ships and equipment necessary for the expedition. His schemes, as always, were novel, far-reaching and original. The stakes were high and his eloquence persuasive; for it was his, designed "to sway all men's fancies, all men's courses".

The Howards, the Blounts, and the Earl of Leicester were contributors, as well as Sir Robert Cecil. It was his contribution that gave it prestige, since it put the official seal to the expedition. He was always avid for any participation in twilight-zone schemes, so long as they were secret and lucrative.

281

Cecil, the Secretary of State, was known to dislike Raleigh, so it is curious that he should have been taken in by this golden lunacy. Small, with a hunchback and thus unable physically to take part in the great Elizabethan adventures, he usually held himself aloof from all of these hair-brained schemes. And the great Raleigh, the first apostle and martyr of the British colonial empire, the founder of what was to be Greater England across the seas, and one who was distinguished for his acuteness and his shrewdness in affairs, so endowed with political realism and wisdom – what had happened to him and, for that matter, to them all?

Finally came the assent of the Queen. Why not offer her Guiana as a key to an overseas empire? It must be certain that Raleigh believed himself in El Dorado, for he sank much of his own fortune in it. The Queen, too, must have been a heavy contributor. This was soon aired about, and the Spanish Ambassador was deeply suspicious of this voyage; to him Queen Elizabeth was the embodiment of dissimulation, indecision, procrastination and, worst of all, parsimony. What was her motive in lending name, prestige and money to search out what was not the Golden City of Manoa? The Spanish Ambassador's summation of her was: "There is more dissimulation in her than honesty and good will: she is best at the game of living."

In her name Raleigh was empowered "to do Us service in offending the King of Spain and his subjects in his dominions to your uttermost power". All who sailed under him, or should afterwards consort with his fleet, are bound to give due obedience in whatever "you shall think meet to direct or undertake for the prejudice of the said King of Spain, or any of Our Enemies", and whatever shall be done under that commission, "as well by sea as by land, for the furtherance of this Our service and enfeebling of Our enemies, the subject and adherents of the King of Spain, you and all such as serve under you in this voyage shall be clearly acquitted and discharged".

Before the main fleet sailed, Raleigh dispatched Captain Whiddon to Trinidad to obtain additional information, acting on the official Spanish documents. But Antonio de Berrio quite rightly, since the lands they wished to explore lay under his governorship, thwarted him, and the information, which of a certainty would have been valuable to Raleigh's success, was denied him. Despite this, Raleigh sailed with his five ships out of Plymouth on 5 February 1595. While yet not arrived, he wrote: "Guiana is a country that hath yet her maidenhood. The face of the earth hath not been torn, the graves have not yet been opened for gold. It hath never been entered by any army of strength and never conquered by a Christian prince. Men shall find here more rich and beautiful cities, more temples adorned with gold than either Cortés found in Mexico or Pizarro in Peru, and the shining glory of this conquest will eclipse all those of the Spanish nation."

So in the spring of 1595, in keeping with the lunacy of this story, Sir Walter Raleigh had four of the ship's boats made ready for the voyage upstream, the larger "bote" carrying sixty men, "the other forty distributed in the other three". They were victualled for one month.

There remained, however, certain practical matters, such as where in all this verdured land *was* the Golden Lake. Raleigh knew that it was "certaine", but not *where* it was. "It was", he learned, "founded upon a lake of salt water 200 leagues long [700 miles] like into Mare Caspium [the Caspian Sea] and for the greatness for the riches and for the excellent seate it farre exceedeth any of the world."

One of the Spaniards obligingly prepared him a map of the location of this lake and El Dorado. The coastline on the map from Cartagena in Colombia to the mouth of the Orinoco is as precise and correct as any map of the time; cities and ports are correctly named as well as the first hundred miles along the river. But the Amazon and Orinoco are drawn as two gigantic rivers running parallel and between – looking like a giant centipede – is the lake of

Manoa, seven hundred miles long and fed by hundreds of streams: "It is landlocked, saline, and around it were the cities . . . of that mighty, rich and bewtiful Empyre of Guiana, that great and golden citie which the Spanyards call El Dorado".

First they had to find the principal stream. They soon found themselves lost in the tortuous maze of the delta of the great river, and, had they not been fortunate in securing an Arawak Indian native pilot, they "might have wandered a whole yeare in that labyrinth of rivers. For I know all the earth", the great navigator writes, without exaggeration in this instance, "doth not yield the like confluence of streames and branches, the one crossing the other so many times, and all so faire and large and so like one to another, as no man can tell which to take; and if we went by the sunne or compasse, hoping thereby to go directly one way or another, yet that waie we are also carried in a circle amongst multitudes of Ilands; and every Iland is so bordered with high trees as no man could see any further than the bredth of the river or length of the breach".

Actually the Río Orinoco extends into Venezuela like a gigantic fishhook; the flattened shank is the delta, while the point of the hook encircles the high granite mountains of Cerro Duida for a thousand miles and comes close to the Río Negro.

Now the eastern trade winds can waft upriver for a hundred miles or so sailboats of shallow draught, until the rock fortress San Tomás, commanding the centre of the river, is reached. After that the cataracts begin. Raleigh admitted that he now knew that his destination was six hundred miles further from the sea "than I was made believe it had beene" by Antonio de Berrio. For the first time Raleigh became aware of the fierce distances, but he "kept [this] from knowledge of my companie who else never have been brought to attempt the same".

The wind began to have less effect upstream, and food began to give out. They were forced to row against the

284

powerful current, and at the larger cataracts they had to portage the large unwieldy boats. As the river began to run violently against them "there were loud voices of dissent". Raleigh, however, refused to return "lest the world laugh us to scorn". Now, as it should be with myths and fancies, Raleigh saw all manners of Beastes and Cannibals "and diverse sorts of strange fishes and of marvellous bigness, and thousands of those ugly serpents called Largartes (crocodiles)".

Once they were beyond the larger cataracts and the land flattened out, Raleigh wrote that "I never saw a more beautiful country, nor more lively prospects, hills raised here and there, over the valleys, the river winding into different branches, plains without bush or stubble, all fair green grass, deer crossing our path, the birds toward evening singing on every side a thousand different tunes, herons of white, crimson, and carnation perching on the river-side, the air fresh with a gentle wind."

But Candide in the wonderful tale written by Voltaire in 1752 did not find El Dorado in the New World "better than the other". They picked up gold, emeralds – and rubies in an ancient country of the Incas. The Spaniards had some vague knowledge of this country which they called El Dorado and about one hundred years ago an Englishman called Raleigh came near to it, but Candide, being a practical young man, was only interested in getting back to his Mademoiselle Cunégonde. So, like Raleigh, Candide never reached El Dorado. Nor did anyone else.

They were still hundreds of miles from the reported fabulous lake as large as the Caspian, but they made no headway. The problems of river transport were beyond them or anyone else. The crowded path to El Dorado began to fare as badly for them as for all others.

The expedition propelled themselves up far enough to see in the hazy distance two mountain peaks of Cerro Duida, each 7,000 feet high, which the Indians said were called Picatoa and Inatac. Beyond this, the Indians said, was the lake of El Dorado.

He did not see it – indeed, no one had ever seen the lake – but Raleigh put it on his maps and there Parima, the Lake of Manoa, remained for one hundred and fifty years. Every cartographer *had* to put the lake on his maps. The small Andean lake of Guatavita had been moved by human imagination, ingenuity and myth from nine thousand feet altitude to sea level and a distance of one thousand miles into the Orinoco's basin.

The printer-geographer, Hondius, who drew his map of Guiana shortly after Raleigh's return from his expedition, locates Lake Parima (=Manoa) or Dorado between latitudes 2° N. and 1° 45 S. and makes it larger than the Caspian Sea. "I have beene assured", writes Raleigh, "by such of the Spanyardes as have seene Manoa, the emperiall Citie of Guiana, which the Spanyardes call El Dorado, that for the greatness, for the riches, and for the excellent seate, it farre exceedeth any of the world, at least of so much of the world as is known to the Spanish nation; it is founded upon a lake of salt water 200 leagues long like unto Mare Caspium." Aaron Arrowsmith, the celebrated eighteenth-century English cartographer, later reduced it to a great inland lake into his maps, seventy miles in breadth, which was supposed to lie between the Amazon and the Orinoco, and such geographical misconceptions persisted to Humboldt's visit in 1799.

So great was the "authority" of Sir Walter Raleigh that the inland sea of Parima endured on all the world's maps until 1800, when the great geographer Alexander von Humboldt pronounced it "fabulous". Yet since in Humboldtian logic all fables have some foundation, where did the idea of a sea as great as the Caspian take root? And why? The Omaguas were, it is believed, an intrusive culture; they

The map of Guiana with the water courses of the Orinoco and the Amazon, drawn by Sir Walter Raleigh in 1595 from information obtained from captured Spanish documents. All is correct except the invention of the Lake of Parima lying between the Orinoco and the Amazon, and appearing to be an outsized centipede. It was meant by Raleigh to be the lake of the Golden City of Manoa. (British Museum)

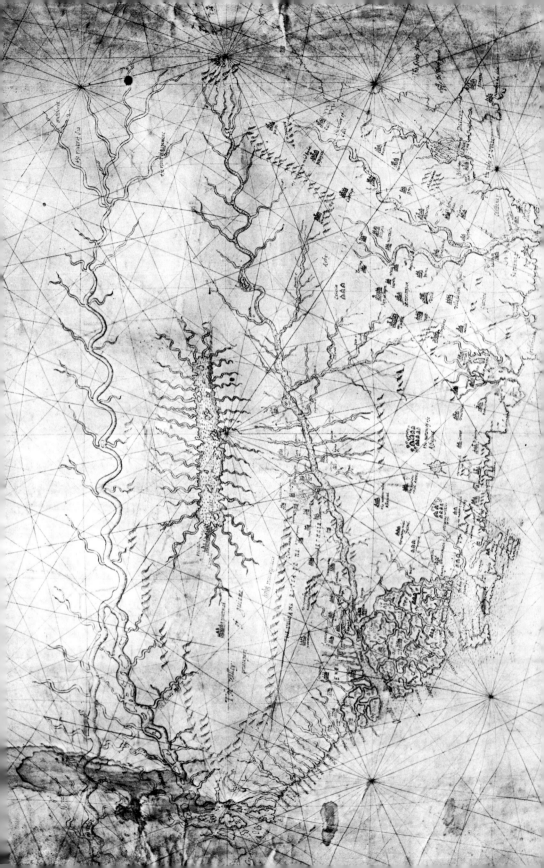

were irresistible in war, they possessed some gold ornaments and they lived in organized communities; they inspired fear and mistrust in all tribes who knew them. It was just this tribe which Philip von Hutten came upon in 1544 which made him believe that this was El Dorado.

Antonio de Berrio, in his search for the Golden City, had come to the southern sources of Upper Orinoco; when the rivers were in high flood, these tributaries overflowed and coalesced to form a large but temporary lagoon. Berrio was told that "in the mountains (of Guiana) there is a very large *laguna* and on the other side are great towns and a vast population with gold and precious stones". So long as the floods lasted and all these over-flowing rivers conjoined, there was the "Great White Sea of Parima", Parima being one of the rivers.

"These rivers", Humboldt observed, "passing through a country entirely flat are subject at the same time to great inundations, so that their real river-bed can hardly be discerned. The Caribs called this swollen river *paraque* which meant in their language 'sea' or 'great lake'." So out of the Omagus, the swollen rivers which formed into a body of water which the Caribs said was a great lake, was born Raleigh's *Mare Caspium*. All who followed Raleigh added their own embroidery to the original fabric of his weaving.

Humboldt had no difficulty in pronouncing "fabulous" these monstrous lakes, sources of rivers and repositories of gold. "I was able to convince myself on the spot".

"Thus we see", he continues, "that the great Mar de la Parima (which it was so difficult to remove from our maps that even after my return from America in 1805, it was still supposed to be 160 miles in length *was reduced by accurate measurements to two or three miles in circumference.*"

Now made aware that there was no chance in the limited time he had given himself – one month – to find the great inland sea and the empire of the Guianas, Raleigh began laying the groundwork for a return in the following year.

He emulated Francisco Pizarro in his conquest of Peru.

288

During his first excursion into the very edge of the Inca realm in 1527, Pizarro left behind two of his company as hostages as well as to learn the language and spy out the lie of the land.

Raleigh did likewise.

He took two of the Topiwari Indian sons of the chieftain Maraquita and left behind Francis Sparrey (he writes it Frauncis Sparrow) and Hugh Goodwin. They were to learn the language, acquaint themselves with the area so as to be useful to Captain Laurence Keymis on his return the following year. Within two years Sparrey was a Spanish prisoner in Spain, whereat he shared his discomfort with another, Captain Jo. Stanley, who, when he was released and brought to Raleigh, told him that Sparrey "found sufficient which the Spaniard knoweth not. He [Sparrey] gave me the reason how [to find the gold] and a map where to find it. I delivered it to Sir Walter at my coming up" – that is, getting out of jail. Later when the public was excited about "the great empire of El Dorado", Francis Sparrey turned author and gave his own account.[1]

The other hostage, Hugh Goodwin, a boy servant, was less fortunate. He slipped away from the Spanish hunt and was hidden by the Indians, adopted by them and became something of an English Juan Martín de Albujar: when he was found by Raleigh twenty years later in 1617, he had forgotten his mother tongue.

This was the extent of Raleigh's "great discovery" of Guiana. He had travelled 150 miles, or if one takes into consideration the sinuosities of the rivers, 250 miles. He did not pursue the way to the great lake of Manoa, nor search for the cities "more rich and beautiful, more temples adorned with golden Images. more sepulchres filled with treasure than either Cortez found in Mexico or Pizarro in Peru". There was a faint-hearted attempt to find gold mines. Raleigh saw "diverse hills", but he knew nothing of the geology of gold. He found a cliff "wherein gold must be found", but admitted that they had neither time nor instruments nor men fit to labour. He sent his Captain Lawrence Keymis with

Indian guides who said they knew where the mines were and in this valley "they saw rocks like unto gold ore and also a mountain of mineral stone." They prised out with mattocks some rock "wherein gold is engendered", and that was all.

The persistence of the fables of El Dorado is explained, obviously, by the gloomy endings to all who searched for it. "The more insurmountable the treasures they guarded," wrote Milton Waldman, one of the many of Raleigh's biographers, "the greater the treasures they guarded." Since so many had set out to find it, since so much time, effort and money and so many lives had been lost, it follows then that it must be true. But why after all this expense and all this talk did not Sir Walter search for it? They were only victualled for one month, although they could have lived off the country as did Antonio de Berrio for ten years, and as did Federmann for an equal number of years. They had trekked for thousands of miles, and he only two hundred. The mines could not be worked, Raleigh said, because during the months of May-September, the Orinoco can rise overnight up to thirty feet – which is true. He was shown stones which they said were "diamonds", and diamonds were eventually found in Guiana, he saw "blue metalline rocks, with a colour unto the best steel ore", which is also true, since Venezuela has in this region opened one of the greatest iron-ore mines on the continent, but of gold. . . .

Then, too, it was the presence of Antonio de Berrio. He constantly was on the lookout for the men he expected Domingo de Vera to bring from Spain. He also expected his son Fernando, aged 17, to arrive with reinforcements from Bogotá some 1,200 miles distant. All this combined to hurry Raleigh's departure.

The original plan, once he gained his ships, was to bring Antonio de Berrio as a prisoner to England, doubtlessly to have the Knight of El Dorado himself explain and confirm the earth-riches of the mighty empire of Guiana. However, in their attack on 6 July 1595 on Cumaná, a well-protected city and harbour on the mainland close upon the Island of

Margarita, in an attempt to sack so as not to return to London with empty coffers, they were beaten off with great loss. This is confirmed by official Spanish documents: "An English Pirate Fleet arrived June 22, 1595, under Milor Guattaral." They landed two hundred and ten men and they lost one-third of them; many were severely wounded so that Raleigh left Berrio and his Captain Alvaro Jorge behind to take care of them, while his four ships took off for raids elsewhere. Because of this miscalculation, Antonio de Berrio won his freedom and a return to his fief and the Kingdom of El Dorado.

All of the miseries of the voyage and the expedition up the Orinoco were as nothing compared with the rolling flood of vituperation he had poured on his head by the Virgin Queen. Where were those riches of El Dorado? Where was this "diadem, this great and beautiful empire of Guiana for her crown"? And her money, where was it? Wasted for some idle dream? By God's death, he, Raleigh, would answer for it. How would she go about the annexation of El Dorado for "the crowne imperiall of the Realme of England"? Did Sir Walter happen to bring back, with his huge unpaid debt, the person of the Golden Man himself so that he could bestow this diadem? Where were the promised riches of so great a sum that – "Our realms would no longer be threatened with any more invincible Armadas"? With astonishing volubility she cursed Raleigh for a gullible fool, a maniac dazzled by fool's gold. A simple and inconvertible ass, he had left more gold in that miserable El Dorado than he would ever bring away.

The wits of London had full play with Raleigh and his El Dorado. Since he had given many a man a feel of his rapier tongue, it was now his turn to receive scorn, rebuke and, what was worst for his pride, ridicule. Some wags suggested that he never left England but hid in Cornwall. He demurred in the book that he was writing, as his apology, *The Discoverie of the Large, Rich, Beautiful Empire of Guiana:* "I had neither hidden in Cornwall or elsewhere as

Map of Guiana, from *Americae Pars VIII*, 1599, with text and illustrations of armadillo, tigers, turtles, deer and wild pig. The fighting Amazons are also shown, and the tribe of headless Ewaipahomas described to Raleigh by a chieftain of the lower Orinoco.

is supposed. They have grossly belied me." He described the malice and revenge of his enemies and he bewailed "that he returned a beggar and withered". He sought out the best-known assayers in London to make a public assay of the ore that he brought back. The results were nil. Then he sought to turn his countrymen's minds toward the acquisition of an empire in South America, beginning in Guiana, as he tried to do in Virginia, and failed to do so. The book as a book is thin, not only in size (175×127 mm) or the number of pages (112) but the contents. One-third is potted history, which he gleaned out of books in his library, which he ill read, for there is little in geography or history that is accurate even by mistake. All of the history of El Dorado and Guiana was taken wholly from Antonio de Berrio so that his own narrative is less than one-third of the book.

Yet it is wholly fair, when dealing with a legend, to hold Sir Walter to the narrow line of truth. Since his apologists say that he should not be judged by his knowledge of the sea, nor his originality as an explorer but in "the greatness of his mind", then he must be judged by his credulity.

The natives seemed to him like something out of another planet. When the Orinoco was in flood stage, the Indians called Tinitinas became arboreal; "they dwell upon the trees where they build very artificial townes and villages". Whole villages in the trees. And then he said there were *acephali,* people who were "headless warriors of Ewaipahomas". Above the River Sipapo, one of the tributaries of the Orinoco, was a tribe which in one of their ceremonies made mammoth masks from bark cloth painted with eyes and mouth that covered their entire heads and shoulders. In the alembic of Raleigh's imagination "they were a nation of people whose heads are reported to have their eyes in their shoulders and their mouth in the middle of their breasts, and that a long train of hair groweth backward between their shoulders. The son of Topiawari, a lower Orinoco chief, which I brought with me into England, told me."

Illustrations of these *acephali* were prepared for his books, and for years and years they appeared in other books, on maps, in histories and in literature; as in Othello:

> And of the Cannibals that each other eat
> The Anthropophagi and men whose heads
> Do grow beneath their shoulders.

Was it really possible that in the age of Rabelais, Machiavelli and Ben Jonson such sheer drivel would find audience?

Yes! People were fascinated by it all. Bankers who had loaned him a sizeable fortune, merely because he wrote of gold and silver, were again made interested. The book went on through three editions in the first year. The Dutch were interested and published. But the edition that made Raleigh popular was the large folio edition (mostly given over to Drake) that appeared in 1599 with superb engravings by Theodor de Bry.

Still it was not the "mightie empyre of Guiana" that saved him from beggardom; it was the threat of a new Spanish Armada that brought Raleigh back into the Queen's grace in the same way as Raleigh inadvertently saved, even though briefly, the offices of Antonio de Berrio.

[1] Alexander von Humboldt came to Guatavita in November 1801. Born in Berlin in 1759, immersed in the studies of geology, botany, and geography, he had been given the royal blessing of Charles IV in 1799; he travelled and collected widely in the Americas, throughout Cuba and Venezuela, and had been poled all the way up the Magdalena, where he arrived at Bogotá. After five years in the Americas, he returned to Europe, where he began in 1803 to prepare the results.

The mere statistics of Humboldt's output are terrifying and will never be repeated again by any one man. He travelled by mule or boat 40,000 miles throughout the Americas and returned with thirty immense cases of material; 1,500 measurements used in his *Recueil d'Observations Astronomiques,* 60,000 plant specimens, of which more than 6,000 were new to science. Botany, which is generously sprinkled with plants which bear the initials of HBK (Humboldt, Bonpland and Kunth), was greatly enriched by him. Out of all this, he wrote thirty volumes – folio, quarto, decimo – (*Voyage aux régions equinoxiales de Nouveau Continent* being his "personal narrative") which consisted of over 150,000 pages and 426 illustrations and maps. The engravings alone cost him 600,000 gold francs, the paper 840,000 francs, the printing 2,753 Prussian thalers. The task of floating and seeing these works through the presses in Paris took him seventeen years.

Humboldt weighed everything in its balance. A fact to be a fact, in the Humboldtean logic, meant both physical and literary research and considerable pondering, but now, at Guatavita, he saw on the low banks of the lake "the remains of a staircase, hewn in the rock and serving for the ceremonies of ablution". He also took note "of the breach which was made by the Spaniards [i.e., Antonio Sepúlveda] for the purpose of draining the lake". When back in Paris, and coming to that section of his scientific travels, he computed that if a thousand Indians a year had made their annual pilgrimage thence to Guatavita for a century, as had been claimed, further, if each had thrown a minimum of five golden trinkets into the lake to honor the resident deity, then there were upwards of 50,000,000 golden pieces buried in the thick black ooze at the bottom of the lake. Humboldt's calculation, taking the price of gold then in 1807, was that the gold in Guatavita would have a current monetary value of some $300,000,000. When this was read by Monsieur de la Kier of the Royal Institute of Paris, he himself revised Humboldt's estimate of the worth of cash value then of the golden Chibcha hoard that lay at the bottom of Lake Guatavita. His estimate: $5,600,000,000.

² *The Description of the Isle of Trinidad, the riche Countrye of Guiana, and the Mightie River of Orenoco* (sic) written by Francis Sparrey left there by Sir Walter Raleigh and in the end taken by the Spaniards and sent prisoner to Spaine and after long captivitye got into England by great sute, 1602. Printed in Purchase. Macclehose edition, Vol. XVL.

CHAPTER XII

'Truth shall... this story say'

Guiana, whose rich feete are mines
of golde,
Whose forehead knockes against the
roofe of Starres,
Stands on her tip-toes at faire England
looking,
Kissing her hand. . . . – Chapman (1599)

AS quickly as canoes and the wind-filled sails of the fly-boats could propel him, Antonio de Berrio moved upward on the Orinoco river to his former seat: the headquarters of the kingdom of Omagua, Trinidad and El Dorado.

This time the Spanish treasury did not stint. All the king's horses and all the king's men rushed up the materials so that Colonel Antonio de Berrio, Knight of El Dorado, could fortify his kingdoms from any future incursions of anyone such as "Milor Gualterreal".

Illustration from Raleigh's *The Third Voyage* . . . (British Museum)

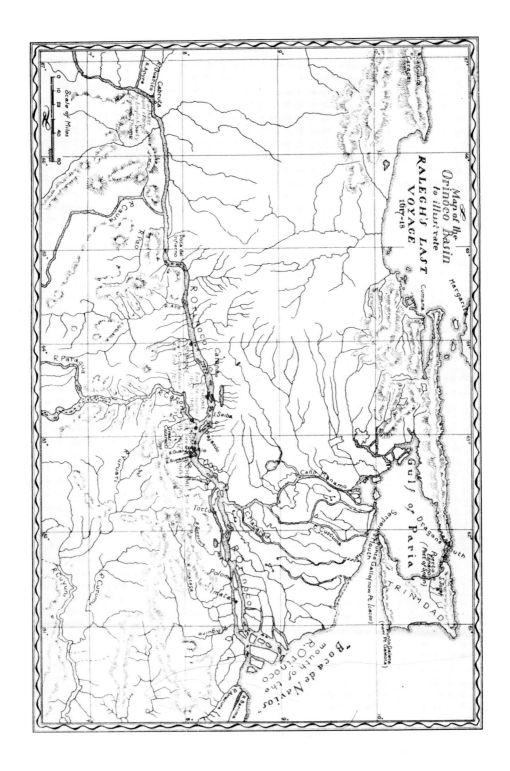

Map of the
Orinóco Basin
to illustrate
RALEGH'S LAST
VOYAGE
1617–18

As the Caroni river seemed to have been the objective of Raleigh, and as it was regarded as the fluvial highway to Manoa and the way to El Dorado, Antonio de Berrio decided to build the fort there. About one hundred and eighty miles from the Orinoco delta, there is a large island, known as the Fajardo, that commands it. There the Caroni makes its furious confluence with the larger Orinoco, and there on a high left, or south, bank, San Thomé fort and town were erected. A Spanish plan of it still extant shows the fort with four cannons guarding the four points. A larger water cistern was in its centre; there were two gates, replete with portcullis landward and another which led to the river-port. The Governor's residence and houses were part of the wall. It was simple and effective. Berrio urged the inhabitants to grow tobacco and develop cattle husbandry so that hides and tobacco became for the moment more lucrative than the gold at the end of the Eldoradian rainbow. Meanwhile, Berrio's son, Fernando, Quesada's future heir, had come overland from Bogotá with more reinforcements.

Fernando de Berrio had "just turned seventeen" and yet at that young age was named "Camp Master" and whether he or the old veteran Captain Alvaro Jorge – who had been held captive by Raleigh – commanded, reinforcements were brought all that distance without notable mishap. So since Berrio was now aged over seventy years, he wrote the King that as the titles to the Province of Omagua and El Dorado were held "in perpetuity" that the King remember to keep his promise that his eldest son Fernando "who is serving with me" be secured in his inheritance.

What other reaction could there have been but pure and unalloyed joy to old Antonio de Berrio to learn that not only had his son been acknowledged the future Knight of El Dorado ["in perpetuity"] but also a message up from Trinidad brought the news that Domingo de Vera, so long absent, had been successful beyond all belief; he was bringing all that Berrio had asked of the King – ships and trade goods as well as people.

300

When Domingo de Vera, as Antonio de Berrio's legate, had arrived in Seville in 1593, he seemed to be out of El Dorado itself. There were Indians with him, he dangled gold and silver objects from his hands, and he was outlandishly clad in a costume of his own devising. "Here," said his impresario, "is the Indian from El Dorado, the land of riches." In his element, where the tongue commanded and reason lay dormant, Domingo de Vera expanded. He gave glowing descriptions of the Lake of Manoa. People of all ranks asked to join; the gentle and base-born rushed to be enrolled. The King's Council turned over the boats asked for by Berrio; funds were allotted. The city fathers of Seville themselves financed five ships and gave five thousand golden ducats. Ten secular monks volunteered and even the Bishop of Seville himself wished to go in order to administer to that great Indian population that lived around the fabulous Lake of Manoa.

Now, also unknown to Antonio de Berrio, Sir Walter Raleigh, while "singeing the beard" of the King of Spain, had animated the Council of the Indies. Whereas Berrio had asked for four small boats, he got a hundred; whereas he asked for a modest contribution, he received seventy thousand ducats; whereas he asked for a few score soldiers and people to aid him in finding El Dorado, the Council of the Indies sent out six hundred bachelors and four hundred married men with wives and children.

For almost a century, as the Council later admitted, "ever since the discoveries of the Indies, there has been talk of the provinces of El Dorado". In most cases the suppliants for aid were given a deaf ear. Now suddenly they were drugged with the golden lunacy.

The gentle reader must have anticipated already what would happen. At first Antonio de Berrio, elated beyond all known human emotion, dispatched to Trinidad forty-four canoes, with paddlers, by which 470 were successfully transported to Fort San Thomé. The next convoy of thirty-three canoes was attacked by Caribs, and all perished. Then

301

Domingo de Vera, hurrying to the rescue in other canoes, ran into a hurricane, which "for my sins God willed it". Forty men were drowned, and all foodstuffs and "all munitions and all arms" perished in the maw of the sea-god Hurricana.

All this was as yet unknown to Berrio. Despite the heat, Antonio de Berrio, in full colonel's uniform, stood out to review the arrival of what he thought were to be his aides in the final discovery. Then he saw canoe after canoe discharge its mixed cargo of men, women and children. "They seemed so comely", wrote the historian, Pedro Simón, "that they were better suited for Seville by reason of their banners . . . rich and costly dresses which were more appropriate for weddings or royal festivals than for the conquest."

To feed the additional hundreds added to those already in residence at the fortress-settlement must have driven poor Berrio to maniacal fury. What he vented on Domingo de Vera's head has not been recorded.

However, to carry on the search, he asked his old comrade Captain Alvaro Jorge, who shared his imprisonment with Raleigh, to attempt an expedition up the River Caroni – that is, southward toward the "great lake of Manoa". They proceeded thirty leagues – that is, a hundred miles – when Alvaro Jorge, old for his sixty years, worn out by climate and mostly by the press of people, died. Discipline evaporated; murder, desertion, rape followed. The remaining survivors were transported back to the fort by a Sargento Mayor. Then Domingo de Vera himself arrived with hundreds more, and upon Vera's head the old Knight of El Dorado rained so much well-earned abuse that Vera "in high dudgeon", he wrote, "departed down the river". Since the King of Spain had personally interested himself in this enterprise, Vera wrote him of the "timorous, dispirited and thoughtless fashion in which the Governor (Berrio) and all the rest had proceeded".

This, too, was Berrio's end. "This enterprise", he wrote in one of his many letters to Philip II, "is costing me more than a hundred thousand ducats and I believe it will end by costing me my life." Antonio de Berrio was fully accurate. In 1597, he died.

And yet not alone in death, for other knights were dying on the Spanish Main. In what must be regarded as a piratical harassment to divert Spanish attention from the real attack on Cadiz, the great port of Spain, Sir Francis Drake and Hawkins were moving in and about the Antilles to fall on ships to attract official attention. It was to be for both of them their last voyages. Drake began, like most freebooters, in slave-trading; then he turned to outright piracy, capturing the outer walls of Cartagena – one of the staging areas in the Caribbean for the conquest of El Dorado. He burnt Portobello and later surprised and captured a mule caravan crossing from the Isthmus from Panama City. It yielded him and his London investors thirty tons of pure silver. Later, in the circumnavigation of the world in the *Golden Hind,* he returned with millions of pounds sterling in loot, which brought him knighthood, and then additional honours for his effective aid in defeating, in 1588, the Invincible Armada.

His death was not knightly; he was infected with dysentery and died of it off the coast of Puerto Rico. And within months he was followed by John Hawkins, another one of the treasured names in piracy, who also began his career by slave-trading. He too "singed the beard" of the King of Spain with innumerable affronts, won fame and ascended to a seat in the House of Commons, then descended again to go to sea. In the same year (1596) he died of whatever one dies of at the age of sixty-three off the coast of Puerto Rico. In the deepest of the seas – more than 14,000 feet – his piratic mates lowered down in a lead casket the body of Sir John Hawkins.

In 1596, Raleigh was to be one of the triumvirate – Lord Howard, the Earl of Essex and himself in that order of rank – to bring the most formidable force ever gathered in an English port to make a raid on Spain itself to destroy the

Raleigh's march inland along the río Caroni above the great cataracts, using Indians to carry his impedimenta. It was from here that Raleigh saw in the hazy distance the peaks of Cerro Duida; beyond that, the natives said, lay the great lake of El Dorado. Engraving by Theodor de Bry, 1599 (British Museum)

new Armada. Whether or not Queen Elizabeth was pleased to have the new equivocal kingdom of Guiana and El Dorado placed on her escutcheon, she was swept along with the public acclaim that greeted the publication of Raleigh's book and eased her stand on his disgrace. The Earl of Essex, although "he liketh him not", generously prepared a love-feast, reconciled himself with Raleigh and begged the Queen to reinstate him as Captain of the Guard, all of which she did.

The actual manning of the crews for the English Armada much delayed the enterprise. Raleigh, once again pampered and elegant, had to run, so he complained in a letter to the Privy Council, from one ale-house to another along the Thames "dragging his finery" to gather his impressments so that the ships could sail with a full complement. Wrote Anthony Bacon to his brother, Francis, who was then passing through the press his volume of *Essays* – witty, pungent pages of epigrammatic wisdom – to be published in that year, 1596, "Sir Walter's slackness and stay [in obtaining men] by way is not thought to be on sloth but upon pregnant design."

Pregnant design or not, the fleet – nearly one hundred and fifty sail – "as beautiful sight as ever the sea beheld" – left on the first of June and within three weeks fell upon Cadiz.

There was – as in all such actions – confusion, collision and collusion. There was a success of sorts; Spanish ships were destroyed, Cadiz was burned, people were killed and the nose of Philip II was unjointed, albeit figuratively. In it all Raleigh gained such honours as there were, making a landing without permission from his superior, the Earl of Essex, whereupon all the bad blood between the two resurfaced. While all this sound and fury was going on, an immense Spanish fleet, forty ships in number, loaded with 12,000,000 ducats of treasure, slipped by and into safety. The hoard it brought was of such quantity that a Fugger News Letter in 1597, which also brought the first news of

305

Drake's death, was able to announce that Philip, King of Spain, in that year of 1597, was going to pay off all of his old debts to the German bankers. The Welser were at long last to get back something of their investments for the twenty-five years of expenditure looking for the Golden Man; they gladly turned over the golden lunacy to the British.

Within two years, intelligence came to Cecil, the Secretary of State, that Spain was building a third Armada on the Atlantic coast in the port of Corunna. Another Cadiz type of raid was suggested. Lord Thomas would be Admiral of the Fleet and the two antagonists, Essex and Raleigh, would share the offensive roles. Now there was reconciliation, and the Queen was persuaded to take Raleigh again into her favour. He was received, Guiana was forgotten and he was permitted once again to resume his duties as Captain of the Guard. Again, and this time in a new suit of armour inlaid with silver, "that dangerous man" stood superb and glittering in the royal ante-chamber in Whitehall.

In the attack on Corunna the Earl of Essex had ill fortune, since a good share of the booty fell into the hands of Raleigh. Essex then wished to redeem himself to the Queen's grace and demanded that he be allowed to settle the Irish question. Essex failed, and that proud man, being unable to understand the contradictory convolutions of the Queen's character, made fierce protest at the affronts delivered to him by the Queen and made an outward form of rebellion. There were Star Chamber proceedings. Francis Bacon, beholden to the well-intentioned Earl in a thousand ways, became his prosecutor. He was condemned to be beheaded. On a cold, mist-filled morning of 1601, Sir Walter Raleigh, as Captain of the Guard, had to be witness. Yet he had the grace to withdraw and watch the proceedings from a window from the White Tower. Did he know that this mirrored his own end? Did it ever cross his mind that the search for the Golden Man and the obsession for

306

Objects from the gold-rich Cauca river (Quimbaya culture). Seen here are stylized animal forms, an anthropological figure and an allegorical effigy.

The Lake of Guatavita lying above 9,000 feet on the bare *páramo* near Bogotá.

gold would bring him to the headsman's axe? Was there not some premonition?

After that day in 1601 the Queen now sat alone in a world of emptiness. She was close to seventy and in the deep winter of her years. All about her observed the oncoming end and all about understood. Their eyes looked toward Scotland for her successor.

The Cecils, long entrenched in the stronghold of power, were in secret correspondence with James of Scotland. They were troubled, and transmitted their fears, by the rise of Sir Walter Raleigh. The Queen had made him Governor of Jersey and even gave him diplomatic missions, so where would this dangerous man lead them? Thus the letters that reached James were filled with envenomed warnings; so much so that James began to feel only loathing for the person of Sir Walter Raleigh, who, in so many ways naïve, apparently suspected nothing.

James, the son of Mary Queen of Scots and Lord Darnley, had a taste for learning. He was highly literate, wrote essays and prepared papers on governing; for one twenty-seven years of age (he had been born in 1566), he was quite a rarity among English sovereigns, a literary prince. James of Scotland had survived. He had since the time of his mother's beheading been pulled one way by the clerics, the other by the nobles. He kept his own counsel. Despite Elizabeth's stern warning, he married, as he willed, Anne of Denmark, and when the Scottish nobility tried to use him, he used them and emerged with a very strong idea of the divine right of kings. Moreover, he thought himself secure since his royal line of descent came from Margaret Tudor, one of the sisters of Henry VIII.

Raleigh, whose pride knew no bounds, rightly believed that the future king must know of his (Raleigh's) poems, his position papers on statescraft, his book on the great and mighty Empire of Guiana; there seemed to be no reason for Raleigh to insert himself personally.

Aside from the dream of El Dorado, which one sees was

always in his thoughts, Raleigh dreamed of being a statesman, a member of the Privy Council, to obtain a position like that of Sir Robert Cecil, that little man, fully conversant with the ways of statescraft who sat patiently among all the men of violence. It was there, Raleigh believed, in these councils of State so long denied him, that he felt he belonged. For he hated the people, but all his life he could command their loyalty, the worship of this baseborn rabble, yet among his peers he was feared and disliked. He must have known it although he seemed oblivious to it, for he prepared a position paper on Spanish policy for James, when he ascended as King, so as to guide him in his affairs. At the same time, so great was his naïveté that he allowed himself to listen to a group of conspirators who wished to raise rebellion and place Arabella Stuart on the throne of England.

Arabella Stuart, a cousin of James, who also was descended from Henry VIII, contended that she had a stronger claim to the throne, for she was actually born in England. There was, too, a genuine fear among the officeholders that they would be eclipsed when James took the throne and he put his threadbare Scots in their lucrative posts. The talk was large, the action little, but Raleigh listened. As Captain of the Guard, Lord-Governor of Jersey and all else, he was an official bound by law and custom to denounce all such.

Life in England was then fraught with cunning and brutality; nearly all were steeped in some sort of intrigue. Bribery was everywhere; a phrase, a sentence of dubious construction, could be taken out of context; a word lightly, carelessly uttered, could be craftily turned and twisted. This could lead one to the Tower and the axe.

Elizabeth died on 24 March 1603. Within the first days of April, James was in London. That things were askew Raleigh understood within moments, for hurrying down to Cornwall where he was on Crown business, he came into the royal presence and was meanly received. He was forbid-

308

den future access to the King's person; his most prized possession, that of Captain of the Guard, was taken from him. A few days later, after a long and tortuous interrogation, Sir Walter Raleigh was conveyed to the Tower. The charge: high treason.

Now the search for the Golden Man had a curious way of wandering from the vaults of bankers to loftily placed lakes where kings gild themselves with gold, to rivers and crocodiles and men "whose heads appear not above their shoulders . . . but have their eyes in their shoulders and their mouths in the middle of their breasts", and the story usually seemed to end at the headsman's axe.

Legally Raleigh's trial was a farce. The accusations that he planned to co-operate with Spain to bring the Pope and Philip's minions to England to assassinate James and place Arabella Stuart on the throne were absurd. But Raleigh misjudged the malevolence of the accusers – as well as the presence of Francis Bacon as a prosecutor for the Crown (who had been promised a knighthood if he obtained a conviction).

"The State of Spain", said Raleigh drily in his defence, "was not unknown to me. I had a discourse which I had intended to present unto the King, against peace with Spain." It was useless. It was futile to talk of justice; for justice involves by its very nature uncertainty, and James could take no risks. The King's new policy was peace with Spain, for both nations during the whole of Elizabeth's reign had spent their life's blood in armadas, raids, reprisals, and where were they? Ireland still remained under England's hand and foot. The English had obtained not even a footing in Spain's America.

France, in King James's policy, was to be England's future enemy (and this was correct reading of history). Therefore he wanted peace with Spain, with a formal engagement of his son Prince Charles to the Infanta of Spain. This being his royal will, he did not want firebrands, such as Sir Walter Raleigh, running about on the Main, "singeing the Spanish King's beard". As for Arabella, his rattlebrained cousin, he had her put into the Tower, where she died from insanity in 1615.

The verdict against Raleigh was, as foreseen, guilty. The sentence: death by beheading with the time-honoured amenities such as castration, disembowelling and quartering. James hesitated when signing the death warrant, giving ear to Bacon's advice that severe measures at this time might bestir public wrath, whereupon he signed a warrant for life imprisonment.

On a day in December in 1604, Raleigh took up

The Tower of London in the sixteenth century, from Visscher's *Panorama of London*. Raleigh was imprisoned in Conqueror's Tower from 1604 to 1616, but was allowed the use of the garden and the company of his wife. It was here that his son, Carew, was born, and that the *Historie of the World* was written. (Mary Evans Picture Library)

residence in Conqueror's Tower. He was then fifty-two. When El Dorado opened the prison door thirteen years later he would really be in the "winter of his years".

Other prisoners have been worsely ill-served. Raleigh had the use of the Tower's garden, his wife Elizabeth came to share his bed and a son, called Carew, was born in the Tower. Many of his books were brought to him.

Time began to be his friend rather than, as before, his enemy. He read, thought and wrote. He would do no small thing. He would be the author of *History of the World,* a book which, when finished, printed and published, would fill 1,354 closely printed pages of a folio volume.

Now although Raleigh's name alone is on the title page, it was not, as most histories usually are, the work of one hand. The greater hand, although unmentioned, was that of Thomas Hariot. Born in Oxford in 1580, he studied at the university in the town of his birth, and some time after coming down met Walter Raleigh. They became friends and remained so until Hariot watched that fine head fall into the red leather case. He knew Kepler, and was a mathematician, astronomer and surveyor. As such he was sent by Raleigh to lay out the first colony of Virginia and in so doing wrote a *True Report of Virginia* which, illustrated with the contemporary watercolours of John White and engravings of Jacques le Moyne, is one of the finest examples of Americana. While Raleigh was in the Tower, it was Thomas Hariot who researched the literary material for the *History of the World.* He collected the books, and took extracts from books, papers and manuscripts. It was he who worked with scribes, proofs and all the rest that belabour authors, especially historians. Thomas Hariot was Raleigh's contact with the outside world.

As Raleigh read and as he wrote, time inexorably passed him by. He was ageing fast. Imprisonment was causing him to waste time, and now time wasted him and made him its numbering clock. The bells sounding the hour in the Tower were clamorous groans which struck upon his heart;

his sighs, tears and groans were as minutes. So time went posting on in the King's proud joy, while he, Raleigh, stood there listening to this jack o' the clock. And while he languished, his friend George Chapman, the poet, sang of:

"Guiana, whose rich feete are mines of golde,
Whose forehead knockes against the roofe of Starres,
Stands on her tip-toes at faire England looking,
Kissing her hand."

For the metallic spirit of the Golden Man was not idle as this great history proceeded, even though it took for the moment a minor place in the dank rooms of the Tower.

Raleigh ordered his friend Captain Lawrence Keymis to make a further survey for that Guiana "whose rich feete were mines of golde". Keymis, with two ships, went down to where they had sailed in 1595, tried to find the two Englishmen left behind but they were not there. He tried to ascend the Orinoco river and found himself blocked by a good posture of defence. Keymis, always the loyal Keymis – whose name, as were most in those times before a dictionary, was spelled in various ways such as Laraunce Kemish – landed on the west side of the Amazon delta, proceeded in this year 1596 along the Guiana coast to the delta of the Orinoco. Self-deprecating, he remained Raleigh's man to the end, and so he surveyed the whole coast and in doing so gave the first systematic outline of the location of tribes, rivers and products. This he modestly published as a *Relation,* with a dedication to Raleigh.[1]

He was described by the Spaniards as a tall slim man with a cast in one eye, who appeared in 1616 to be about sixty years of age. He had the appearance of gentle birth and was of grave demeanor. That is the Keymis for whom an unworthy end was marked.

Raleigh then ordered another, a certain Captain Berrie, to go out, which he performed in 1596 and left a published record.[2]

While Raleigh languished and wrote in the Tower, others were resuming his plans for the colonization of Guiana. Time was indeed making Raleigh his numbering clock. In his first year of prison, 1605, there occurred the Gunpowder Plot. James was not amused – nor particularly appeased by a signed copy of Bacon's new book *The Advancement of Learning,* which implied too an advancement of Bacon, for he was knighted the same year by the King.

Then Raleigh learned that a new continent called Australia had been discovered in 1606, and in the following year King James had agreed to the founding of Jamestown and the settlement of Virginia. The same year (1611) that James produced the Authorised Version of the Bible, Henry Hudson was sailing in the Arctic into the bay that bears his name. Due to Hudson's earlier discoveries, the Dutch would found Manhattan two years later. Quebec had already been set up in 1608 and gradually the French would inhabit the ripe lands that Raleigh in his position paper had long suggested be colonized by Britain. Things were happening outside that Raleigh still felt belonged to his era. While he was looking over the final pages of his *Historie* before it was sent to the printer, the first newspaper appeared in Frankfurt, and William Harvey – the same physician who found the delicate light hazel eyes of Sir Francis Bacon "as like the eye of a viper" – announced what was then startling enough, the circulation of the blood.

Despite all this, the spectre of the Golden Man and the Golden Cities haunted Raleigh and would not leave. He seemed to feel "certaine" that out there somewhere in that "large, rich and beautiful Empyre of Guiana" the figure of El Dorado was waiting.

How could he emerge out of this wretched confinement and continue the search? The ploy of the Golden City could no longer be used; the wits had laughed that voyage to its death. Nor would King James, this royal Stuart who was planning his son's marriage to an Infanta of Spain, consider using another expedition to Guiana as a means of seizing the Orinoco basin and destroying Spanish overseas power.

What the *New Atlantis* was to Bacon, the Guianas would be to Raleigh. There, in his solitude, he unravelled it . . . the mines, the rich mines of Guiana. This was the chosen bait to free himself. Raleigh believed that the soil of Guiana was highly auriferous. However, the ore samples that he had brought back were found by the royal assayer to contain no gold. Raleigh's well-tried friend, Keymis, assured Raleigh that there was gold. Raleigh seized on this, and it became a mania; now "Guiana was a mountain covered with gold and silver ore".

How would the gold be obtained? "We would ride at anchor 3 or 4 months in the river [Orinoco] carrying with us six great bellows . . . we would melt down the mineral into ingots." Melt down into ingots! One mines silver but one wins gold; and to win gold even today it takes 15,000 tons of high grade ore, followed by a complex chemical treatment, to produce one single ingot of gold the size of a brick!

Next he wrote to Queen Anne and asked her to beg her liege to allow him out of the Tower to go to Virginia – "to perish there". Then he plagued the King: "Your Majesty refused a most easy way of being enriched." He turned to the Earl of Holderness seeking his aid to get him released to go to Guiana: ". . . it is a journey of honour and riches. I offer you an enterprise feasible and certaine . . . and if I not bring them to a mountain cover'd with gold and silver let the commander cut off my head then and there".

At last the King consented. "Raleigh", a friend noted, "has now left his Mansion in the Tower on this 19th of the month (March 1616). He is enlarged out of the Tower and to go on his journey but remains unpardoned."

In this dithyrambic history one is dealing with so much that is incredulous and with such an abundance of madness that one might ask, and expect a reasonable answer, why the King allowed him his freedom. An answer is certainly

314

not cogent. Raleigh remained under the sentence of death. He was not, said the royal instructions, to wound or harm anyone or thing in the areas laid claim to by the King of Spain. But the famous "gold mine" lay 150 miles up the Orinoco, dominated by two forts, hundreds of Spanish settlers farming tobacco, raising cattle, and how could he with hundreds of men undertake an intrusion into Spanish-held territory, work a gold mine within sight of their fort, without provoking retaliation?

There was, however, in all this one notable fact. Even the word "fact" is almost an intrusion in this short, brief, history of calculated lunacy. The King's Council was of two factions: one favoured a Spanish marriage for Prince Charles to which the King openly leaned and so wished not to provoke Spain; the other favoured a French marriage, so that those who helped to release Raleigh to go after the gold of El Dorado hoped to have him provoke precisely what the King would avoid. Raleigh could sink, swim or lose his head, no matter, so long as it provoked Spain into armed conflict and thus ended the proposed Spanish marriage and alliance. To the secretary, Winwood, Raleigh admitted: "I am unfitt and I feare me unable to undergoe so great a Travail." The thirteen years in the Tower had aged him even more than his sixty-six years, yet his dream prevailed. At the back of his mind he envisaged the marching with a great American Indian army (headed, of course, by English officers) to hammer at the gates of Manoa and receive the homage of El Dorado, the Gilded King. The first harsh winds of reality to blow against these vapours were made known to him when he tried to put together crew and captains for the voyage, from the scruff and scrum of the waterfront. For what lay on the voyage? No war, so no prize money – no sacking or ransom. Who on God's earth wanted to go on such a voyage?

The ten ships with that of Raleigh's own *Destiny*, the flagship, 500 tons burthen, went to Plymouth port, and four additional ships joined them.

The *Destiny* (the name itself a symbol of Raleigh's rise and fall) and the other part of the fleet were costly. He mortgaged his last estates, called in money which earned good interest, and his own Lady raised money from her private property; the total sum for this fated enterprise was £30,000. Many subscribed to the business; some of those who had lost a modest fortune in the first voyage, scenting gold and El Dorado, came in again.

All this was made broadcast. The Spanish Ambassador, the astute Diego Sarmiento de Acuña, Count of Godomar, one of the architects of Anglo-Spanish amity, was alarmed. It was preposterous to profess friendship with Spain, to make plans for a royal marriage and at the same time send a fleet into a land which belonged to the King of Spain; and if Raleigh was only searching for mines and it was a peaceful expedition, why the arms? So James, according to this logic, exacted a promise and then proclaimed it: Raleigh would not inflict in his enterprise any harm on any subjects of the King of Spain; if he did, his life would be forfeit. Raleigh had everything to lose. If mines actually were discovered, why should the Spaniards allow him free access into their own territory? He was running a fearful risk. But the image of gold, upon which everything hangs in this all-hating world, would never leave him, and as usual Raleigh had a novel plan.

On 21 September 1616, after remaining weather-bound by contrary winds for several weeks in Cork, the fateful and last voyage to seek the whereabouts of the gold mines began.

The King of Spain had been well informed. James of England made no secret of his detestation of Sir Walter Raleigh, and betrayed all that was of sufficient importance to the Spanish Ambassador in London, who dispatched all that he learned to Spain: "London, 26th June 1617 . . . Gualtero Rale has set forth with [fourteen] ships indifferently equipped both as regards men and provisions but with very good guns and munitions of war."

These dangers had awakened the Council of the Indies that long ago had taken measures. "Ever since the first discoveries of the Indies", the president had written to the King in 1599, "there has been talk of the provinces called El Dorado: that they are peopled by great numbers . . . contain vast riches . . .". The report perorated on the various expeditions. It wrote of Antonio de Berrio's various attempts to find it and how in 1596 a thousand or more people had been sent out and the "greater part were wasted or perished". The Council sought to know if Raleigh had actually discovered a gold mine as he claimed, for now the Flemings were talking of it, and the Dutch. "If the enemy (that is, the British) should people it, it would be extremely inconvenient; and to drive them out would entail heavy expense". So it was advised that the whole area be "put into a posture of defence".

In the cold atmosphere of El Escorial where the King regulated the world, he endorsed the suggestions. "Let every effort be promptly made . . . I, the King."

The new Knight of El Dorado, Antonio's son and Quesada's heir, young Fernando de Berrio, scarcely twenty, took over the fort, the colony on the Orinoco and the title of Governor of Guiana, Manoa and El Dorado. "He presided over his post," wrote that theological historian, Fray Pedro Simón, and although the young man governed well in peace and quietness for some years, "he meanwhile kept up the search for the great lake of Manoa and the golden cities with the usual result and the usual discontent.

"There were no lack of complaints and eventually this reached the ears of the King and Council" and, as usual, an official took up a *residencia* – that is, a court of impeachment, the result being that the last knight of El Dorado, he who had obtained it as if by a form of apostolic succession, was momentarily displaced. Yet only for a while, but it was in this *while* that Sir Walter Raleigh's second voyage began. Whereupon the King of Spain informed all of his governors in and about the Caribbean that it "has pleased us to place in command, as my Governor and Captain, General, Diego de Palomeque."

In this manner the fates had woven a strange pattern, for had Diego de Palomeque not displaced the last Knight of El Dorado, Fernando de Berrio, then he would not have been killed in the coming affair. Moreover, such in the concatenation of cause and effect that had Don Diego not been there, neither would have Christoval Guayacunda, his Indian servant of Sogomosa. For so inextricably woven were the threads in the tapestry of the Golden Man that a representative of the Chibcha tribe – the very people who had supplied both the fact and the myth of El Dorado – was to be present at its most dramatic dénouement.

Now Sir Walter Raleigh knew that it was virtually impossible to seize and work a gold mine in the areas controlled by Spain without invasion of Spanish territory and without injury to Spanish vassals. Raleigh even failed to bring along those "six immense bellows" with which he would reduce the ore to golden ingots; there were none among them who knew about mines or mining, only John Talbot who was called a gold assayer.

Why then all the ships, the host of people, the great arms? The plan, wrote one of Raleigh's many biographer-apologists,[3] that came out of Raleigh's "nimble brain", was to bring in the French, who, not being under such orders as he himself, were to carry out very hostile action against the Spanish which he himself was strictly forbidden to do. The French intervention, over which there was considerable secret negotiation, was that they were to pull the golden chestnuts out of El Dorado's fire, and so Raleigh would then sail up, with the Spanish out of the way, and look into golden mines and golden men.

Even the extremely clever Richelieu, then Cardinal-Secretary of State, was aware of these negotiations and was at first fascinated by the proposal "that Raleigh had a great and signal enterprise in hand from which he hoped great advantage". "Seeing myself", Raleigh secretly wrote, "so

318

evilly and tyranically treated by my own King . . . and I make this to the King of France, your master. . . ."

Raleigh, no matter how hard he tried, never could behave with the Machiavellian calculation which guided one like Francis Bacon. He trusted everyone. This credulity was fathomless. He confided in people without examination and who betrayed him at the first moment. It was one of his strange inconsistencies of character that this worldling trusted almost everyone. Is it even thinkable that Richelieu would allow a French squadron to do away with the Spanish so that Raleigh could undertake his so dubious second voyage "and bring great advantage to France"?

From the very beginning, nature conspired with fate to make Raleigh's way down difficult. A gale, which he describes as if he were writing *Twelfth Night,* widely dispersed his ships. He had difficulty watering at the Canaries, and there and on the high seas an epidemic broke out on ship, leaving fifty men unfit for service. They were struck by a hurricane near the Cape Verde Islands, then death began to collect its harvest; forty-two died on shipboard, including Fowler who was to be the one of the assayers of the ore; then John Talbot, the same who had shared his imprisonment in the Tower: "He was my honest friend: an excellent general scholar . . . I lost him to mine inestimable grief." He also lost the only one who claimed to be able to assay gold – the real gold from the fool's.

On 4 December 1616 the ships lay off Cayenne – the capital of present-day French Guiana. Raleigh himself was so ill he had to be carried about in a chair and he thought himself about to die. For 1616 was a fatal year for geniuses. Will Shakespeare expired in that year. Miquel de Cervantes, who gave the world *Don Quixote de la Mancha* ("that wisest and most splendid book in the world" was Raleigh's comment), died in Seville. In the same year, too, El Inca, Garcilaso de la Vega, who, with his *Royal Commentaries,* would begin the cycle of the "Noble Savage", also left the world. It would have been best for Raleigh had

Seal of the Welser.

he too died in that year that saw depart men who were in the country of his mind.

Instead of which, it became evident that Raleigh was too ill to command; the faithful Captain Lawrence Keymis would lead and, in addition, Raleigh had his cousin there as Sergeant-Major, and his well-loved son, heir and namesake "having just rounded seventeen", the tempestuous young Walter Raleigh.

It took the pinnaces about twenty-one days to go up the 180 miles of the Orinoco until they reached the junction of the turbulent Río Caroni. There on the left or south bank of the Orinoco and the Caroni was the newly-built, palisaded village-fortress of San Thomé; the gold mines, according to Raleigh's divining rod, although neither he nor anyone else of his party had ever seen them, were "three or four miles from the town". It contained more gold then there existed in Peru or Mexico, and the source was out of Raleigh's fervid imagination. Why would not the inhabitants of San Thomé have worked it? Further, why should the Spaniards allow the English to enter their territory, work the mines and depart with the gold, should it have existed?

The lunacy of the Golden Man must have destroyed all of the deductive reasoning of Sir Walter. It seems hardly possible that one so intellectually talented, one who could write *A History of the World,* should be so lacking in elementary logic to suppose that a mine, if found, could be worked with the pitiful supply of mattocks, shovels and spades that were carried along, and without the presence of the assayers, both of who had died. He whom the gods would destroy they first make blind. Obviously blind, as observe the final instructions to his cousin, George Raleigh: he was to throw out a covering party between the "miners" and the anchored ships. "If you find the Mine Royal, and Spaniards begin to war upon you, YOU, George Raleigh, are to repel them." To Keymis: "If you find the Mine be not so rich as many persuade and to the holding of it . . .

321

you shall bring out a *basket or two* [of the ore] to satisfy His Majesty that my design was not imaginary."

Was it for this basket or two that Raleigh raised £30,000, prepared a fleet and put so many lives in jeopardy, not to mention the Anglo-Spanish treaty of friendship, and, moreover, his very life? The King stated very emphatically that should he imperil the lives of Spanish subjects his head would answer for it, and also Raleigh pledged to the Earl of Holderness that if he did not bring back gold, his own captains could behead him; he would be willing to order his own execution.

Everything hangs on gold, said the poet. But does it? There was about the whole expedition an aura of desperation that curiously seemed not to hang on gold. The expedition decided to eliminate the fort of San Thomé. Since the defenders were outnumbered ten to one, it was not a great enterprise. Raleigh had written in another Order of the Day: "It is rumoured that Spanish reinforcements are already posted on the river; if this proved to be true so that without manifest peril of my son and the other captains, you cannot towards the Mine then . . . attack. For I know, a few gentlemen excepted, what a scum of men you have, and I would not for all the world receive a blow from the Spaniards to the dishonour of our nation."

"The manifest peril" came soon enough. Young Raleigh, trying to live up to the reputation of his name, dashed forward in "unadvised daringness" with his pikemen, and had his brains blown out for his trouble. Five others died. The palisade was breached, the place was sacked, and – the usual thing when English attacked all Spanish possessions – burnt down. Keymis then set out for the mine "three miles from the village". It became three leagues and more. They were gone for twenty-one days. Then, having left the burdensome mattocks and spades in the jungle, they returned to the waiting boats and set off down the river toward Trinidad.

The Spaniards who survived told all of it in detail, for

the reason if for no other, that they were to be compensated for their losses by the King of England. It was a night attack on Friday the 12th of January. "One Englishman, getting ahead of the rest, came along singing 'Victory, Victory' and he was given a sword thrust in the gullet that sent the heretic to re-echo his song in Hell." The Governor Diego de Palomeque put on his breast-plate and murrain, entered the fray and was killed. The fort was stormed, the English entered, burned and pillaged. They carried all the treasure that had been stored in the Governor's strongbox. Taken was a collection of embossed silver plate . . . security for money owing to the Exchequer by Doña Andrea María de Berrio (the niece of Gonzalo Jiménez de Quesada) for a deed of indenture involving a considerable sum of money. Other treasures were an ingot of pure gold belonging to Corporal Ycola, an ingot of pure gold owned by Captain Brea, and an image of gold in a casket *garnished with emeralds.*

No doubt the gold of the ingots had been collected over a period of years from the alluvial gold that is found in many rivers, but not from mines. The emeralds were from Colombia, 1,200 miles distant. As minor as the loot was, it convinced Raleigh that he had found gold mines and he carried these ingots even to the Tower. His men also brought away a particular treasure: testimony, living testimony, of the mine's existence, an Indian named Christobal.

It was he who identified the body of the Governor, Diego de Palomeque, from among the dead, and it was he who sat by him faithfully and arranged his burial. When questioned through an interpreter, he had answered that he had been the Governor's faithful servant, and that he was a native of New Granada – that is, the lands of the Chibcha.

That narrative was quite enough. He was brought down and away. The Spanish records are very definite on this point. "Two Indian men who spoke Spanish joined the enemy, one by force, the other voluntarily, for one was Christobal [Guayacunda] a Mosan Indian from Sogomosa

(n) of New Granada." He was brought to Raleigh, placed in good quarters on the ship *Destiny,* and brought to England "*Fro ye towr* . . . Sr. W. R. saith of one Christofero [Cristoval Guayacunda] that he brought home with him now, was the Governor's man . . . who will even if upon his life . . . to shew us 7 or 8 mines of gold."

Guayacunda, known as Christobal, "had been born in Sogomosa (the Chibcha trading centre), famed for its great religious temple and the same place where Quesada had found the sacred mummies of the Chibchan chieftains, with eye sockets, mouths, ears, navels, plugged with emeralds, and thousands of pesos-weight of wrought gold". This place had, in time, become a sizeable town, and was on the edge of the "place where the land fell away" – that is, the down-going entrance to the *llanos.* Guayacunda had taken part in many of the great treks from there to San Thomé on the Orinoco. Now he was destined to go to London, give his information on all the valuable mines, of which "he knoweth not", and then to be present at the beheading of Sir "Gualtero Rale". What an odyssey, what a train, this real tribal son of the Golden Man was to have: afterwards the Spanish Ambassador sent him to Spain, where he told his story. Then in one of the returning Spanish fleets he went back to America, disembarked at Cartagena, and went up the great river, where, after much walking, he came to rest at his own village. It was here that Pedro Simón, the first to formally record the conquest of New Granada, found him "where he now dwells in this year 1622 in his native place at Sogomosa".

Raleigh, waiting anxiously on the deck of the *Destiny,* must have sensed that the project had been disastrous. They had only been gone for one month and a half; no victory bunting was to be seen. His telescope searched in vain for the face of his son. Such was the poignant contrast between illusion and reality; he dreamed of sailing home with a cargo full of gold ore, and in his triumph press upon the King and public the manner to found an Anglo-Guiana

324

kingdom, with himself as general leading native troops to make conquest of all South America.

When Lawrence Keymis stood before him in his cabin, he prepared himself for the worst. This unexpected relaxed attitude seemed to lighten Keymis' load of anguish, and he was glad that Milord was so armed to bear the tidings of calamity. So it was told – the death of his son, the burning of San Thomé and the non-existence of the gold-mines. It all had gone worse than he had power to tell.

"Too well, too well have you, Keymis, told a tale so ill," said Raleigh.

"I told him that he had undone me and that I would not favour or colour in any sort his former follie", wherein he said that the gold mines did exist. "He then asked me whether this was my resolution; I told him it was." Keymis answered: "I know then, Sir, what course to take."

They found him dead a half-hour later with a knife through his heart.

The expedition turned homeward. One by one the ships deserted. At St. Kitts, one of the Windward Islands, Raleigh sat down to write the events to his lady. Well, all too well, did Lady Raleigh, that mild-natured and trusting lady, deserve his affection. She never pretended she could understand him. His oblique ways were beyond her own unsubtle mind. She was never able to follow the grandiose patterns of his imagination, yet she loved him, and she accepted with resignation all of the terrible effects of his actions. When he thought in 1603 that he would die since he was sentenced to death, he wrote one of the saddest, loveliest letters.

"My love, I send you this that [you] may keepe it when I am dead and my counsel, that you may remember it when I am no more. I would not with my last will present you with sorrows, Dear Besse. Let them go to the grave with me . . . bear my destruction gently and with a heart like yourself."

He had not perished then; now, at St. Kitts, he had to

NEVVES
Of Sʳ. Walter Rauleigh.

WITH
The true Defcription of Gᴠɪᴀɴᴀ:

As alfo a Relation of the excellent Gouernment, and
much hope of the profperity of the Voyage.

*Sent from a Gentleman of his Fleet, to a moſt
eſpeciall Friend of his in* London.

Frem the Riuer of Caliana, *on the Coaſt of* Guiana, *Nouemb.* 17. 1617.

LONDON,
Printed for *H. G.* and are to be fold by *I. Wright,* at the figne of the
Bible without New-gate. 1618.

present her with new sorrows: "I was loathe to write because I know not how to Comforte you. And God knowes I never knewe what sorrow ment till now." And he told about the death of their son, the rape of San Thomé, the lost illusion of the mines: "my braines are broken and it is a torment to me to write."

"No sooner had the ships arrived", said a contemporary account, "upon the coast of Ireland, but the Taking and Sacking of Saint Thomé . . . and putting the Spaniards there to the Sword was noised abroad in all parts and was by special Advertisement come with knowledge unto the knowledge of Count de Gondamor: Who Thereupon Desiring Audience of His Majesty said he had but one word to say. His Majesty much wondering what might be delivered in one word. When he came before him he only bawl'd out: 'Pirates, Pirates, Pirates.'"

Thus, when Lady Raleigh met her liege in Plymouth already the walls were plastered with Broadsides: "By the King! A Proclamation declaring His Majesties pleasure concerning Sir Walter Raleigh and those who adventured with him. . . ."

All concerned were to "repair unto some of our Privy Council and to discover and make known . . . under Paine of our high displeasure and indignation that We may thereupon proceed in Our Princely Justice. . . ."

Raleigh, having flouted the King in this regard, was rearrested on the original charge of 1604 for which he had been sentenced to be beheaded. The Lord of Verulam, none other than Francis Bacon, was again the prosecutor, as he had been in a similar trial on his patron, the Earl of Essex. So Sir Walter, who vexed the King, must now with Bacon's prosecution be led to the headsman's axe. To give double certainty that it was rightfully done, Bacon appealed to posterity with a booklet of subtle design: *A Declaration of the Demeanour and Carriage of Sir Walter Raleigh, Knight as well in this voyage.*

The trial was short, precise and final. For his "same

treasons by them adjudged he was to be drawn, hanged and quartered according to the laws and customs of this our realm of England". The King entertained only one plea for mercy; the sentence would be changed to beheading only.

"Upon Thursday, the 29th of October, 1618, Sir Walter Raleigh was conveyed by the Sheriffs of London to a Scaffold in the Old Palace at Westmoreland . . . at Nine of the Clock in the Morning. . . ."

With "smiling Countenance", Raleigh saluted all Lords, Knights and Gentlemen. The highest-placed people of the land were on hand to witness the end of a man who had listened all too well to the siren voice of El Dorado. Did it seem possible that that small lake of Guatavita had been the origin of all this? One can follow the causality: the lake; the ceremony; the salt and emeralds; the gradual development of the myth; the conquest; then the manner in which the environment of El Dorado's whereabouts shifted from a small mountain tarn to an inland sea the size of the Caspian. What a train, what a regulation, what a concourse of pre-established harmonies, what a proof of man's inherent folly!

Standing in the shadows of the headsman's axe – for the sun shone briefly – was the figure of Christobal Guayacunda shivering and out of sorts. The spirit of the times demanded that there should be a dignified formality. As the beheading approached it went through a long series of ornate, pious commonplaces.

Poor Christobal Guayacunda could not understand it all. He lived in a world where one ate one's enemies, where legs, arms, heads were chopped off like branches of trees. The long ceremony he never understood. He gathered that the man who had brought him to England had upset his chieftain and he was to die. But before him stood Gualtero Rale, saluting everyone, as if he were going on a tour,

The execution of Sir Walter Raleigh which took place in the Old Palace of Westmoreland, 29th October, 1618. Among the by-standers was Christobal Guayacunda, a native of the Chibcha trading centre of Sogomosa, who was brought to London to report on the treasure to be had. (Mary Evans Picture Library)

328

SIR WALTER RALEIGH

beheaded in Old Palace Yard.

smiling, bowing, gentle spirited. The talk of which Guayacunda understood nothing was overlong. No one seemed to raise a voice, so that the words must have been good medicine. "There was a Report that I meant not to go to Guiana. . . ." And at that word, Guayacunda became alert.

The peroration now stopped. Raleigh stood before the block. Then he begged the pardon of all those present, since "I have a long journey to go and therefore will take my leave". He passed through the final ritual, putting aside his costly gown and doublet, and asked to see the axe. On thumbing its edge he remarked: "This is sharp Medicine, but is a physician for all Diseases." Then he arranged his head on the block.

Suddenly it ended. Christobal Guayacunda witnessed the axe coming down. In two blows the head was off. The great dark eyes of Sir Walter Raleigh were still open as if he had not got over his surprise of having head sundered from body. It was lifted up by his hair by the headsman, and showed, dripping blood on all around, that justice had been done.

The head of Raleigh was then actually put into a red leather bag, but, figuratively, it rolled down the sides of its rim into the lake of Guatavita, into that tarn which fecundated the myth that held out for so many and for so long a time the dazzling hope of a Golden Utopia.

[1] *A Relation of the second voyage to Guiana.* Performed and written in the yeare 1596 by Lawrence Keymis Gent. London 1596. 32 leaves.
[2] *The Thirde Voyage set forth by Sir Walter Raleigh to Guiana with a pinesse called the Watte in the yeare 1596* (commanded by Leonard Berrie. Written by Thomas Masham, a gentleman of the companie).
[3] V. T. Harlow. *Raleigh's Last Voyage.* London, 1832. (With documents).

The cosmographer Diego Ribeira's final map of South America after the search for El Dorado. (Vatican Library, Rome)

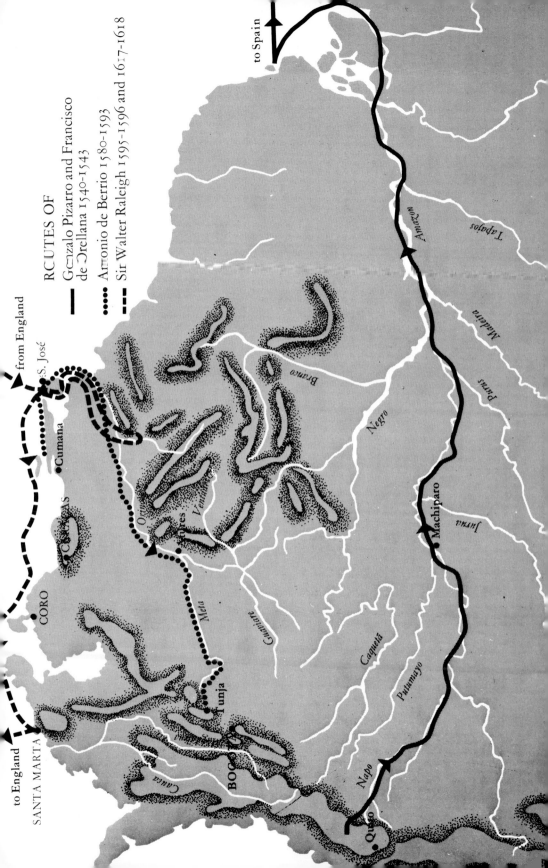

ROUTES OF
Gonzalo Pizarro and Francisco
de Orellana 1540-1543
Antonio de Berrio 1580-1593
Sir Walter Raleigh 1595-1596 and 1617-1618

to Spain

from England

to England

SANTA MARTA

CORO

S. José

Cumana

CARACAS

BOGOTA

Tunja

Quito

Napo

Putumayo

Caqueta

Guaviare

Meta

Orinoco

Andes

Venet

Branco

Negro

Amazon

Madeira

Purus

Tapajos

Juruá

Machiparo

Cauca

BIBLIOGRAPHY

Acosta, Joaquín. *Compendio histórico del descubrimiento colonización de la Nueva Granada en el siglo décimosexto.* Paris, 1848.

Aguado, Pedro de. *Historia de Santa Marta y Nuevo Reino de Granada,* 2 vols. Madrid, 1916–7.

Arciniegas, Germán. *El Caballero de El Dorado.* Buenos Aires, 1942.

Arrubla, Gerardo. "Prehistoria colombiana. Los Chibchas", *BHA,* 11 (1923)
"Las ruinas prehistóricas de San Agustín y sus rutas migratorias, *BHA,* 17 (1929).

Bandelier, A. F. A. *The Gilded Man.* New York, 1893.

Baessler, Arthur. *Altperuanische Metallgeräte.* Berlin, 1906.

Bayle, Constantino. *El Dorado Fantasma.* Madrid, 1930.

Bennett, W. C. "Archaeological regions of Colombia. A ceramic survey", *YUPA,* 30 (1944).
"The archeology of Colombia", *HSAI,* II (1946).
"Andean Highlands," in *Handbook of the South American Indians.* Washington, 1946.

Bergsoe, Paul. "The metallurgy and technology of gold and platin among the Pre-Colombian indians," *Ingeniørvidenskabelige Skrifter,* XLIV (København, 1937).

Bose, F. "Die Musik der Chibcha und ihrer heutigen Nachkommen," *IAE* XLVIII, 2. (1958).

Burland, C. A. "Chibcha Aesthetics," *AAnt* XVII, 2. (1951).

Castellanos, Juan de. *Historia del Nuevo Reino de Granada,* 2 vols. Madrid, 1886.
Elegías de varones ilustres de Indias, Biblioteca de autores españoles, 4. zit. Madrid, 1847.

Codazzi, A. "Ruinas de San Agustín," in *Geografía física y política de los Estados Unidos de Colombia,* ed. by Felipe Pérez, vol. II. Bogotá, 1863.

Cubillos Ch., J. C. y Bedoya, V. A. "Arqueología de las riberas del Río Magdalena, Espinál-Tolima," *RCA* II, 2 (1954).

Cunninghame-Graham, R. B. *The Conquest of New Granada.* London, 1922. (Being the life of Jiménez de Quesada)

Duque Gómez, Luis. *Colombia: Monumentos históricos y arqueológicos.* 2 vols. Mexico, 1955. (Instituto Panamericano de Geografía e Historia. Comisión de Historia 72.)

Duquesne, José Domingo. *Disertación sobre el calendario de los muyscas.* Santafé, 1795.

Ernst, A. "Zu Nikolaus Federmanns erster Reise in Venezuela (1530–1531)," *ZE* 4 (1872).

Federmann, Arnold. *Deutsche Konquistadoren in Südamerika.* Berlin, 1938.

Federmann, Nicolaus. Indianische Historia. // Ein schöne kurtz. // weilige Historia Niclaus Fe // dermanns des Júngern von // Vlm erster raise-so er von Hispania vn // Andolosia auss in Indias des Occea- // nischen Nörs gethan hat / vnd // was ihm allda ist begegnet biss auff sein // widerkunfft inn Hispaniam / auffs /// kurtzest beschriben / gantz // lustig zu lesen. // MDL VII. (Colophon).

Viaje a Las Indias del Mar Océano. Buenos Aires, 1946.

Fernández de Navarrete, Martín. *Colección de los viajes y descubrimientos que hicieron por ma los Españoles desde fines del siglo XV, con varios documentos inéditos concernientes a la historia de la marina castellana y de los establecimientos españoles en Indias.* 5 vols. Madrid, 1829–59.

Fernández de Oviedo y Valdés, Gonzalo. *Historia general y natural de las Indias, islas y tierra firme del mar océano,* 4 vols. Madrid, 1851–5.

Fernández Piedrahita, Lucas de. *Historia general de las conquistas del Nuevo Reino de Granada.* Antwerpen, 1688.

Fresle, Juan Rodríguez. *El Carnero.* Madrid, 1636.

Friede, Juan. *Ambrosius Dalfinger Erester Gouverneur von Venezuela.* Ulm, 1957.

Los Welser en la conquista de Venezuela. Caracas, 1961.

Los Quimbayas bajo la dominación española. Bogotá, 1963.

Invasión del País de Los Chibchas. Ediciones Tercer Mundo (n.d.)

(Editor and translator) Nicolas Federman: *Historia Indiana.* Bogotá, Colombia (n.d.)

Friedrichsen, L. *"Sir Walter Raleighs Karte von Guayana im 1595," Hamburgische Festschrift zur Erinnerung an die Entdeckung Amerikas,* vol. II Hamburg, 1892.

Fugger, Anton. *Götz Freiherr von Pölnitz.* JCB Morh, Tübingen, 1958. 2 vols.

Giraldo Jaramillo, Gabriel. "El verdadero descubridor de la cultura agustiniana," *Boletín de la Sociedad Geográfica de Colombia,* XV, 56 (Bogotá, 1957).

Haebler, Konrad. *Die überseeischen Unternehmungen der Welser und ihrer Gesellschafter.* Leipzig, 1903.

Hagen, Victor W. von. "The Bitter Cassava Eaters." *Natural History Magazine* (March 1949).

"The Search of the Gilded Man," *Natural History Magazine.* American Museum of Natural History, New York, 1951.

"The Valley of the Emeralds." *Think Magazine* (IBM) October, 1953.

"The Incas of Pedro de Cieza de León." trans. by Harriet de Onís and ed. by Victor W. von Hagen. University of Oklahoma Press, Norman, 1959.

The Ancient Sun Kingdoms of the Americas. Cleveland and New York, 1961.

Haury, Emil W. "Some thoughts of Chibcha culture in the high plains of Colombia," *AAnt* XIX, 1 (1953).

Haury, Emil W. y Cubillos, Julio C. "Investigaciones arqueológicas en la sabna de Bogotá, Colombia (cultura Chibcha)," *University of Arizona Bulletin,* XXIV, 2 (Social Science No. 22. Tucson, Arizona, 1953).

Hernández de Alba, Gregori. "Descubrimientos arqueológicos en tierras chibchas. Laguna de Fúquene," *Boletín del Museo Arqueológico de Colombia,* III, 1 (Bogotá, 1944).

"Descubrimientos arqueológicos en tierras de los Chibchas," *AAnt,* XI, 2 (1945).

Herrera, Antonio de. *Historia general de los hechos de los Castellanos en las islas y tierra firme del mar océana.* Madrid, 1726–30.

Humboldt, Alexander von. *Vues des cordillères et monuments des peuples indigènes de l'Amérique.* Paris, 1810.

El Dorado. Aus der Geschichte der ersten Amerikanischen Entdeckungsreisen, Mitteilungen der geographischen Gesellschaft. Hamburg, 1889.

Jijón y Camaño, Jacinto. *Sebastián de Belalcázar,* 2 vols. Quito, 1936–8.

Jiménez Arbeláez, Edith. "Los Chibchas," *Boletín de Arqueología,* Bogotá, Colombia, Tomo II, March–April, 1945.

Koch-Grünberg, Theodor. *Südamerikanische Felszeichnungen.* Berlin, 1907.

Klüpfel, Kalr (Hrsg.) *N. Federmanns und H. Stadens Reisen in Südamerika 1529–1555.* Stuttgart, 1859.

Krickeberg, Walter. *Märchen der Azteken und Inka-Peruaner, Maya und Muisca.* Jena, 1928.

Kroeber, Alfred L. *The Chibcha. HSAI,* II (1946).

"The Chibcha", *Handbook of South American Indians,* Vol. II. Washington, 1946.

Lanegg, F. A. Junker von. *El Dorado, Geschichte der Entdeckungsreisen nach dem Gold-lande El Dorado im XVI and XVII Jahrhundert.* Leipzig, 1888.

New edition, Akademische Verlagsanstalt, Graz, 1973.

Lehmann, Henri. "Archéologie du sud-ouest Colombie." *JSA,* 42 (1953).

Lehmann, Walter. "Die Sprachen Zentral-Amerikas in ihren Beziehungen zueinander sowie zu Süd-Amerika und Mexico," in *Zentral America*. Berlin, 1920.

"La antiguedad histórica de las culturas gran-mexicanas y el problema de su contacto con las gran-peruanas," *El México Antiguo*, IV, 5–6 (Mexico, 1938).

"Uber das Alter der amerikanischen Kulturen," *IAA*, 17 (1943–4).

López de Gómara, Francisco. *Hispania Victrix: Primera y Segunda Parte de la Historia General de las Indias*, Medina del Campo, 1553; London, 1578 (as *The Pleasant Historie of the Conquest of the West India*, now called new Spayne, Atchieved by the worthy Prince Hernando Cortez); reprint, Biblioteca de autores españoles 22. Madrid, 1852.

Lothrop, S. K. "Coclé, an archaeological study of Central Panama," *Museum of American Archaeology and Ethnology*, Mem. 7, 1 (Cambridge, Mass., 1837.)

"Archaeology of Southern Veraguas, Panama," Peabody Museum of Archaeology and Ethnology, Mem. 9, 3 (Cambridge, Mass., 1950).

Mason, J. Alden. "Archaeological researches in the region of Santa Marta, Colombia," *ICA*, XXI, 2 (Göteborg, 1925).

Archaeology of Santa Marta, Colombia: the Tairona Culture, Field Museum of Natural History, Publications 20, 1–3, Anthropological Series. Chicago, 1931–9.

Meggers, B. J. and Clifford, Evans. *Archaeological investigations at the mouth of the Amazon, Smithsonian Institution, Bureau of American Ethnology, Bulletin 167*. Washington, 1957.

Métraux, Alfred. *La civilisation matérielle des tribus Tupí-Guaraní*. Paris, 1928.

"Weapons," *HSAI*, V (1949).

Museo del Oro (Banco de la República). *El Museo del Oro*, 2nd ed. Bogotá, 1948.

Nachtigall, Horst. *Tierradentro, Archäologie und Ethnographie einer kolumbianischen Landschaft*. Zürich, 1955.

Alt-Kolumbien. Vorgeschichtliche Indianerkulturen. Berlin, 1961.

Neale, J. E. *Queen Elizabeth I*. London, 1934 (reprint, Penguin, 1960).

Ochoa Sierra, Blanca. "Los Panche," *BdA*, I, 4 (1945).

Oviedo y Valdés, G F. de.

Historia general y natural de las Indias, vol. XXVI. Madrid, 1851–5.

Panhorst, K. H. "Das Kolonisationsunternehmen der Fugger in Amerika," *IAA*, II, 3 (1927).

Deutschland und Amerika. München, 1928.

"Uber den deutschen Anteil an der Entdeckung und Eroberung des Chibcha-Reiches durch Gonzalo Jiménez de Quesada," *IAA,* VII, 2 (1933).

Park, Willard. "Tribes of the Sierra Nevada de Santa Marta (Colombia)," *HSAI,* II, (1946).

Pérez de Barradas, José. "Interpretación de un mito chibcha," *RA,* I, 4 (Bogotá, 1936).

Los Muiscas antes de la conquista, 2 vols. Madrid, 1950–1.

Poseda, E. "Laguna de Guatavita," *BHA,* 8 (1912).

Preuss, Konrad Theodor. *Die Begäbnisarten der Amerikaner und Nordostasiaten.* Königsberg, 1919 (Unpublished dissertation.)

Raleigh, Walter. *The discovery of the large, rich and beautiful empire of Guayana, with a relation of the great and golden city of Manoa (which the Spaniards call El Dorado),* etc. 1595. Reprinted by Robert H. Schomburgk, London 1848.

Reichel-Dolmatoff, Gerardo. *Datos histórico-culturales sobre las tribus de la antigua gobernación de Santa Marta.* Santa Marta, 1951.

Colombia. Thames and Hudson, London, 1967.

Reichlen, Henri. "Contribution à l'étude de la métallurgie précolombienne de la province d'Esméraldas," *JSA,* 33 (1941).

Restrepo, Vicente. *Los Chibchas antes de la conquista española.* Bogotá, 1895.

Restrepo, Tirado, Ernesto. *Historia de la provincia de Santa Marta,* 2 vols. Bogotá, 1953.

Robledo, Jorge. "Descripción de los pueblos de la provincia de Ancerma," *Colección de Documentos Inéditos,* vol. III, pp. 389–413. Madrid, 1865.

Rodríguez Fresle, Juan. *Conquista y descubrimiento del Nuevo Reino de Granada de las Indias occidentales del mar océano, y fundación de la ciudad de Santa Fé de Bogotá.* Bogotá, 1859.

Röthlisberger, Ernst. *El Dorado. Reise- und Kulturbilder aus dem südamerikanischen Columbien.* Bern, 1897.

Santesson, C. G. *A report in brief on an examination of Chocó Indian poisons.* 1935.

Sarmiento, Pedro. "Replación del Viaje del capitán Jorge Robledo a las provincias de Ancerma y Quimbaya," *CDI,* II. Madrid, 1864.

Saville, M. H. *The antiquities of Manabi, Ecuador,* 2 vols. New York, 1907–10.

Schuller, Rodolfo R. *The Ordaz and Dortal expeditions in search of El Dorado.* Washington, 1916.

Simón, Pedro. *Noticias historiales de las conquistas de Tierra Firme en las Indias Occidentales,* 5 vols. Bogotá, 1882–92.

Sitwell, Edith. *The Queens and the Hive.* London, 1962.

337

de la Torre y del Cerro, José. "Gonzalo Jiménez de Quesada," *BHA,*
XXIII, 258 (1936).

Triana, Miguel. *La civilización chibcha.* Bogotá, 1951 (Reprint of 1922
edition).

Uhle, Max. "Verwandschaften und Wanderungen der Tschibtscha,"
ICA, 7 (1888).

Wessén, Henry. "Algunos datos del comercio precolombiano en Colombia," *RCA,* 4 (1955).

Zahn, John Augustine. *The Quest of El Dorado.* New York 1917.

Zerda, Liborio. *El Dorado, estudio histórico, etnográfico y arqueológico
de los Chibchas.* Bogotá, 1833.

INDEX

340

341

344

25765   913.3
                               Von

Von Hagen, Victor W.
     The Golden Man: a quest
for El Dorado.

25765
                                     913.3
          Von Hagen, Victor W.   Von
AUTHOR

              The Golden Man: a quest
TITLE
       for El Dorado.

DATE DUE	BORROWER'S NAME	ROOM NUMBER